GROW YOUR OWN
VEGETABLES

GROW YOUR OWN
VEGETABLES

Carol Klein

contributing editor
Fiona Gilsenan

MITCHELL BEAZLEY

Grow Your Own Vegetables
Previously published as *Grow Your Own Veg*
by Carol Klein

First published in Great Britain in 2007 in association with
The Royal Horticultural Society by Mitchell Beazley,
a division of Octopus Publishing Group Limited,
2–4 Heron Quays, London, E14 4JP

An Hachette UK Company

www.hachettelivre.co.uk

Distributed in the US and Canada by Octopus Books USA:
c/o Hachette Book Group USA, 237 Park Avenue, New York, NY 10017

www.octopusbooksusa.com

Design and layout copyright © Octopus Publishing Group Ltd 2010

Text copyright © Octopus Publishing Group Ltd 2010

Photography copyright © The Royal Horticultural Society 2007,
unless otherwise stated on page 224

ISBN 13: 978 1 84533 551 9

Mitchell Beazley

commissioning editor Helen Griffin
project editor Joanna Chisholm
senior art editor Juliette Norsworthy
designer Victoria Easton
production controller Sue Fox

Created and produced for Mitchell Beazley by
The Bridgewater Book Company Ltd

A Cataloging-in-Publication record for this book is available
from the Library of Congress

Typeset in Frutiger

Color reproduction by United Graphics, Singapore

Printed and bound in China by Toppan

Contents

Why grow your own?

In a world where we are becoming increasingly alienated from what we eat, growing our own food is a fundamental way to reassert the connection between our gardens and what we cook. Much of our food is grown many miles away, and then transported by planes, trains, and trucks to sit on supermarket shelves before we bring it home (in the car) to our kitchen tables. When you grow your own, you know exactly where it came from, and it's as fresh as possible.

Supermarket selections

We all know vegetables are good for us, but what a difference there is between those we buy and those we grow. Bought vegetables are selected for uniformity and their ability to be packaged neatly to fit supermarket shelves. Their production and distribution are governed by logistics often on a global scale. Vegetables may be kept in cold storage, irradiated, washed in chlorine to destroy bacteria, and treated with preservatives to prolong their shelf life. Plant breeders' priorities are to produce agricultural crops with high yields that ripen simultaneously so machines can move in with the greatest efficiency and harvest the lot. But when convenience is everything, freshness, taste, choice, and seasonality often go out the window.

Year-round food

In real life, you don't want all your vegetables to mature at the same time. By growing your own, you can stagger your sowings to lengthen the season and deliberately select varieties that offer their leaves, roots, and seedpods or fruits over a long period. With a bit of planning, you can learn what grows best in your area and plan your meals in a seasonal pattern. In Southern California, you may still be picking tomatoes off the vine in November, when gardeners in Maine are harvesting frost-kissed kale. By drying, storing, pickling, freezing and canning, you can make your harvest available for even longer.

Know what you grow

When you grow your own produce, you know exactly what's been done to each vegetable at every stage of its existence. If you grow without the use of chemical-based fertilizers, you know that it is a combination of humus-rich soil that you have enriched with amendments, water, and perhaps an occasional feed with compost tea or liquid seaweed that has made your vegetables grow and flourish. If you have to combat pests and diseases, you get to make the decision whether to do so with the help of pesticides and fungicides, or to go with more natural methods of control.

Another of the great advantages of growing your own is that you get the final say in what you grow and eat. In your own garden, you can produce unusual vegetables that supermarkets don't stock. This might be fresh borlotti beans, a spicier version of arugula, or heirloom tomatoes that, although imperfect in shape, have so much flavor you can eat them like apples. There are also many different varieties of vegetables that you never see in the grocery store, with a fascinating range of different flavors, colors, and shapes to choose from. There is now enormous interest in heirloom and rediscovered

WORK TOGETHER with butterflies, bees, and other beneficial insects when tending your own vegetables and enjoy the seasons and the natural rhythms of life.

THERE IS GREAT JOY to be had in planting your crops and watching them grow into bountiful crops that you then transform for the family table.

varieties, and it is fascinating to find the ones that do well in your region, and then to grow them, eat them, and save seed to pass on to others.

Just-picked freshness

When you harvest your crops, they are totally fresh and taste completely different than store-bought produce. The only distance they've travelled is from the garden to the table so there are only food inches involved. There's no degradation of flavor or nutrition. And don't forget that growing your own means working outside too, providing invaluable exercise.

But it's not just your physical health that's improved by growing and eating your own. It is immensely good for the soul—therapeutic in every way. One of the greatest joys of harvesting your own crops is to feel part of the natural world around you. Gardening of any kind provides an opportunity to re-establish a relationship with the soil. Putting back what you take out by feeding the dirt makes you an active participant. Modern living often erases the link we have with the earth or at least disguises it so much that we can't see or feel it any more. Yet growing food has been the most basic common activity of every civilization. It is fundamental to human existence and to get back down to earth re-establishes our roots.

Wildlife in the garden

To watch the drama of the seasons unfold and to be directly affected by it through what you grow builds a deep connection with the real world. You feel the sunshine on your face as you tend and water, and watch the birds getting ready to depart as you harvest. You learn which plants attract pollinating insects such as butterflies and hummingbirds, and you see how ladybugs work as miniature pest control experts. You feel part of the cycle of the growing

GROWING IN HARMONY: COMPANION PLANTING

Native Americans planted beans and squash between maize, and gardeners today continue to do so with their 'three sisters bed'. In this, they are emulating a traditional practice in which three important staple crops—beans, maize, and squash—were grown together in a perfect symbiotic relationship. The soil was gathered into a series of mounds a stride apart. In the top of each mound was planted a seed of maize; two weeks later, the soil would be drawn up further and a bean seed would be pushed in beside the maize. When both had germinated and started to grow, in would go a squash seed at the foot of the hollow created by building the mound. As the corn grew, the bean would use it for support while at the same time fixing nitrogen in the soil and feeding itself, the corn, and the squash. Meanwhile the squash would benefit from the cool conditions created by the other two, while its large leaves suppressed weeds.

There are many ways to practice such companion planting in modern gardens. Taller plantings such as beans can shade lettuce from bright sun. Nasturtiums can be planted around cabbage to draw away harmful caterpillars. Carrot-family plants like dill and parsley can be planted to attract beneficial insects like ladybugs, spiders, and predatory wasps and help keep other crops free of aphids and mites. Experiment to see what combinations can be mutually beneficial.

year. Cultivating your own food presents you with a more meaningful measure of time—removed from the pressures of work, school, or everyday worries. Participating in the full circle from making compost to sowing seed to eating what you have grown, and then collecting your own seed and starting all over again, are what life is really all about.

A family affair

Gardening, preparing food, and eating together are multigenerational activities. Most children are naturally fascinated by the miracle of seeing tiny seeds turn into full-grown plants. They like to have their own patch of garden in which to grow favorite and easy plants such as sunflowers, peas, and tomatoes. And gardening is an activity that can be enjoyed by seniors, as well. There are many ways to make vegetable gardens accessible to people of all ages, from building easy-to-reach raised beds and generously proportioned paths, to using special tools that are smaller or more ergonomically designed for those with limited movement or strength.

Gardening in the community

In urban and suburban areas, there is strength in numbers and there are many opportunities to get involved with edible gardening even if you don't have your own garden in which to plant. Community gardens are on the rise, with citizens finding places to raise vegetables in unused public land, in empty lots, on rooftops—all the way to the White House. These gardens take many forms: They may be collections of individual plots similar to allotments, large plots run as cooperatives or educational centers, or a productive space dedicated to urban agriculture where the produce is grown for distribution through the community or at a local farmer's market.

LOCAL NURSERIES and garden centres offer transplants at the right planting time for your region. Plant them or pot them as soon as possible after arrival.

Preparation and techniques

- Growing in a small space
- Knowing your site
- Building the garden
- All about growing
- Extending the season
- Dealing with problems
- Planning what to grow

Growing in a small space

For new gardeners who want to grow vegetables at home, one of the first questions is, 'Do I have enough room?' The answer is 'Yes'—even if you have a tiny space, or no garden at all, you can find a way to grow edibles. Among the best ways to take advantage of limited space is to build raised beds. In the smallest yard, you can use containers to raise favorite herbs and vegetables.

Making a raised bed

Traditionally, vegetables were grown in long rows on flat soil, with space between the rows for harvesting. In a raised bed, the growing area is above the ground, and the sides are usually made of lumber or another building material. By using such a bed, gardeners sidestep a host of gardening challenges ranging from poor soil to limited mobility. A raised bed in a sideyard or even on a patio or deck can increase the range and quantity of vegetables grown.

Choosing the size and shape

Ideally beds should be no wider than 4ft. (1.2m) so that you can reach into them from both sides. If the bed is being positioned against a wall or fence, make it 24in. (60cm) wide. The maximum convenient length for a bed is probably 10ft. (3m). Square or rectangular beds are easiest to construct.

Deciding on materials

You can buy pre-fab raised bed kits (made of plastic or sometimes recycled lumber), which have the great

ADVANTAGES OF A RAISED BED

• The growing area is concentrated in a permanent bed with easy access from a permanent path.

• The soil dries out and warms up quite quickly. This is a considerable advantage on cold, wet soil, and in areas with short growing seasons. Also, the soil can be worked for more days of the year, and in bad weather.

• There is ample growing depth, which is especially useful for root vegetables.

• You can fill the bed with the most appropriate soil for your chosen crop.

• Raised beds drain well, which means that they can make a productive garden space even on rocky or clay soil, or on a slope.

• Gluts of any vegetable are less likely because the produce is being grown in short rows or small blocks, giving smaller harvests at a time.

• Beds can be made to almost any shape. Different materials can be used to match the style and size of the garden, and need not be expensive.

• Portable hoop houses, protective netting, and plant supports are easy to manage in a raised area.

• You can plant with closer spacing and get good yields, even on small beds, because the planting and sowing are concentrated in deep soil with high fertility, and there is extra light from the sides. The paths also give good access, so the soil won't be

RAISED BEDS may be as low as 12in. (30cm) in height, or up to 3ft. (1m), depending on your needs. Even a low bed offers advantages.

compacted by treading, thereby damaging its structure, hindering drainage, and making it harder to warm up in spring.

DISADVANTAGES OF A RAISED BED

• There is the initial time, expense, effort, and skill needed to build a rasied bed, and you may need to pay someone to do the work.

• Raised beds are less useful in hot-summer climates, where they dry out more quickly than open-ground beds, requiring extra watering and mulching. An irrigation system (see page 32) makes the job of watering raised beds much easier.

• Once in place, beds cannot be moved easily.

• There are plenty of hiding places in the sides for potential pests, such as slugs and snails.

advantage of being easy and quick to construct and are ideal if you want only one small bed. However, building a bed yourself is cheaper and gives you design flexibility. The sides are most commonly made of wood, but you can use any material that suits your landscaping, such as timbers, brick, interlocking landscape blocks, or stone. If you are using wood, you may prefer to use untreated lumber for the sides, where the soil will come into contact with the wood. This eliminates any chance of chemicals leaking into the soil and possibly being absorbed by the crops. (Do not use old railroad ties, or any lumber that may contain creosote.) Hardwood, such as cedar or redwood, is good for up to 20 years; softwood, such as pine, lasts about five years and is less expensive.

Building a simple raised bed

If you are making more than one raised bed, sketch out plans on graph paper to scale to ensure that they fit the site. This will also help when buying the materials as it will give you a clear idea of the quantities and sizes of the materials you need. Then mark out the area for the raised beds in the garden.

For the simple bed shown below, 2 x 6in. (5 x 15cm) boards for the sides are held together with 2in. (5cm) square corner stakes, 12in. (30cm) long. Longer beds will need extra staking along the sides to prevent the weight of soil bending the boards. Use screws to hold everything together securely. Pre-drilled holes prevent the wood from splitting.

Once the frame is assembled and placed on the soil, hammer the stakes into the ground. Tap each corner into the soil just a few inches at a time to avoid twisting the frame as the stakes go in.

To prevent weeds from growing on dirt pathways, lay permeable landscape fabric beneath the bed soil using metal staples, then cover with a layer of mulch such as wood chips 2in. (5cm) deep. This makes the bed accessible even in bad weather.

Gardening without a garden

Recent years have seen a rapid rise in the popularity of community gardens in the United States and Canada. Although allotment gardens have been

MAKING A RAISED BED

1 ASSEMBLE THE FRAME of the raised bed by attaching the long sides and short ends to the stakes using galvanized screws.

2 HAMMER THE CORNER STAKES of the frame into the ground with a mallet. Use an old piece of wood to protect the frame.

3 LOOSEN THE GROUND in the bottom of the raised bed before filling it with soil. This will help drainage.

A COMMUNITY GARDEN offers opportunities to grow vegetables alongside your neighbors in any size community.

a familiar site in European towns and cities for many years, they have been less common in North America since the era of the Victory Gardens of the Second World War. At that time, vegetable gardens were seen as a way for ordinary citizens to contribute to the war effort, raising food to feed the troops and keep down the cost of fresh fruits and vegetables. Eleanor Roosevelt planted a Victory Garden in front of the White House in 1943, which inspired millions of Americans to follow suit. In 2009, more than half a century after this first Victory Garden, Michelle Obama followed Roosevelt's example and planted a new vegetable garden on the White House grounds.

A community garden is typically on publicly owned land and takes the form of a collection of individual plots, available through some kind of selection process. They may be run as a cooperative venture, either by a non-profit group or by a public agency or branch of the municipal government. However, there are many variations on the theme.

FINDING COMMUNITY GARDENS

It's relatively easy to discover a community garden in your town or city—just take a walk or bike ride until you spot one, then introduce yourself to a gardener. Or you could contact your local municipal government to inquire about public gardens in your community. The American Community Gardening Association (www.communitygarden.org) has links to community gardens across Canada and the US.

OTHER PLACES TO PLANT

Apartment dwellers, or those who live in condominiums or cooperative housing, can speak to their landlords or housing boards about starting a shared garden on common land. This might even be on a rooftop, as various kinds of green roofs are becoming a more common feature in urban settings. Another place you might be able to start a garden is at a local school or hospital. Why not ask there?

Making the most of your space

Especially if you are gardening in a limited space, it is easy to get carried away when looking through seed and plant catalogs, so choose the crops that give you the biggest bang for your buck, then gradually experiment with new choices. Likewise, if you have a limited amount of time to spend caring for your vegetable garden, you'll find that a little pre-planning and some time-saving techniques can ensure that you get the most out of your garden no matter what its size or situation.

Select varieties carefully

When starting out as a vegetable gardener and trying to decide what to grow in your area, consult with knowledgeable local sources first. Ask your neighbors and fellow gardeners what works in their gardens. Visit some community gardens and see what is thriving and what combinations of edibles are being grown. Consult your local Cooperative Extension Service, which provides a wealth of information not only on varieties that do well in your local region, but also on timing—when to sow or transplant different crops. The staff can also give advice on pest and disease identification and control.

In a small garden, consider growing dwarf varieties and bush forms rather than rambling crops such as pumpkins and zucchini. Ignore anything too big for your space (such as perennial vegetables like artichokes and asparagus) or that needs elaborate preparation and cultivation (such as celery). Remember, too, that slow-growing plants such as cabbage take a long time to mature and take up precious space all season.

Local garden centers and nurseries make transplants available at the appropriate time for planting. Although this is often a good way to start experimenting with edibles, you'll find a wider selection through seed catalogs, which carry many unusual and heirloom varieties. All-America Selection (AAS) winners are chosen for their ability to perform well in many different areas.

Start with the easy ones

Some plants require a certain amount of expertise to grow successfully. They like their conditions to be just perfect, or they won't produce a good crop. If you are starting out as a gardener, try some of the more fool-proof plants first. In general, easy-to-grow edibles include: leafy greens such as lettuce, arugula, and Asian greens; mustard greens; kale; broccoli; beets; radishes; fava and other beans; garlic; peas; Swiss chard; tomatillos; and tomatoes. Start with these and

ABOVE LEFT: BEETS can be sown directly into the ground in early spring and are ready to harvest as soon as they are large enough to handle.

LEFT: FAVA BEANS are among the easiest crops to grow for beginner gardeners, sprouting quickly from seed.

then, as you get to know your garden conditions and gain confidence, you can move to more demanding plants.

Extend the seasons

Although many edibles can readily be grown from seed, your vegetables will spend less time in the ground before maturity if you start them from seed indoors, or plant from nursery containers such as six-packs. In addition, you'll avoid losses to pests such as slugs or cutworms, for whom young seedlings are nothing more than a snack. Gardeners in short-summer areas can further extend the growing season with the use of cold frames, hoop houses, and greenhouses (see page 40), which help you get plants in the ground earlier and keep them there for a longer period.

Maximize the growing space

Make the most of existing walls and fences for growing vining plants, such as beans and peas, or provide free-standing supports made from canes wired together. Any spot in the garden that is shady might be suitable for plants that don't like a blast of sunlight at midday, such as lettuce and other salad greens. If your soil is poor or rocky, consider putting in a few raised beds and filling them with good-quality planting mix.

Mixing edibles and ornamentals

Try growing vegetables and herbs that are ornamental as well as edible; vegetables certainly don't have to be dull. Many lettuce and salad leaves come in red, green, and purple, while basil can be dark red, and carrots have attractive, feathery foliage. Artichokes make stunning, sculptural plants in a perennial border, while peppers, tomatoes, and eggplant are dramatic choices for tall or wide containers.

When planting edibles in the ornamental garden, give extra thought to soil preparation. Clear the bed well in advance and dig over the soil thoroughly. Mix in plenty of well-rotted organic soil amendment, such as compost. Work the compost into the soil and then smooth over the surface before planting.

EDIBLE HERBS and flowers can be squeezed into beds alongside other crops, for the kitchen and to add color.

Mulch is the gardener's friend

No matter what size your vegetable garden is, mulch makes growing easier, by retaining moisture in the soil, helping prevent soil from crusting, and keeping weeds at bay. Finally, mulch makes your vegetable garden look tidier.

In natural landscapes, organic material accumulates on the ground and slowly decomposes into the earth, adding nutrients and texture that will improve the quality of the soil. You can mimic this process in your vegetable garden by putting down a good layer of mulch throughout your beds.

Many materials make good mulches, depending on local availability. Compost is an excellent choice for general purposes. Dry materials such as pine needles and straw can be useful when you want to keep plants away from wet soil, especially for crops such as tomatoes or squash, which can rot where they remain in contact with the ground. Shredded bark and wood chips in various sizes are all commercially available, either in bags or in bulk from landscape supply companies.

Apply mulch up to several inches thick, but keep it 2in. (5cm) away from the stems of your vegetables so that insects cannot use it as a hiding place and so that it does not encourage stem rots.

Making a container garden

A deck or patio garden can be filled with assorted pots, tubs, and window boxes in which to grow produce from herbs to ~~potatoes~~. Cherry tomatoes, chili peppers, and other dwarf varieties have been bred specifically for container culture. Arrange the containers in groups near the kitchen.

Types of containers

A huge range of shapes and materials are now readily available, the most popular being plastic, terra cotta, metal, and wood. All have different characteristics, advantages, and disadvantages, though a lot will depend on your garden style and preferences.

Clay and terra cotta look very attractive, but tend to dry out more quickly than plastic, and need more regular watering. To combat this, line the inside walls with thin plastic to reduce moisture loss, being sure to pierce the plastic in the base for sufficient drainage. In cold-winter areas, look for frost-proof rather than frost-resistant pots unless protection can be given over winter. Stand pots on 'feet'—which can be bricks or tiles—to avoid waterlogging and keep drainage good, and to prevent freezing.

Plastic pots are lighter than clay (an important consideration when you are moving pots about), dry out less easily, don't break, and aren't affected by frost. Imitation terra cotta pots that look similar to the real thing are now available.

Metal containers have a contemporary look. They are frost-proof, can be heavy or lightweight, and won't dry out like clay. Their main potential problem is that they heat up (and conduct the cold) quickly.

HERB POTS can be stuffed full of kitchen herbs and you can experiment with different types of a single kind, such as basil.

Wooden planters can have a limited lifespan because the wood will rot, though this can be slowed down by lining the inside with plastic sheeting or landscape fabric with drainage holes pierced in the bottom. Planters made of cedar or redwood will last longest, and old wine barrels also seem to resist rot for a long time.

Recycled materials Almost anything can be reused as a plant container, from old kettles, large tins, and wooden boxes to buckets and wooden crates (lined with pierced plastic).

Vegetables in containers

Size Ensure that the container size is appropriate for what you want to grow. Root vegetables such as carrots need deep pots, while beets sit near the top of the soil and need less depth. Shallower pots are also fine for lettuce and other salad greens. Big plants such as tomatoes and eggplant require large pots to accommodate their roots. For tall plants that need a stable base, such as beans, use a heavy pot and fill with soil-based potting mix.

Drainage No vegetables thrive in waterlogged soil, so good drainage is essential. Check that there are

---

REGIONAL RECIPE POTS

Try planting up pots with the ingredients from a particular country, or for a specific kind of recipe.

- Italian—plum or cherry tomatoes, basil, chard, sweet peppers, and flat-leaf parsley.

- Greek—eggplant, tomatoes, and Greek basil.

- Indian—peppers, Asian greens, and coriander.

- French—tarragon, peppers, and tomatoes.

---

enough drainage holes in the base of the container. If there is only one, drill more. (Stick masking tape over the area to be drilled to prevent terra cotta or clay from cracking.) Cover the base of the pot with broken pots or stones to aid drainage, and raise the pots on 'feet' to let the water drain.

Watering Potting soil needs to be moist at all times. Do not rely on rainfall because it may not penetrate the leaf cover of the plants, or be heavy enough to soak down to the roots. If it is allowed to dry out, it is often difficult to rewet and your crops will suffer as a consequence. To make the job easier, mix water-retaining crystals into the soil when planting. The crystals swell when wetted, and then release water gradually back into the soil. Large containers take longer to dry out than smaller ones. Mulching the surface with gravel or other decorative materials looks good and helps minimize evaporation.

If you have many pots, it might be worth installing an automatic irrigation system. Feed spaghetti tubing to each pot and use small emitters set at the base of the plant, or coil tubing with in-line emitters around the soil surface and peg it in place with metal staples.

To check if a plant needs a drink, scrape away the surface or mulch to see how moist the soil is. You can also use a moisture gauge with a probe that penetrates down about 6in. (15cm) to check below the soil surface.

If the water simply runs down the sides of the pot rather than trickling through the pot, the potting mix in the container has become compacted, and needs to be replaced with fresh mix.

Potting mix It is important to use a light, free-draining potting soil mix for your vegetables: This should be a water-retentive soilless mix or a soil-based medium. A good-quality mix will improve the quality of your plants. You can make your own potting mix by blending good-quality loam, peat moss, and vermiculite or perlite. Renew your potting mix every year, putting the old mix into the compost bin. Fresh mix will also ensure that your plants have plenty of nutrition and are disease-free.

Feeding The relatively small amount of potting mix in a container will have limited nutrients for plants and, if the plant is frequently watered, the nutrients may quickly be flushed out. Incorporating a slow-release

fertilizer on planting will help; otherwise use a balanced fertilizer regularly—one that contains nitrogen (N), phosphorus (P), and potassium (K) in equal proportions. Either use a liquid formula, or apply in the form of granules; you must thoroughly water in any granular fertilizer to be sure it reaches the root zone and to avoid burning plant stems.

For fruiting crops such as tomatoes and zucchini, use a high-potassium fertilizer once the flowers begin to appear; this encourages more flowers and fruit formation. Nitrogen-rich fertilizers aid leafy growth and are good for leaf crops such as spinach, chard, and lettuce. Phosphorus-rich fertilizers encourage root growth so are suitable for root crops. In practice, any balanced liquid feed is satisfactory.

Position The advantage of containers is that they can be moved in or out of the sun as required, especially if they're on a base with wheels. In general, though, they are too heavy to keep shifting about, so choose your position with care. Avoid windy areas when growing vines, and remember that an open, windy site can dry out a pot as quickly as one in hot sun—and all vegetables dislike heavy shade.

CONTAINERS are also very useful when it comes to sowing seeds of early crops indoors, for later planting out.

Knowing your site

Soil is the raw material of all gardening, but especially vegetable gardening. It is teeming with beneficial bacteria, fungi, and other microscopic creatures that recycle organic matter and use air, water, and minerals to make compounds that plants can convert to food. Without healthy soil, plants cannot produce good crops. But the good news is that you can always make your soil better.

Taking a look at the soil

Before you decide what you want to grow in your garden, you need to know about its soil. To do this, dig a narrow, sharp-sided hole about 24in. (60cm) deep, and check the color of the sides. There should be a dark topsoil layer above a paler subsoil. The topsoil should be open and friable, ideally with plant roots visible to their full depth. Hard, compacted soils block growing roots and drainage, so careful cultivation is required to open up the soil.

Subsoils might be hard clay, or bedrock, possibly coarse, stony material, or even deep sand. In the arid West and Southwest, they may be a rock-hard compacted layer of calcium carbonate called caliche. There is not much you can do about your subsoil, but at least you can be aware of the degree of drainage it offers and what potential there is for plant roots to grow.

The advantage of a porous subsoil is that it allows the plant roots to explore for nutrients and, during periods of dry weather, for water. If you have solid subsoil, think about making a raised bed to increase the drainage and depth of good soil.

IS YOUR SOIL ACID OR ALKALINE?

Measuring the pH of your soil enables you to determine whether the soil is acid or alkaline. A pH of 7 is neutral, less than 7 is acid, and more than 7 is alkaline. Vegetables grow best in a slightly acid soil with a pH of 6.5, although pH7–7.5 helps reduce clubroot disease in the cabbage family.

Although a laboratory test is best (and not hugely expensive), soil test kits are available from all good garden centers. A test kit can quickly give you an indication of your soil's pH, using a simple color system to show the pH level. Acid soil usually turns the testing solution an orange-yellow color; neutral changes it to green; and alkaline makes it dark green. Your local Cooperative Extension Service can also test your soil. The staff there will often look for deficiencies that are common in soils in your area and suggest appropriate amendments.

TESTING THE pH OF YOUR SOIL USING A KIT

1 PUT A SMALL SAMPLE of your soil into the pH testing kit test tube.

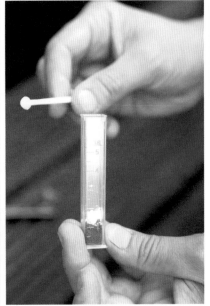

2 FOLLOW THE INSTRUCTIONS carefully by adding testing chemicals to your sample.

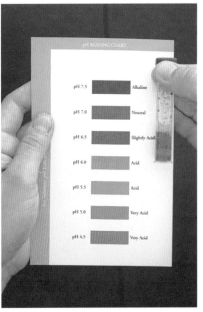

3 COMPARE THE COLOR of the resulting mixture with those on the supplied color chart. The best match indicates your soil's pH.

Checking the drainage

Once you have taken a look at the soil in your hole, fill it with water, cover, and leave overnight. If the water is still there the next day, drainage is poor and raised beds or some kind of drainage system might be needed. Excess water excludes air from the soil and roots can't survive long without air.

Identifying the elements

Roll some of the topsoil between your hands. If it flakes and crumbles, it is low in clay. If it feels gritty between finger and thumb, it is sandy. A soapy or silky texture suggests loam. And if it is easy to roll into a firm ball, it is clay.

Soil structure

When growing vegetables, the better the soil structure, the better the crop. Soils consist of minerals, clay, sand, and loam, which are coated in and bound by organic materials. These elements give structure to the soil and prevent it from becoming a solid mass impenetrable to roots.

Soil particles have air spaces between them, which allow oxygen, water, and roots to enter the soil. The roots then extract water and nutrients from the soil. Working or trampling on your soil, especially when it is wet—construction workers are common culprits!—compacts the soil. On the other hand, digging in well-rotted organic matter, such as garden compost or manure, applying mulches, and working your soil only when it is reasonably dry, preserves and enhances the soil structure.

Adding well-rotted organic matter is good for all soil types, whether you have clay, sand, or loam. It improves the soil structure, makes clay soils more free-draining and sandy soils more water-retentive. Well-rotted organic matter—and indeed excellent gardening generally—is also good for soil wildlife. It boosts the number of soil organisms, and they in turn feed larger ones, including insects and worms, which eventually feed the likes of lizards, toads, and birds.

SOIL TEXTURE

The size of particles in soil determines its texture. These include large particles of sand, tiny ones of clay, and in-between ones of loam.

SANDY SOIL

Sandy soil drains easily in winter and warms up quickly in spring, but it holds few nutrients and dries out in summer. It is good for cool-season crops, but later ones often need extra watering.

CLAY SOIL

Clay soils, also called heavy soils, are rich in nutrients, drain poorly in winter, and are slow to warm up in spring. But they are usually moist in summer, and can grow good crops of most types of vegetable.

LOAM

In between clay soil and sandy soil comes the crumbly soil—loam. It combines most of the best features of clay and sand and has excellent texture.

DIG IN organic amendments when the soil is reasonably dry, to preserve and enhance your soil's structure.

The effects of weather

Frost and wind

Even the best soil is no good if it is in the wrong place. Your crops will need as much sun as possible, and few are worth growing where buildings or trees limit the summer sun to less than six hours a day. Windy conditions also slow vegetable growth and make floating row covers hard to keep in place. Hedges and evergreen shrubs make good windbreaks, being cost effective and good refuges for wildlife; fences are an alternative in small gardens and where you need to construct a quick windbreak. Porous fences (with 50 percent spacing between boards) are best because they slow the wind, whereas solid barriers force the wind up, over, and down, creating a buffeting effect. Frosts can be damaging and are worst in low-lying sites where cold air collects. Because cold air is heavy, gardens at the foot of a hill are likely to suffer the worst frosts, as are areas where walls and hedges prevent the cold air from moving through to lower levels. Nearby high trees and buildings are also sources of cold air because they leak heat into the night sky, chilling the air which then sinks to the ground.

SIMPLE HOOP HOUSES, greenhouses, cloches, and floating row covers all protect your crops from wind and frost, but they too are best in sheltered locations, away from frost pockets.

The last frost in late spring marks the beginning of the growing season, and the summer growing season ends—except for some hardy plants—with the first frosts in early fall. The longer the growing season the better, especially for frost-sensitive plants such as pumpkins and corn. Gardens in frost pockets

WILDLIFE

A garden can be an oasis for wildlife even in urban areas. If there are forests, parks, and rivers or lakes nearby, an even wider range of wildlife will benefit from the shelter and food your garden provides. Bird feeders, thick organic mulches, sources of water such as ponds and birdbaths, leaving plants to go to seed, and using cover crops (see page 31) all attract beneficial wildlife to the garden.

Some wildlife needs to be kept away, using deterrents and barriers. Raccoons, for example, can make a mess in your pond or vegetable garden, as can deer, foxes, squirrels, rats, and—in the South—armadillos and opossums.

BIRDS are attracted by berry-bearing shrubs and trees, sheltered places to nest, and sources of water.

LOW RAISED BEDS and a greenhouse assist in extending the growing season in cold-climate gardens.

experience a much shorter growing season than gardens where cold air can move freely.

In general, inland and upland areas are colder than coastal regions, and urban areas are usually warmer than the rural ones, as the warm masonry and paving emit heat at night. Conditions are obviously cooler as you move north. The growing season gets shorter the further you go, and eventually crops such as heat-loving okra and peppers cannot be grown outdoors.

Wet winters, dry summers

Mediterranean conditions on the West Coast and in the Pacific Northwest present a range of opportunities—and some challenges—for gardeners. Wet winters make harvesting and preparing the soil difficult, and can spoil the produce even if there is good drainage. While gardeners in wet districts can lay planks across the ground in winter so that they don't damage the soil, a good alternative is to build raised beds that drain well, warm up earlier in spring, and can be worked from paths. But winter rains are not all bad: They fill the soil with water until it can take no more (usually around midwinter). The surplus then drains away, but the stored rain is available for plants during early summer.

MULCHING adds a layer of organic matter to the soil surface, which helps to reduce evaporation from the soil.

Dry summers can greatly reduce the quantity and quality of crops. Raised beds help gardeners in areas prone to summer droughts, because the greater depth of fertile soil gives plant roots an increased area to explore for water, though in the warmest regions, they may simply dry out too quickly. An irrigation system is invaluable, as it allows you to control and automate the amount of water your beds receive, without wasting scarce resources. Adding well-rotted organic matter, by mulching or digging in, and avoiding compacted soils increase the moisture-holding capacity of the soil—enough to keep plants going during periods of drought.

PROTECTING TENDER PLANTS

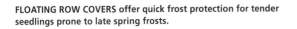

FLOATING ROW COVERS offer quick frost protection for tender seedlings prone to late spring frosts.

HOOP HOUSES made from clear plastic sheeting over wires or PVC tubing are a cost-effective way of extending the season.

Growing for your climate

Every area brings its challenges and rewards. Crops that do well in hot or humid zones, such as sun-~~loving beans, fiery chili peppers, may wilt in northern~~ gardens, failing to reach ripeness during a too-short growing season or in areas where summer brings too many overcast days. That's why it's helpful to understand the climate in your area—not just your USDA climate zone, with which most gardeners are familiar, but also other variables such as frost dates and the length of your growing season.

Seasons of growth

If you were to go by what you see in the aisles at the supermarket, you might think all vegetables grow year-round. But it's not the case. To a great extent,

no matter where you live, tomatoes can't ripen in February and peas will wilt in mid-August. Most of the produce at the grocery store or supermarket ~~has been grown thousands of miles away and then~~ ~~shipped or flown there so that you can enjoy food~~ that bears no relation to seasonality.

Vegetables fall into one of two categories, being either cool-season or warm-season plants. When and how you grow these plants depends not only on your climate, but also on how much work you are willing to do to provide the conditions that the plants need to produce a crop. With some extra effort, an understanding of your climate, and careful selection of plants and varieties, it's possible to grow a wide variety of vegetables in most climate zones throughout the United States and Canada. Even

USDA HARDINESS ZONES

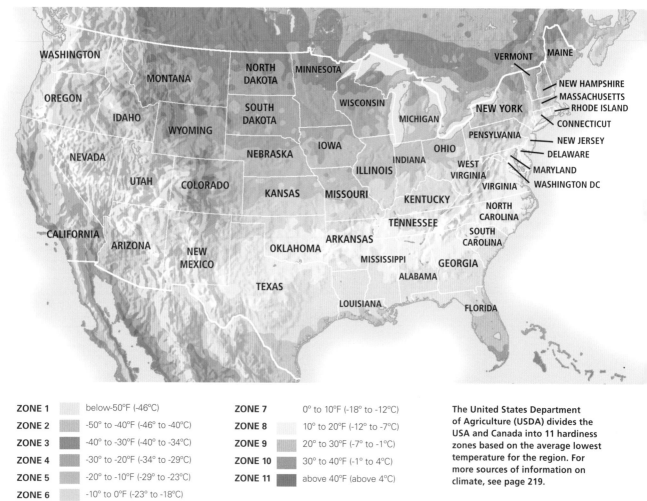

ZONE 1	below-50°F (-46°C)	**ZONE 7**	0° to 10°F (-18° to -12°C)
ZONE 2	-50° to -40°F (-46° to -40°C)	**ZONE 8**	10° to 20°F (-12° to -7°C)
ZONE 3	-40° to -30°F (-40° to -34°C)	**ZONE 9**	20° to 30°F (-7° to -1°C)
ZONE 4	-30° to -20°F (-34° to -29°C)	**ZONE 10**	30° to 40°F (-1° to 4°C)
ZONE 5	-20° to -10°F (-29° to -23°C)	**ZONE 11**	above 40°F (above 4°C)
ZONE 6	-10° to 0°F (-23° to -18°C)		

The United States Department of Agriculture (USDA) divides the USA and Canada into 11 hardiness zones based on the average lowest temperature for the region. For more sources of information on climate, see page 219.

if you stick strictly to what grows well in your area, it is essential to know your local conditions so you can plan appropriately.

Warm-season crops

The traditional vegetables of summer, such as beans, corn, cucumbers, peppers, tomatoes, and zucchini, are warm-season plants. They need warm soil and sunlight, along with high temperatures to germinate, grow, and then ripen their fruit. They are sensitive to frost and cannot be left outside when there is a danger of frost in spring (they will nip back developing seedlings) or in fall (when low temperatures can turn fruit into mush).

Cool-season crops

Broccoli, Brussels sprouts, cabbage, cauliflower, chard, collards, kale, leeks, most salad greens, peas, and spinach are cool-season crops that need to complete their growth cycle when temperatures are moderate—typically 55–75°F (13–24°C). They can tolerate varying amounts of frost. In fact, the taste of some—such as kale and cabbage—may actually improve when subject to mild fall and winter frosts. Some cool-season vegetables can tolerate a certain amount of summer heat—collards, for instance— but success with most of them relies on bringing them through their growth cycle during the cooler weather—with temperatures 10–15°F (5–8°C) lower than those preferred by warm-season vegetables. When temperatures start to rise, most cool-season crops will grow bitter, or produce flowers and then seeds, a process known as bolting.

Cool-season edibles need to be planted in late winter or early spring so they can grow before the hottest temperatures of summer set in, or again in late summer for a harvest in fall or early winter.

An exception to this rule is in the mild-winter climates found in Southern California, through parts of the Southwest, Texas, and up through coastal regions of southern states such as Louisiana, Alabama, Georgia, Florida, South Carolina, and North Carolina. In these areas, many cool-season crops can be harvested right through winter and early spring.

Climate zones

The United States and Canada are classified by the United States Department of Agriculture (USDA) into 11 broad hardiness zones. Plants are assigned a hardiness zone based on the lowest temperature they are able to survive in winter. Hardiness zones are important when deciding whether you can grow perennial plants, including edibles such as artichokes, because these plants need to survive the winter where they are planted. Hardiness zones continue to be refined as more data become available and the effects of climate change are assessed.

First fall frost

Like the last frost date, the first frost date of fall is an average, which can come anytime from August to December (in some areas, such as southern Florida, frost-free winters are common, but the occasional freeze does happen, usually in January or February). Fall frost dates can assist you in determining when the summer harvest is coming to an end and can help you plan for fall planting and harvesting of cool-season crops.

Growing season

Calculations for the length of the growing season are based on the last spring frost and the first fall frost. It varies from 60 days to more than 240 days— quite a difference! This number helps you figure out what crops you can grow. If a vegetable is listed as requiring 85 days from seed to maturity, for instance, you need a growing season at least this long to plant the crop outdoors from seed and let it mature to harvest (bearing in mind that you also need the temperatures preferred by the plant).

If your season is shorter than this, you'll have to use methods to extend the season (see page 40), or choose varieties with a shorter growing-season requirement. Fortunately, there is usually a wide range of varieties from which to select any given crop.

Day length

The number of hours of daylight varies according to your latitude and the season. Vegetables respond differently to day length, depending on their stage of growth: Short-day plants grow and set seed only if day length is less than 12 hours; long-day plants need more hours of sunlight to grow properly. Day length can affect planting times and variety selection for some vegetables. In the North, for example, the short days at the end of summer are needed to trigger cauliflower to develop. In Southern gardens, you may need to grow short-day onions in order for them to set bulbs successfully.

Building the garden

The kind of edible garden you create will depend on a few factors: what you are hoping to grow, your garden conditions, and how much room you have. If you want the maximum amount of fresh produce from a small space, try raised beds. If the plot is part of an ornamental garden, consider bed edging and decorative paths. And don't forget about providing easy access to your vegetables.

A SPACE-SAVING ROW of tall containers placed along the length of a hedge provides a home for leafy greens.

Initial decisions

Unless you are developing an already established kitchen garden, you will need to plan the shape, size, and look of your plot, and decide where it should be positioned to best suit your requirements. Is it to be a practical area designed to produce as much as possible for the kitchen?

Traditionally, a vegetable garden has neat, well-tended rows of crops set in bare, well-tilled, weed-free soil. In an informal setting, try scattered patches of crops among showy plants, with teepees of peas and beans dotted here and there, and pumpkins scrambling over compost bins and even low walls. In geometric and more minimalist gardens, a formal potager with neatly edged beds might be better, perhaps with individual tomatoes and obelisks of climbing beans in a carpet of salad greens or a regimented block of red cabbage or beets. You can get as creative as you like with the design.

Positioning your site

Of most importance is the garden's exposure, as most vegetables need at least six hours of direct sunlight per day. You can place a vegetable garden adjacent to a south- or west-facing wall or fence, which can act as a support for climbing vegetables. Soil in the rain shadow of walls and fences, however, can be dry, so create beds at least 24in. (60cm) wide, and amend them generously with well-rotted manure or compost so that they retain moisture well.

In warmer areas, you may need to provide some shade or protection from the sun during the hottest part of the day. Tall crops, such as corn or beans on a trellis, can provide shade for lower-growing plants, or you can take advantage of an existing feature such as a large tree that casts dappled shade at midday.

Accessibility

Working in the vegetable garden can be fun, but some gardening tasks such as mulching can seem like a chore if your garden is awkward and difficult to reach. Position it as close as you can to the kitchen, so you can easily harvest fresh produce, especially crops such as salad greens and herbs that you'll use almost daily. Make sure you have access to watering equipment, and to tools and supplies. Keep pathways wide enough to walk comfortably and to move equipment such as a wheelbarrow.

Tackling the weeds

Although it is handy to break up very compacted dirt, rototilling a weedy site to clear it is not a good idea, because the blades chop up perennial roots into many pieces—all of which then take root and regrow. It is best to remove weeds either by hand, or by treating with herbicide (see page 47). Perennial weeds such as bindweed, blackberries, quack grass, or Bermuda grass are very challenging to remove even with repeated applications of a root-killing herbicide such as glyphosate. An alternate method is to cover the proposed garden area with plastic or impermeable landscape fabric and leave it in place for several weeks during the heat of summer. Any pernicious perennial weeds in the proximity of the beds can still return, however, and may call for continued control.

Annual weeds such as groundsel, purslane, and oxalis are best hoed off as they emerge, before they can set seed. Don't add perennial weeds, or annuals weeds that have set seed, to the compost, as they can survive the composting process and resprout in your garden after months or even years.

Improving your soil

If you can, add bulky organic matter such as compost or well-rotted manure, every second year, to half or one-third of your vegetable garden. Some crops, such

as carrots and parsnips, are best grown on soil that was enriched the previous year. As a rough guide, one bucketful of amendment to every square yard (or meter) is enough, but double this amount could be used for thin, poor soil and for hungry crops.

Bulky amendments are not always enough on their own. Heavy feeders, such as brassicas, beets, spinach, and celery, need the boost of a balanced fertilizer containing roughly equal amounts of nitrogen, phosphorus, and potassium. Other crops, such as tomatoes, may need extra potassium. Advice for individual crops is given in each entry in this book.

Now is also the time to amend your soil or adjust its pH in line with the results from a soil test (see page 21). If the soil is too acidic, lime in the form of calcium carbonate, dolomitic limestone, bone meal, or wood ashes will help to raise it. If your soil is too

---

TOOLS

Having the right tools for the job makes vegetable growing much easier and leaves more time for you to enjoy the end result. Good inexpensive tools are sold at garden centers and home supply stores, and are widely available second hand—check local garage sales. Make sure you clean your tools and store them carefully after every use. That way they will last longer and be a pleasure to use. A typical starter kit for growing vegetables includes:

- a spade, shovel, and fork
- a rake
- a long- and short-handled hoe
- a pair of pruners
- a trowel and hand fork
- boots and gloves.

SOME CROPS really benefit from extra nutrients added to the soil before planting.

COVER CROPS

These are also known as green manures, because they are plants grown for the sole purpose of improving the soil. Typically planted in fall so that they overwinter when the ground is otherwise bare, cover crops are then chopped down and dug into the soil in early spring. Cover crops improve soil texture and water retention, and often add nutrients to the soil.

Legumes such as fava beans, field peas, and other beans make excellent cover crops, as their roots supply nitrogen. Other choices include mustard, clover, and vetches. Garden supply catalogs also offer cover crop seed mixtures that combine several different types of green manure.

A GREEN MANURE CROP feeds the soil, keeps weeds at bay, and makes an excellent addition to the compost pile.

alkaline, as in many parts of the West and the Midwest, you'll need to add sulfur in the form of calcium suflate, iron sulfate, or aluminum sulfate.

Making your own compost

Composting can be one of the most rewarding gardening tasks, and is a great 'green' activity. In essence, it is just gathering organic waste—scraps from the kitchen and prunings from the garden—then allowing naturally occurring organisms to break down the waste to a rich soil conditioner. There are plenty of techniques advocated by various gardeners for composting—everyone has their favorite—but the basic process is relatively straightforward.

Compost bins of various kinds are widely available. Check with your local municipality. Many offer low-cost or free compost bins to residents in an effort to keep waste out of landfills. Or you can build simple wooden enclosures—typically measuring 2–3ft. (0.6–1m) in width, height, and depth. A layer of chicken wire or hardware cloth underneath an open-bottom composter will keep out rats and other pests that may burrow up into the compost from below.

If you have the room, use two compost bins or piles: One to fill up while the other is rotting down. When you have emptied one, shovel the contents of the second into the first as a way of turning the pile.

Add a mix of organic waste from the garden and kitchen to your compost. Kitchen waste should be from vegetable sources only; do not add meat, fish, or dairy products. About a third of the waste should be nitrogen-rich material such as kitchen waste and grass clippings; the rest should be strawlike or woody carbon-rich material, such as spent crops and dried leaves. (Large pieces of bark or excessively twiggy material, however, should not be included.) Keep adding material until the pile is full, and sprinkle with water if the contents look dry. Then leave to rot. Turn the pile with a fork occasionally to mix in air. Add water, more green waste, or more carbon-rich waste as required in order to speed up decomposition and improve quality.

In small or urban gardens, worm composting might be a better bet. Bins can be quite small, and use special worms—usually red wrigglers. Both bins and worms can be bought from specialty suppliers.

Watering and irrigation

All vegetables need a steady supply of water for optimum growth, to set flowers, and to develop fruit. Without water, most vegetables soon succumb to drought stress, failing to thrive and eventually dying. Learning how much and when to water your crops are an important part of vegetable gardening.

How often to water

All young seedlings and transplants need plenty of water—sometimes constant moisture in order for them to develop root systems. Once plants have started to grow, their watering needs vary—and also depend on the weather and your soil.

Soil types and water

The ability of soil to absorb and retain water is closely related to its makeup (see page 22). Loose sandy soils have large particles with air spaces between them. Such soils absorb water quickly and then drain just as quickly. Clay soils, on the other hand, have small, dense particles that absorb water slowly and then hold onto it for longer. The same amount of water also penetrates differently depending on the soil.

In clay soils, water is distributed widely and shallowly under the surface. In sandy soils, it will penetrate in a more narrow, deep fashion. Loam soils are in between.

Mounds and basins

Whenever you plant vegetables on a hill or mound, water will pool in a depression around the mound. To direct water toward the root zone of the plant, create a moat or basin around the planting mound so that water does not run off far from the mound.

Using hoses

Watering with hoses is time-consuming and you need to be consistent. Buy good-quality hoses to make the job easier. Reinforced vinyl hoses are kink resistant and not too heavy, which is important because you usually need to haul the hose around the garden. Rubber hoses are durable, but also heavy. They work best in cold weather. Reinforced rubber-vinyl hoses are tough, flexible, kink resistant, and moderately lightweight. Look for reinforced brass fittings. To help keep the fittings in good shape and prevent leaks, install female brass couplers on the hose and male couplers on the end of different spray heads or hose-end sprinklers that you attach to the hose end.

HOW MUCH TO WATER

Many plants wilt during the hot daylight hours when the sun is shining directly on them. This may not mean that you aren't watering enough. Overwatering, especially in clay soil, can lead to sodden roots that can't get enough oxygen, and to problems like root rots or fungal diseases. Plants may develop yellow leaves and darkened, dropping stems and branches. On the other hand, plants suffering from drought stress may be wilted in the morning and evening as well as at midday. Under long-term stress, plants wilt, growth slows, and developing flowers and fruit will drop—indicating that you may not be watering plants sufficiently, or that you are watering frequently but too lightly, soaking only the top inch or two of the ground.

TO DETERMINE whether your irrigation system is delivering enough water, use a water gauge: 1in (2.5cm) per week is an average need for most edible crops, but in dryest areas, plants may require twice that.

IRRIGATION IN YOUR GARDEN

A MICROIRRIGATION system can be fitted with drip emitters, which deliver measured amounts of water to the base of plants.

SPRAYER HEADS are good for covering larger areas, which can be handy for seedling beds or leafy greens.

WATERING BY HAND is time-consuming but allows you to check on the condition of your plants as you water.

Automatic irrigation

The most efficient and time-saving way to irrigate your vegetable garden is with an automatic or semiautomatic irrigation system. This comprises a network of rigid and flexible tubes that deliver water to your plants via sprinkler heads and drip emitters. A simple setup will ensure that plants get water evenly and consistently—especially important for seedlings and leaf crops such as lettuce.

Microirrigation systems are extremely flexible and can be tailored to water individual plants or to distribute water over a larger area. You can reconfigure the setup depending on the crops you are growing and the time of year. An inexpensive timer can be set to turn the water on and off to a schedule so that you don't need to worry about plants going thirsty. You can design your own system or hire a specialist provider to install a system for you.

A basic microirrigation setup starts with a faucet or hose-bib attachment that is essentially a series of valves to prevent backflow into the house plumbing,

to filter the water, and to control the water pressure. These valves are designed with 1in. (2.5cm) or ¾in. (2cm) connections; from this connection you attach supply lines of either rigid poly pipe (for subsurface installations) or flexible ½in. (1cm) tubing (for running on top of or just below the surface of the ground). If you live in an area where the ground freezes, flexible tubing may be the best option as it is easier to check for leaks and to repair damage caused by freezing pipes. To protect the tubing, you can bury it a few inches below the soil surface and cover with mulch.

Run the supply lines to your vegetable garden, then attach risers to bring the tubing up over the edge of any raised beds. Attach either ¼in. (0.5cm) drip microtubing or ½in. (1cm) tubing with microemitters (drippers and sprayers). For larger plants such as tomatoes, you can arrange the emitters so that they are roughly at the base of each plant. For leaf crops, coil the tubing for more overall coverage. If you want a light spray of water on your leaf crops, you can fit risers up to 18in. (45cm) high with sprayer heads.

All about growing

Raising strong and healthy seedlings is a critical part of growing your own edibles, whether you are germinating your own seed or buying seedlings in cell packs that have already been started by a nursery. All good crops depend on a solid start, after all. Seed can either be sown directly where it is to grow or sown in cell packs or trays and then the plants are put out later.

Where to start

When planning your crops, you need to decide whether you are going to grow from seed or from plants bought from a specialty supplier by mail order or from a local nursery or garden center. The range of plants available—and of sources—is growing all the time. There are pros and cons to seed sowing as well as using transplants: You will have to weigh what suits you and your available space.

Perennial crops can be grown from seed, but it's a lot less effort to buy young plants. Potatoes are grown from 'seed potatoes,' and alliums, except leeks, are usually started from 'sets' or bulbs. If you want to grow from seed, there are two ways—either in flats or cell packs for later transplanting, or by sowing direct into drills made in the soil. Which method you choose depends on the crop as well as the growing conditions. You might, for example, decide to sow in flats because you have problems with hungry mice or birds, and the young plants require some growth before they are exposed.

Germinating your seeds

Seed germination is related to temperature. Carrots sown in cold soil in late winter for harvesting in early summer might take 21 days or more to germinate, but if they're sown in midspring for a summer crop they should come up in 14 days.

SEEDLINGS

Small seeds makes small seedlings, and these take a long time to put on good growth (carrots and onions are good examples), whereas large seeds (such as peas and fava beans) produce large seedlings that get off to a flying start.

Warm-season crops usually need high soil temperatures to germinate well, and that's why tomatoes, peppers, and eggplant, for instance, need to be started indoors in cooler climates. If you sow them indoors in early spring, they'll start growing quickly, and have a growing season that's long enough to produce a good crop before the fall frosts. Large-seeded beans, corn, zucchini, pumpkins, and squash can be sown outdoors in late spring or early summer and, being large-seeded, grow fast and have enough time to crop well, especially in warmer areas.

Seedlings are vulnerable to fungal diseases such as damping off, which can kill young plants. You can minimize the risk of an attack in your plants by sowing at the optimum time, when the soil is warm and not too wet.

Use clean containers and clean water. Wash all cell packs and seedling trays with a dilute bleach solution. Above all, make sure that any potting mix is sterile. Providing good air circulation for seedlings also helps to minimize diseases.

Sowing direct in the soil outdoors is quick and easy, and the seedlings look after themselves, developing strong root systems that resist drought and disease. The downside is that they are vulnerable to pests, diseases, and the weather, and to competition for space and food from weeds.

THE SMALL SIZE of seedlings means that many can be sown closely together, but they will soon need to be thinned if they are to have space to flourish.

WHEN DIRECT SOWING, use a string to help you plant in a straight row. This makes watering and weeding easier after germination.

Seeds of heat-loving warm-season plants require warm soil to germinate. If started indoors, use a heat mat to warm the soil up to 20°F (11°C) higher than room temperature. Edible crops also need bright light to develop properly. If you grow seedlings in a windowsill, you'll often notice that those closest to the window will be taller and stronger, while those receiving less direct light can be spindly and weak. If you don't have a greenhouse or other well-lit place for seedlings, try growing them under fluorescent grow lights, available through garden suppliers.

Sowing seeds outdoors

To create the right conditions for sowing, you need a seedbed in which the previously cultivated soil is raked level to create a smooth layer of finely divided soil over firm, but not too hard, underlying soil. This can be done only if the soil is dry. Spread a light dressing of a balanced fertilizer on the soil before raking to ensure that the emerging seedlings aren't short of nutrients.

Make a groove, called a drill, in the surface just deep enough to cover the seed to about twice its diameter or, in the case of small seed, as shallow as possible but still enough to cover it. The large seeds of peas, beans, and corn need a drill about 2in. (5cm) deep, the moderate-sized seeds of the cabbage family, spinach, and beets require a 1in. (2.5cm) drill, and the fine seeds of onions, carrots, parsnips, and lettuce, a drill no more than ¾in. (2cm) deep.

The groove can be made using the corner of a hoe or rake or, better for small seeds, by using the length of a broom handle pressed into the soil. Water the drill and place the seeds in it in a sparse, continuous flow. Alternatively, sow five or six seeds wherever you want a plant (such as lettuce or turnips), later thinning to one plant. Then carefully draw back the soil with the hoe or rake to fill the groove.

The seed and soil must be in close contact if the seed is to take up moisture from the ground. The easiest way to make sure this happens is to firm down the soil by pressing on it with the head of the rake. Do it firmly if the soil is dry, and lightly if it's moist. Some soils pack down under rain so solidly that the seed cannot emerge; if this is a danger in your seedbeds, cover the seed instead with fine potting soil.

Transplanting young plants

Young vegetables can be carefully dug out of their original seedbeds and replanted in a fresh spot. This is a traditional way of raising leeks and members of the cabbage family. They are set at the same depth as in the seedbed or, in the case of the cabbage, are buried up to the depth of the lowest leaves.

YOUNG SEEDLINGS, such as these basil plants, need to be well watered until their root systems develop.

SOW FAST-GROWING CROPS into all available spaces to increase the productivity of your garden.

Seedlings can be left to grow where they germinate, although they usually need to be thinned to their final spacing. In most cases, you can always sow more seed or move seedlings to fill any gaps. Root crops like carrots and parsnips don't like to be moved. Give any transplants plenty of water to help them settle.

Watering before and after transplanting limits the shock of moving from container to open ground. Most plants are best transplanted as soon as you can handle them, but leave cabbage until it has five true leaves, and leeks until they are pencil thick. Trimming leaves and roots makes the plants easier to handle but slows recovery, and is best avoided.

Sowing in containers

Raising plants in flats and cell packs involves more work and expense than sowing directly in the ground, but it saves seed since you just sow one or just a few per pot. Excess seedlings of expensive seeds can be transferred as young seedlings to another pot or bed, to avoid waste. Sowing indoors usually leads to a higher germination rate than sowing in the ground, where there is more risk of diseases, pests, and

weather damage. In cooler regions, there is little choice with some crops such as tomatoes and peppers: These need to be germinated under cover before it is warm enough for planting out. Vegetable seed is undemanding, and any good potting mix—peat-based or peat-free—is suitable. Don't use home-made soil starting mix unless you have thoroughly sterilized it to remove contamination from any pests, diseases, or harmful nutrient levels.

Once seedlings have grown to a few inches, you may want to pot them up in individual pots.

Hardening off

When the root system binds the soil together and the last frost date has passed, seedlings can be planted out. But before you do this, you must gradually accustom the seedlings to life in the outdoors: Set the flats or pots outdoors during the day, then bring them back into shelter at night for at least a week before transplanting the seedlings to the garden.

Repeated sowings

Some plants, such as Brussels sprouts and tomatoes, crop continuously while others, such as potatoes and carrots, can be stored. Repeated sowings at intervals, called 'successive sowing', is necessary for a continuous supply of other crops, such as peas, beans, lettuce, and cauliflower. If you sow no more than you are likely to need over a two-week period each time, and then start again when the first plants are 2–3in. (5–7.5cm) high, you will avoid waste and seldom be without produce.

If you are fertilizing seedlings, use a dilute liquid fertilizer specially formulated for them. Soilless mixes will need more feeding and watering. Some potting mixes come with fertilizer pellets mixed in, but the nutrients are quickly taken up by the growing young plants.

TRANSPLANTS brought home from the garden center should be planted as soon as possible as they will soon run out of nutrients in their cell packs.

INTERPLANTING fast-growing crops, such as radishes, in between corn, is a good way to make the most of any spare space among vegetables that take longer to mature.

Interplanting

Some plants develop slowly but eventually become large, and you can use the space between the growing vegetables for one more quick crop before the larger vegetables block out the sun. For example, peas sown in midspring need 24in. (60cm) of space on each side so that the pods can be gathered, but they won't cast much shade until early summer. In the meantime lettuce, spinach, and arugula can be grown near the peas. Such a technique is known as 'interplanting'

Where a crop is gathered early, or planted late, there are opportunities to grow crops before and after. This is called 'catch cropping.' So, fava beans sown in late winter can be cleared away in midsummer, leaving time for a row of pole beans (in warm areas) to be sown for harvest in early fall. Leeks planted out in midsummer leave time for a row of lettuce to be planted in early spring and gathered before the leeks need setting out.

ROTATION OF CROPS

Growing each crop on a different piece of land by moving it each year can help reduce the effect of soil pests and diseases. Where possible, aim for a two- or three-year rotation but if serious diseases such as clubroot of cabbage-family crops strikes, you may want a longer crop rotation. Divide the vegetable bed into equal sections and choose which crops you want to grow. Group them by plant family (by pests and diseases), then soil requirements and soil benefits (such as nitrogen fixing by legumes). For example, grow potatoes and tomatoes on a specific area in year one; peas, fava beans, carrots, parsnips, onions, shallots, leeks, and garlic in year two; and in year three (after adding lime if necessary) the cabbage family. Other crops suffer fewer soil problems, and can be grown wherever is convenient.

Extending the season

In cool climates, vegetable gardeners are in the habit of extending the season of their crops by raising seedlings indoors; it gives plants a head start while it is cold outside. Even so, not much can be gathered from the garden until midsummer. To really extend the season, you will need some extra tricks, such as warming the soil in spring or using a greenhouse or cold frame.

AN UNHEATED PROPAGATOR acts like a mini-greenhouse and is perfect for germinating seeds of cool-season vegetables.

Sowing in the warmth

Most crops can be started off early in a greenhouse or indoors, in a warm, well-lit place. Greenhouses can also be used to extend the season well into fall for crops that respond well to a long season, such as tomatoes and eggplant, where they can be raised in containers or grow bags. A sunny windowsill is suitable for starting off young plants, but the light quality may be uneven, so it is not practical for large numbers of seedlings. Windows provide less light than you might think, but you can always supplement with grow lights. A heat mat under the cell pack or seedling tray will also provide the extra warmth needed to germinate warm-season vegetables.

Moving your plants outside

Use a hoop house or a cold frame as a halfway house to acclimate plants gradually to the outside world. When the plants are first put out in the vegetable garden, protect them with floating row covers. This acclimatation process is called 'hardening off.' It avoids sudden changes in airflow, humidity, and temperature, which can lead to poor growth and, often, premature flowering.

A GREENHOUSE means you can start seeds indoors or even grow a crop entirely under glass.

Warming the soil

Early crops can be sown outdoors by taking advantage of plastic mulches. Covering a seedbed with plastic (use clear or black; clear gives most warmth, black suppresses weeds) for at least six weeks before sowing warms the soil enough to risk early sowings. A covering such as this enables seed to be sown up to four weeks earlier than usual. For example, it's risky to sow carrot seed before early spring, but, if a seedbed is prepared and covered in midwinter, seed sown in late winter has a good chance of success. After sowing, the plastic can be replaced by floating row covers, which are invaluable in mild-climate gardens. They are essentially lightweight blankets made of spun-bonded polypropylene. When placed over your plants, they allow in light and rain, and retain warmth in the soil. Sowings can be made under row covers about two weeks before seed sown

in open ground, if the material is suspended over the soil on hoops. Beneath the row cover the plants are protected from the worst frost and flying pests, including birds. Slugs and weeds also appreciate the shelter, so keep an eye out for both. In cold weather, use a double layer of cover, reducing it to a single layer as soon as possible.

SUNNY, SHELTERED PATIOS are almost as good as greenhouses. The bricks and pavers emit heat at night as they cool down.

GLASS CLOCHES are single-plant solutions for the gardener without a greenhouse.

TOMATOES are ideal crops for greenhouses, and they can be grown in containers or grow bags.

Protection with row covers for the early part of the crop's life also encourages an early harvest. When transplants are covered they should mature about two weeks before uncovered crops.

Cloches are really pint-sized greenhouses, about 20in. (50cm) tall, and can be used in the same way as row covers. Use them to protect individual tender plants such as eggplant, bush tomatoes, zucchini, okra, and peppers, in summer. Cloches can make all the difference in Northern gardens. Traditional cloches are bell-shaped glass jars, but you can also get plastic models, and even ones that have double walls that can be filled with water for a further insulating effect.

Gardeners lucky enough to have a glazed porch, sun room, or even just a picture window can grow tender plants such as eggplant, peppers (especially chili peppers), and tomatoes in pots 18in. (45cm) diameter or larger, or in grow bags. In fact, a sunny balcony or patio can be a useful sun trap nearly as good as a greenhouse for growing these heat-loving crops.

COLD FRAME DOORS can be propped open on hot spring days and closed at night when frosts are still possible.

Dealing with problems

Vegetables are just as attractive to pests and diseases as they are to people. The tender texture and mild flavors probably make crops vulnerable, but plants do have built-in mechanisms for resisting pests and diseases. There are also many beneficial insects and other organisms that prey on pests or inhibit disease. Keep your plants well nourished and watered to help them to ward off attacks.

Coping with pests

You can't miss the likes of snails and slugs, caterpillars, and beetles; other pests, such as red spider mites, are barely visible, and some are invisible without a microscope. Insects are by far the most prolific pests. They feed on plants by sucking (aphids attack fava beans and leaf miners are often seen on beets and celery) or by tunneling into tubers. Insects also spread viral and bacterial diseases; cucumber beetles, for instance, can spread bacterial wilt, a potential deadly disease of squash, pumpkins, and other cucumber-family plants.

Helping plants to fight

Gardeners should boost natural countermeasures; avoid harming helpful organisms and do not wage war directly on pests and diseases. A certain level of disease and pest attack has to be tolerated, especially if the edible part of the crop is not directly affected.

The first line of defense is knowing that well-grown plants with sufficient water and nutrients fend off insect attacks much more readily than stressed plants. Second, make life inhospitable for the pests, removing hiding places and limiting access by getting rid of debris and weeds, and raking the soil level to deter slugs, for example. Large pests such as tomato hornworms can be removed by hand, but this can be time-consuming. Third, prevent pests reaching the crop by erecting barriers and traps. Many beetles,

A WEED-FREE SOIL means that insects have nowhere to hide.

MANY KINDS OF BEETLES like to feast on vegetable crops, but they can be kept at bay with natural controls.

caterpillars, and loopers can be excluded with floating row covers. The carrot rust fly travels low down and cannot fly over a barrier more than 20in. (50cm) high, so erect one using plastic sheeting. The best way to counter cutworms or cabbage maggots, which lay their eggs at the foot of brassicas, is to put a 3–6in (7.5–15cm) collar around the base of the plant. Sticky traps can be helpful for small flying pests such as whiteflies. Pheronome-based traps, which contain an attractant to particular insects, are of mixed value. In some cases, such as with Japanese beetles, they may attract more pests to the garden than would be there otherwise.

Where possible, choose seed varieties that resist attack. Although mixing plants, for example onions and carrots, to confuse pests is often advocated, there is little evidence that it is effective. Similarly, plants with strong odors such as marigolds are believed to protect vegetables from pests.

Encouraging beneficial insects and other predators is a must for every vegetable gardener. Ladybugs, lacewings, predatory wasps, ground beetles, assassin bugs, and praying mantid all eat damaging insects, typically when the pests are in their larval stage. Birds, toads, and lizards are also voracious consumers of insect pests. Beneficial nematodes, applied to the soil, can counter weevils and other soil-dwelling pests.

The final remedy is to apply an insecticide. This should only be used as a last resort. Sprays with a physical action (such as horticultural oil, insecticidal soap, and fatty acids) will do least harm to beneficial insects. Of those that poison insects, ones with natural ingredients such as pyrethrum and *Bacillus thuringiensis* (Bt) are short-lived and have mild toxicity. If all else fails, a synthetic insecticide can be tried, but consult your local Cooperative Extension Service before taking this step to be sure that you are using a pesticide that is recommended for your pest problem and that is approved for use on edibles.

Dealing with slugs and snails

Gardeners in moist climates often feel that slugs and snails are their garden's worst enemies. Slug pellets and bait containing metaldehyde give good control, but they are not organic and some gardeners are uneasy about using them. Alternatively try iron phosphate powder. Copper barriers may be helpful for container-grown crops or raised beds; these are available as a kind of tape that you can use to entirely encircle the pot or bed. Diatomaceous earth, the sharp, jagged remains of microscopic creatures, can be sprinkled around vulnerable seedlings. Handpicking, especially in the evening, is a reliable method. Take a flashlight with you and a spray bottle filled with a mixture of vinegar and water, or sprinkle the pests with salt if you are squeamish about picking them up. (Don't spray vinegar or salt on your young vegetables, however.) Other remedies such as beer traps and half-grapefruit skin traps are unreliable, and you should expect to lose some of your crops.

Plant diseases

Diseases are caused by infections of bacteria, viruses, and especially fungi. Again, plants grown in good conditions are better able to fight off infection than those under stress. Where possible, choose plants that have some resistance to disease. For example, there are potatoes resistant to potato blight, peas that resist powdery mildew, and certain cabbage-family plants that resist clubroot. Good air circulation, crop rotation, and scrupulous garden hygiene can help keep diseases under control. Many have spores that overwinter in the soil and reinfect in spring.

A BEER TRAP can be used to attract and drown slugs.

Fungal diseases are greatly influenced by the weather. Powdery mildew, for example, is a fungal disease that leaves a powdery white or gray coating on leaves, stems, and fruit. It is more common in humid weather but needs dry leaves to develop.

Downy mildews also strike in wet spells. Younger leaves (such as spinach) are usually unaffected, as are lettuce hearts. Late blight (which also attacks tomatoes) is one of the most common diseases, but it needs the warmth and moisture that generally occur in wet spells in late summer and early fall. Fusarium wilt can live in the soil for many years; it affects the water-conducting tissues of plants and is most common in warm temperatures. Verticillium wilt can cause entire plants to turn brown and die.

When these fungal diseases are suspected, you can use fungicides such as sulfur, neem, or copper—in the form of copper sulfate or Bordeaux mixture—but be sure you have correctly identified the problem before resorting to chemical control.

Clubroot of brassicas and onion white rot cannot be treated with fungicides. Crop rotation (see page 39) is the first line of defense. Scrupulous destruction of infected material reduces the soil spore levels and, for clubroot, raising the pH of the soil with lime will reduce the severity of the disease.

Bacterial diseases such as potato scab and viruses such as tobacco mosaic virus cannot be treated with chemicals. Plant resistant varieties, practice crop rotation (especially of tomatoes and potatoes), and destroy infected plants.

Growing healthy plants

It is in your interest to make sure that your vegetables are well grown, as robust ones are not prone to disorders. Most vegetables are hungry crops, and should be fed with all the nutrients they need.

Fertilizers may be from natural (organic) or chemical (synthetic) sources. Natural fertilizers are obtained from the remains of living organisms and include blood meal, bone meal, fish emulsion, and animal manures such as bat guano. Typically, organic fertilizers are slower-acting than synthetic ones and contain lower amounts of nutrients, which can be determined by reading the N (nitrogen), P (phosphorus), and K (potassium) listed on the package label of all fertilizers.

Most apparent disorders in vegetable crops result from insufficient nitrogen, which affects the rate of plant growth and the yield. Some plants are heavy feeders, especially cabbage-family plants, Asian greens, leeks, potatoes, and spinach. Fruit-bearing vegetables initially need plenty of nitrogen to develop but then require more potassium as fruit is forming.

On sandy soils in particular, yellowing between the veins can be caused by lack of magnesium. Spraying the foliage with Epsom salts—8 tablespoons (120ml) to 2.5 gal. (10l) of water—should fix this. Chlorosis (a deficiency of iron) appears as yellowing leaves with thin, green veins. Checking soil pH and, if needed, adding sulfur to correct alkaline soils, can help. If not, apply chelated iron.

In the longer term, the remedy for many nutrient deficiencies is to increase the amount of soil amendments you apply; fertilizers really offer only a quick fix. Well-rotted compost and manures are best applied to the soil in fall or early spring.

Keeping weeds in check

Vegetables are quickly ruined if there is competition from weeds (see page 30), especially at the seedling stage. Weeds can easily take hold because vegetables are grown in widely spaced rows with areas of bare soil. Few vegetables cast enough shade to deter or block out weeds.

Most perennials weeds are easily removed by digging and hoeing, but those with persistent rhizomes, such as quack grass, horsetail, and bindweed, can be troublesome. If digging them out doesn't work, you can use a glyphosate herbicide when they are in full growth in summer.

Annual weeds, on the other hand, can easily persist among vegetables. They do this by shedding huge numbers of seeds—sometimes shooting them quite a distance. These seeds remain dormant, but through light and fluctuating temperatures they can 'sense' when they are near the surface and when conditions will probably result in good growth. Their ability to detect high-nitrogen levels ensures that they germinate at the right time.

Older gardens usually have large numbers of dormant weed seeds in the soil. In new gardens, this is much less of a problem, and if you are careful never to let weeds set seed you may avoid a weed problem indefinitely. Hoeing, raking, and hand-weeding to remove all weed seedlings amongst young crops is the first step. Keep checking that none survives to set seed, and if they appear, pull them out by hand. As weeds may continue to develop after being pulled up, they should be disposed of and not left lying around or added to the compost pile. Where weeds are numerous, some crops, including cucumbers, zucchini, garlic, onions, pumpkins, shallots, squash, corn, and tomatoes, can be grown through holes made in black plastic or other landscape fabric that covers the soil. A thick organic mulch will suppress weeds, otherwise.

PLANT THROUGH a black plastic mulch for low-maintenance weed control. The plastic also warms the soil.

Planning what to grow

Start with your favorite vegetables and those in which freshness counts, because you can't grow everything in your first vegetable garden. Tomatoes are on most gardeners' wish lists, as are salad greens, herbs, peas, and beans. After you gain confidence and get to know your local conditions, you can expand your repertoire to more exotic and challenging choices.

What crops to grow?

First of all, consider your needs. Do you want to grow crops that are readily available and cheap to buy? Do you want to experiment with exotic varieties, or those that are expensive to purchase from the supermarket (such as asparagus) or the ones that taste so much better eaten fresh (such as tomatoes)? Once you have made a list of what you like, decide how much time and effort your plants require. Tomatoes, for example, need staking and training, and they crop outdoors for only a few weeks in late summer, while beans crop abundantly over a long period. On the other hand, once established, asparagus almost looks after itself, and needs only routine annual maintenance in exchange for up to 10 years of abundant produce. If you prefer to avoid periods of intense work, select crops that require sowing, planting, thinning, and weeding over a long period so the work is spread out. Finally, consider the timing of the harvest. Make sure you plan crops that will be ready for picking all through the year.

Your climate is also hugely important when deciding what to grow in your vegetable garden. Learn about your climate zone, your first and last frost dates, and the length of your growing season (see page 26). In the South and West, you can easily grow heat-loving crops that you might have to fuss with in more northern areas.

Next, consider the available space, and your soil. If you haven't created raised beds filled with decent soil and have cold clay ground, then early crops will be tricky to grow because the soil is slow to warm up. Sandy soil, on the other hand, is good for producing early crops but can be dry and unproductive later. So if you have clay soil, consider raising early crops in containers; if you have light soil, try growing late-maturing crops in shallow trenches so that you can give them a good watering.

Above all, consult other local gardeners and your Cooperative Extension Service for help and advice on what kind of vegetables do well in your area.

Buying seeds and transplants

Having settled on what you would like to grow, check out the catalogs and websites of suppliers of vegetable seeds and transplants (see list of seed suppliers, page 219). Good local garden centers and nurseries will also offer a selection of seeds and can give you advice on planting and variety selection.

Seed packets usually have some kind of expiration date and, though it is true that old seeds are less likely to germinate than new ones, most are likely to be viable for several years, so keep the surplus.

A LARGE PLOT allows for plenty of scope, but still needs careful planning for year-round cropping.

Early spring

Clean start Double check that old crops and weeds have been removed. In warm climates, harvest the last of the winter crops.

Cover crops Dig under any remaining cover crops.

Weeds Hoe young annual weeds the moment they appear. It is worth preparing the seedbed just to encourage weed seeds to germinate so that you can kill them now. Once the surface weed seeds have germinated and been removed, few others will sprout and you should have a clean bed.

Raking As soon as the soil is dry enough, rake it level and create a fine tilth.

EARLY SPRING is the time to start sowing the first seeds in the ground.

Feeding Most vegetable gardens need feeding. Once the winter rains have stopped, spread a balanced fertilizer, according to package directions.

Compost Turn the compost and add the last of the winter crops to it.

Germination rates The soil is still often rather cold yet for good results. If in doubt, wait until weeds begin to emerge; when they germinate, so will your seed. It is better to wait a week or two than to sow in poor conditions.

Soil covering To keep the soil weed-free, moist, and ready for sowing, cover it with black plastic.

Containers Fill containers with potting mix, ready for sowing vegetables.

Sowing in the ground
In all but the coldest regions, fava beans, broccoli, early carrots, salad greens, onions, parsnips, peas, radishes, early beets, turnips, Asian greens, spinach, spring onions, turnips, and herbs such as parsley, dill, and chervil, can be sown where they are to grow. If frost threatens, cover the sown area with floating row covers or cloches.

Carrots and cabbage All carrot and cabbage-family crops benefit from floating row covers to exclude soil pests, cabbage worm moths, and carrot rust fly, which are on the wing in midspring.

Successive sowing Once the first sowings are a few inches tall, it is time, in many cases, to make further sowings to get a continuous supply of crops. Peas crop for about two weeks in summer; to cover the whole period, you can sow up to four times in spring for a regular supply. Because salad greens become unappetizing very quickly, sow seed little and often.

Watering With the soil still moist from winter, you seldom need to water in spring, but cold, dry winds can parch seedbeds, so light watering is helpful.

Thinning As soon as seedlings can be handled, start thinning them out where they are too thick and, where appropriate, transplant to fill gaps.

Indoors Ideally in a greenhouse, or indoors, sow warm-season crops such as beets, celeriac, celery, eggplant, sweet and chili peppers, tomatoes, and tender herbs (such as basil).

Crowns, tubers, and sets Plant asparagus crowns, rhubarb, tubers of early potatoes and sunchokes, onion sets, and shallots.

Ordering If you have decided not to raise your own plants from seed, order transplants from mail-order suppliers as early as possible. Or inquire at your local garden center to see what vegetable starts they will be stocking.

Poor results Failures will occur. If this happens, sow again with fresh seed. This is why you should always hold some seed in reserve.

Pests Control slugs, snails, and cutworms to protect seedlings. Nets will help exclude birds from seedbeds, where they can be very destructive.

Late spring

Second batch In northern regions, finish planting or sowing cool-season vegetables and continue to do successive sowings in milder regions.

Warm-season crops If the last frost date has passed in your area, sow seeds of warm-season crops in the ground. These include zucchini, cucumbers, beans, squash, pumpkins, and corn. If your last frost is still weeks away, sow indoors.

Successive sowings Remember that by the time these crops mature in later summer you will want less of them because warm-season crops, including beans and tomatoes, will then be ready. And in the heat of midsummer the likes of lettuce, spinach, and radishes won't stay in good condition for more than a few days and will quickly deteriorate.

Transplants Start transplants, including cabbage and cauliflower for fall, spring, and winter, and broccoli, in pots, cell packs, or flats.

Hardening off Many of the transplants sown earlier in spring will be ready to go outdoors after hardening off. Brussels sprouts, salad greens, broccoli, cauliflower, and cabbage in particular appreciate early planting out.

Greenhouse plants In short-summer areas, tender crops, such as eggplant, peppers, and tomatoes, can be planted in the greenhouse in containers or grow bags. Those for growing outside need a few more weeks under glass before being moved out.

Buying plants If you have not raised your own plants, garden centers are usually well stocked with cell packs of summer vegetables and herbs. The best ones sell quickly, and those that don't soon deteriorate under garden-center conditions, so buy as soon as possible even if you have to keep them in a cold frame or on a sunny windowsill until you are ready to plant.

Catching up There is still time to sow and plant any crops that should have been raised earlier in spring. They invariably catch up. In fact, with badly drained gardens in cold, exposed sites it is worth waiting until late spring; early sowing is too risky.

HOE AS YOU GO. Remove the heads of weeds as they emerge to give your young plants the best advantage.

Pest protection By now, seedlings should be pushing up well. Because carrots, parsnips, and cabbage-related crops are still vulnerable to pests, keep them covered with floating row covers for as long you can.

Support Peas need to be provided with sticks or mesh to climb up, and fava beans often require support from stakes and string.

Potatoes Pile up the earth around potatoes as shoots emerge to prevent the tubers from turning green.

Weeding Weed growth is at its peak. Hoeing on dry days reduces hand-weeding to a minimum.

Thinning Crops can be growing very fast, so thinning is a priority to avoid spoiling all the hard work you've already invested.

Smart and beautiful Vegetable plots should look good, so keep weeding and tidying edges and paths, and removing debris. Tidiness helps prevent accidents in the garden (leaving less around for you to lose or trip over), and deprives slugs and other pests of areas in which to shelter.

Irrigation systems Before plants get too big, check that all irrigation systems are working well. Replace any broken or damaged sprinkler heads and drip emitters. Make sure that there are no leaks or kinks in supply lines. Also check that hoses and sprinklers are in good repair.

Compost The compost pile or bin should be turned now, as temperatures are starting to rise. Use a garden fork or a special aerating tool.

Early summer

First crop The first ~~baby~~ ~~beets, fava beans~~, Asian greens, and peas are ready in early summer. Because their freshness declines with age, harvest immediately. This also frees the space for later crops.

Cut-and-come-again Salad greens can be harvested on a daily basis. Use scissors to clip off the new leaves and allow the crown to send up new leaves until temperatures get too hot.

Act early Long days, moist soil, warm temperatures, and a high sun give excellent growth. By late summer, conditions are much less favorable, so it makes sense to get everything planted and in full growth well before midsummer.

Keep planting As space becomes available, lightly cultivate the ground, add fertilizer, and sow or plant.

Outdoor sowing Zucchini, cucumbers, beans, pumpkins, squash, and corn can be sown outdoors in sheltered, mild regions, where they are to grow. Being sown in the ground, they develop superior roots systems which help them grow fast; they won't require as much watering as transplants.

Warm-season plants raised indoors In the coldest areas, these can also be planted out after hardening off. Eggplant, tomatoes, and peppers may still need extra protection outdoors if late frosts threaten.

Avoiding bolting By the end of early summer, crops that bolt if they encounter cold nights and/or short days can be sown. These include chicory, endive, fennel, and Asian greens.

Mounding Potatoes can be given their final mounds of earth around the stems.

Staking Canes and cages should be inserted to support taller crops such as climbing beans and tomatoes. Help guide peas and beans up their trellises by winding them around the supports. Tie indeterminate varieties of tomato loosely to their supports and pinch out the growing tips, to encourage bushy growth.

Weeding Weed growth should slow down in summer, but survivors of a spring weeding session

TIE UP tall plants such as tomatoes and pole beans.

will need pulling out before they can set flower and scatter their seed.

Feeding Giving crops more fertilizer is often worthwhile. Greedy cabbage-family plants, beets, celery, celeriac, and leeks benefit from supplementary feeding. Container-grown vegetables require a regular liquid feed.

Pest protection Take precautions against carrot rust fly. Insect pests, including aphids, caterpillars, beetles, and leaf miners, begin to cause damage in summer. Red spider mites thrive in hot, dry conditions, causing leaf loss on beans. If damage threatens to become significant, act promptly.

Diseases From midsummer, fungal diseases are a threat. In dry seasons, powdery mildew can be damaging to zucchini, cucumbers, peas, and squash. Watering to keep the soil moist can limit damage.

Wildlife There should be plenty of wildlife in the garden now. Attract pollinators by planting companion plants. Fill hummingbird feeders and keep birdbaths topped off with water. You may need to erect fences of chicken wire or plastic netting to keep deer and rabbits off your young crops.

Late summer

Frequent picking The more you pick zucchini, beans, and tomatoes, the more will be produced.

Herbs Keep removing the flowers on herbs to gain extra leaves.

Garlic, onions, and shallots The leaves will turn yellow and topple, and the produce can be gathered, dried, and stored.

Harvest quickly Clear spent crops promptly to eliminate pests and diseases, and to expose weeds.

Beans and tomatoes Train growth to supports. Continue to remove sideshoots and tops of vining tomatoes, and pinch off the tops of climbing beans as they reach the top of their support.

Cole crops Tall winter crops such as Brussels sprouts, kale, and collards can be made more secure using soil or a stake.

Extra crops As soil becomes free, sow quick-growing crops of beets, beans, kohlrabi, radishes, winter salad leaves, and turnips. Plant out seedlings raised in early summer. Also plant new potatoes for fall.

In warm areas Sow cool-season crops for fall and winter harvest, including cabbage and broccoli.

Pest and diseases Attacks often decrease in hot, dry weather, but caterpillars can be very damaging to cabbage-family crops if they are allowed to develop. Late blight remains a risk during wet periods. Affected potato crops should have their foliage removed and disposed of; the potatoes should be lifted two weeks later. Don't ignore carrot rust fly—it's still a potential problem and an infestation can ruin the roots.

Potatoes As soon as they are ready, store potatoes in a dark, cool place to avoid slug damage.

Green manures If you have spare time and space and the soil is sufficiently moist, sow cover crops such as legumes and mustard, to improve soil fertility and the workability of compacted ground.

PINCH OFF sideshoots and tops of tomatoes to concentrate growth on fruit development.

ENJOY THE HARVEST. Crops are best picked when they are young and sweet; this will also promote further cropping.

Fall

Plant In mild-winter areas, transplant cool-season crops such as arugula, chard, kale, salad greens, mustard greens, radishes, short-day onions, and spinach for late-fall harvests. Sow fast-growing Asian greens in the ground. Plant cabbage and broccoli for late winter or spring harvest.

Harvesting Remove the dying tops of pumpkins and squash, and cure the fruit in a warm, sunny place for a week or two before storing in a dry, frost-free site.

In warm areas Summer crops such as beans and tomatoes may continue to produce. Where harvests have slowed, pull up plants and compost them.

Protection In warmest areas, protect newly transplanted cool-season crops with shade cloth.

Root vegetables Most are best left in the ground and gathered as you need them, but in case a cold spell prevents harvesting or even damages them, a portion can be lifted and stored in a frost-free shed. Celeriac and turnips are especially frost sensitive.

Carrots left in the ground benefit from being insulated under straw or cardboard, with a plastic sheet to shed rain.

Clearing up Remove spent stems and debris to avoid harboring pests and diseases, and to expose slugs and other pests to the birds and weather.

Garlic Plant garlic cloves.

Leaves Keep fallen leaves off the vegetable garden, as pests use them as hiding places.

Mulch Apply an organic mulch over roots of perennial vegetables such as artichokes.

BOTTOM: TIDY AWAY old plants once they finish cropping and add them to the compost pile.

INSET: WORMERIES are good for small gardens that produce just small amounts of waste.

Winter

IMPROVE YOUR SOIL by adding plenty of well-rotted organic matter such as your own garden compost.

Harvest In cool areas, winter vegetables such as kale, broccoli, Brussels sprouts, and cabbage may be at the peak of their flavor after a few frosts.

Asparagus Leave ferns until they die back, then cut them down and mulch the beds.

Mulch Cover the crowns of perennials vegetable with a protective mulch.

Tools Clean and sharpen tools. Rub wooden handles with linseed oil. Clean and oil the metal on digging and cutting tools. Replace pruner blades if needed. Check irrigation systems and repair any broken or missing emitters and spray heads.

Wildlife Keep bird feeders full of winter food and make sure birdbaths are ice-free.

Planning and ordering In cold regions, draw up plans for next year's vegetable garden, and order seed packets. When seed arrives, store in cool, dark, dry conditions. Check you have sufficient canes, stakes, netting, and fertilizer. Keep in mind that mail-order suppliers and gardening clubs and societies may offer significant savings over retail outlets.

Pre-spring checks In late winter, dig over vacant ground, spread compost, incorporate cover crops, check the pH and amend if required. Keep weeding.

In mildest-winter regions Plant cool-season crops for late winter harvest. Beets, carrots, chard, kale, lettuce, peas, radishes, and spinach can be sown.

Raising under glass By late winter, there is an almost irresistible temptation to start sowing early crops under glass. Fava beans, Brussels sprouts, cabbage, broccoli, cauliflower, leeks, onions, peas, radishes, shallots, spinach, and turnips can be started indoors or in greenhouses.

Storage Check all vegetables in storage, such as cabbage and potatoes, for signs of rot or mold.

Growing your own

- Garlic, leeks, onions, and shallots
- Cabbage family
- Beans and peas
- Perennial vegetables
- Root and stem vegetables
- Salad vegetables
- Spinach and chard
- Squash, pumpkins, and corn
- Heat-loving vegetables

Garlic, leeks, onions, and shallots

With their spherical shape and layers of flesh sheathed in a golden or crimson skin, onions are a masterpiece of natural design. Gentle cooking brings out the sweet, aromatic taste of shallots—ideal for adding flavor to sauces and side dishes. Garlic, whose juicy, fresh bulbs are the most flavorful of all, is an essential element of dishes from pasta sauces to salad dressings. And it's an easy crop, demanding little effort to grow and suffering from few problems. Leeks, a wonderfully tasty addition to soups and stews, can be harvested all through winter and early spring in many areas.

Garlic

Few crops are as easy and satisfying to grow as garlic. Each separate clove planted in the ground will yield, just a few months later, a great clump of 20 or more cloves. Despite its associations with Mediterranean and Asian cuisine, garlic is perfectly suited to cultivation as a cool-season crop in all except the coldest zones. Cultivated culinary garlic must have summer sun. The more it gets, the faster it develops and the chunkier the bulbs grow.

Although supermarket garlic can be planted, it's best to buy garlic bulbs, or sets, from a nursery or garden center. Nurseries categorize garlic in several ways.

Softneck, or artichoke, types have up to 20 small cloves per bulb. These are the kind most often sold at the market or grocery store. They are easy to grow and store well. Silverskin varieties are smaller softneck garlic; they store the longest.

Hardneck types—also called purple-striped, porcelain, or rocambole garlic—have thicker, purple and white bulb wrappings than softneck garlic. Hardneck types grow well in colder areas but do not store as long as softnecks.

GARLIC BULBS can spring up unexpectedly if left in the ground from a previous crop. Bees love the flowers.

Elephant garlic (*Allium ampeloprasum*) produces impressively large bulbs, up to twice the size of other types. The flavor, however, is typically mild.

The process of planting garlic could not be simpler. Lower individual cloves into holes deep enough to just hide their tips, and cover with soil, patting gently. This encourages roots to grow rapidly and, at this stage of any bulb's existence, that is the most important task; only when a good root system has developed can nutrients and water be transported into the bulb.

Green, or spring, garlic is simply garlic that has been lifted while it is still growing, before the cloves have started to mature and the leaves are still green. Just lift a whole bulb, separate a few cloves, and, when you are ready to use it, squeeze the clove out of its pappy covering, new and pristine. It has a much milder flavor than stored garlic, and a creamier texture. Roast it whole with other vegetables or bake it and then blend into dips based on chickpeas or puréed beans.

Garlic's health-giving and healing properties have been recognized for millennia, and there are references to its medicinal properties in texts from Roman, Egyptian, and other ancient civilizations. But whether you are growing it for health or for the kitchen, from summer until the end of fall after it has been lifted it retains its fresh, creamy quality. It will last beyond that, depending on the variety, but the flavor will change as the cloves age, becoming stronger and harder. Garlic is prone to rot when stored if it is not sufficiently dried or if it is bruised, so handle the bulbs gently.

Garlic

Allium sativum

Garlic is one of the oldest and most valued of plants. In herbal medicine, a host of ailments are said to be curable by garlic—and so potent are its properties that the ancients believed it had supernatural powers. It is extremely easy to grow, and produces so many fat, juicy bulbs that it will transform your cooking, and you won't ever want to go back to supermarket garlic.

Where to grow

Because warmth is needed to ripen the bulbs, garlic must be grown in a sunny site, in rich soil that is moisture-retentive but with good drainage.

Planting cloves

In most areas, garlic can be planted in fall, a few weeks before the first frost, for an early summer harvest. In the South, plant from November through January. In cooler areas, try planting in early spring, as soon as the soil can be worked, for a fall harvest. If your soil does not drain well, amend it with plenty of organic matter or make a raised ridge of soil to plant on. Just before planting, thoroughly rake the top few inches of soil and incorporate a balanced fertilizer. Gently split the bulb into individual cloves, and use a trowel to plant each one with the pointed end up, spaced in rows 14–18in. (35–45cm) apart with 4–6in. (10–15cm) between cloves. The tips of the cloves should be hidden just below the surface. (Plant elephant garlic with the tips about 2in. (5cm) below the soil surface.) Cover with soil, patting gently.

PLANT EACH GARLIC CLOVE in the ground about an inch deep with its pointed tip up and just below the surface.

Caring for the crop

For the first month or so after planting, regularly check the garlic bed for signs of bird or rodent

Selected varieties

California Late
This popular variety is grown commercially around Gilroy, California, the 'Garlic Capital of America.' A softneck garlic, its skin has a purple or pink hue and it stores well.

Spanish Roja
An heirloom variety with a strong, spicy flavor; good for cold regions. The medium-sized bulbs store well and the cloves are easy to peel.

WHEN HARVESTING GARLIC, cut off the stems of the bulbs unless you plan to braid them together, to hang up.

ONCE THE BULBS have dried out, you can gently split some of the individual cloves apart for planting your next crop.

damage; any uprooted bulbs need to be pushed back into the soil, before they dry out. Because garlic has shallow roots and little foliage cover, weeds quickly take root. Hoe regularly to remove weeds, taking care not to damage the garlic bulbs. In cold areas, cover with several inches of mulch during winter. In spring and early summer, an occasional thorough watering during dry spells will improve yields. Don't water once the bulbs are large and well formed, because this could encourage rotting.

At harvest time

Varieties mature from late spring to late summer, and plants are ready to harvest when the stems begin to yellow and bend over. Use a fork to loosen the bulbs from the soil, and then spread them out in the sun to dry, ideally on chicken wire or hardware cloth so that the air can circulate around them. Keep them dry.

Storing and cooking tips

To store bulbs, gently knock off the dry soil and place on a rack, or braid the stems to form a rope of bulbs. Although a garlic rope in the kitchen makes an attractive decoration, a cool, dry shed or garage is by far the best place for storage. Garlic can be stored for months but check the bulbs occasionally for rot or mold.

Garlic wrapped in foil with a few drops of olive oil can be cooked on the barbecue or roasted in the oven. Squeeze the soft contents of each clove out of the papery wrapping onto a piece of bread, sprinkle on some salt, and enjoy. When adding garlic to a stir-fry, don't let it burn in hot oil because it becomes bitter.

Pests and diseases

Disease is unlikely in good growing conditions, but mold or rust may occur if drainage is poor. Dig up and discard any badly affected bulbs; add organic matter to the soil to improve drainage.

If the foliage yellows and wilts, look for the fluffy, white growths of pink or white rot on the bulbs. Throw out any infected ones, and avoid growing garlic or onions in the same site again for several years, to give the diseases time to die out.

GREEN GARLIC is harvested before the bulb has formed into individual cloves. The flavor is still recognizably garlic, but milder, and it becomes sweeter with cooking.

Leeks _Allium porrum_

Grown for its stemlike shanks, the leek is a versatile and useful vegetable that's easy to grow in the right soil conditions. But 'easy' doesn't mean low maintenance: Leeks need transplanting and hilling or blanching. They may take up space in the vegetable garden for a long time, but their big advantage is that they can be harvested over a long period—from fall to late winter.

Where to grow

Leeks do best in a sunny site on any reasonable soil that doesn't become waterlogged in winter, although the ideal soil is rich and moisture-retentive. In sandy or well-drained soils add plenty of well-composted organic matter, to enrich the soil. Prepare the planting bed in fall or winter, then rake over before planting, and incorporate some balanced fertilizer. Set out leeks in furrows so you can gradually mound the soil around them as they grow. Do this over a period of time rather than all at once. A single large mound of soil on young plants can lead to rot rather than blanching.

Sowing and planting

Leeks are a transplanted crop that can be sown in containers or in a seedbed before being moved to their final growing position. They are easy to raise from seed, but if you miss the sowing time or don't have a place to grow seedlings, buy transplants at the garden center. Leeks should be set in the ground after the last frost date in your area or, in warmer zones, you can also plant in fall for a spring crop.

If you are growing leeks from seed, start them about six weeks before spring planting, sowing them in cell packs in a greenhouse or heated potting shed. Thin

ABOVE: AFTER TRANSPLANTING, water the young leek plants thoroughly. Repeat during long, dry spells—but sparingly.

LEFT: HOE YOUR LEEK bed regularly to keep the weeds at bay.

the seedlings so they are spaced about 2in. (5cm) apart, and continue growing them under cover before hardening them off in a cold frame for planting out in early spring.

Alternatively, sow directly outside in early spring. Rake the soil to a fine tilth and sow thinly in furrows 8in. (20cm) apart and ½in. (1cm) deep.

The time to transplant is when the young leeks are about pencil thick. Water thoroughly the day before transplanting and lift using a fork. Make wide, deep holes—6in. (15cm) deep and 2in. (5cm) across—and drop a single seedling in each. Don't backfill with soil, but simply fill each hole with water to settle the soil around the roots.

Selected varieties

Ashton
Dark green leaves on an upright plant that grows strongly. Pure white medium stems are easy to peel.

Tadorna
Frost-tolerant variety that is good for cold regions. Has blue-green stems that can be blanched to 8in. (20cm). Easy to clean.

Pancho
A good-quality, summer leek with 6in. (15cm) stems. Consistent and tasty producer.

Caring for the crop

Planting leeks in deep holes will produce white shafts of a good length, but for even longer ones 'hill up' by gradually mounding soil around the stems during the growing season. This process, known as blanching, makes the stems white and mild. Continue to weed regularly as the plants grow. During long, dry spells, water thoroughly but sparingly—a good soaking every 10 days will do. If growth slows in summer, feed lightly with a nitrogen-rich fertilizer.

If the growth of leeks is disrupted by a sudden change in temperature or lack of moisture, they may bolt, forming a typical allium flower. If this happens, you should pull up the bolted plants and put them in the compost pile. Small bulbils may appear in the flowerheads, and you can try planting these for harvesting later in the season.

At harvest time

Leeks are simple to harvest; just lift them as required when the stems are sufficiently thick, and trim the leaves and roots. Although 'baby' leeks for salads can be pulled from early summer, it's more usual to wait for the stems to thicken to ensure a harvest of good-sized plants from late summer for soups, casseroles, and other dishes.

Storing and cooking tips

Wash leeks thoroughly by slicing in half lengthwise and holding them upside-down under running water so any dirt washes out easily. Take care when cooking leeks in hot oil: Like garlic, they can burn easily and become bitter. Cook them gently until they are soft and translucent.

You can keep leeks for a week in the refrigerator. If you have a bumper crop, leave some of them in the ground until you are ready to harvest.

Pests and diseases

Leek rust, seen as orange pustules, is a disease that may occur in damp weather. When harvesting leeks, make sure that you dispose of affected plants (do not compost them) and, in future, look for varieties that have some resistance to this disease.

Onions and shallots
Allium cepa and A.c. aggregatum

In the kitchen, onions are essential for dishes ranging from pasta sauces to soups to burgers. Shallots are more delicate in flavor and perhaps less well known, but they are equally versatile. In the garden, both require similar conditions, although shallots grow to form clusters of small bulbs rather than a single large bulb. Scallions, also called spring or bunching onions, are simply white onions that are harvested before the bulb has developed.

Types of onions

Correct variety selection is essential for onions, which form bulbs in response to the number of daylight hours. Suppliers usually classify onions as short, intermediate, or long, depending on the day length required. Generally, short-day varieties are suitable for southern gardens and long-day onions suit northern zones. In mild-winter areas, short-day varieties can also be planted in fall for spring harvest. Planting time is also important. If planted too early, onions may bolt or fail to form bulbs. A knowledgeable local nursery, a good seed catalog, or your local Cooperative Extension Service can advise on suitable varieties for your region, as well as the best time to plant.

Where to grow

Onions need cool conditions following planting and then hot, dry weather when the bulbs are maturing. Grow onions in a sunny, sheltered site in soil that is moisture-retentive but has good drainage. Onions like fertile, well-drained soil that is not too acidic; if a soil test shows a pH of less than 6, grow in raised beds with a suitable planting mix. The soil should be free of rocks and soil clumps, so use a rake to create a fine, smooth texture. Ideally, you should avoid growing onions on the same site every year, as pests and diseases can build up in the soil.

Sowing and planting

Onions and shallots can be grown from seed or transplants, but the easiest and quickest way to raise them is by planting sets, or baby onions. These are available typically without variety names but may just be listed as red, white, or yellow onions. They grow rapidly and are particularly useful when the growing season is short. If you have grown onions successfully from sets for a few years, you may then want to try growing from seed, as more varieties are offered through seed catalogs.

In colder zones, onion sets are usually planted in early spring a few weeks before the last frost date. In the South and warmest regions of the West, plant onion sets in fall. Prepare the soil by adding organic

THE BULBS begin to swell during early summer. It is essential to keep them well watered and free from weeds at this stage in the plants' development.

matter such as compost and some balanced fertilizer. Mark out rows 10–12in. (25–30cm) apart, and push the sets into the soil with 3–4in. (7.5–10cm) between each one, the pointed end up and the tip just visible. Shallots need earlier planting and wider spacing between plants—6in. (15cm).

In mild regions, onions and shallots can also be grown from seed sown in spring, as soon as the soil is workable, to give a late summer crop, or in late summer for an early summer crop the following year. Sow in rows 12in. (30cm) apart, and thin to the above spacings. Or sow indoors in late winter and plant out the young seedlings in spring when the soil can be worked.

FRESHLY HARVESTED SHALLOTS should be separated into their individual bulbs and laid out in the sun to dry. The roots and shoots will shrivel up and can be trimmed off before storing.

Selected varieties (onions)

Milestone
Extra large, globe-shaped, long-day onion with beautiful skin. Good for medium-term storage. Resistant to bolting.

Ruby Ring
Extra hard, firm, globe-shaped bulbs with red skins and firm, red and white skin. Long storage life.

Tokyo Long White
A Japanese bunching type onion with 12in. (30cm), white stalks and a sweet, mild flavor.

Verrazano
Bronze-colored, disease-resistant, medium bulbs with firm skins. Has average storage.

Walla Walla
A favorite sweet variety with large, flattened, ultra-mild, sweet bulbs. Originally a short-day onion but has been bred so it can be widely planted in the US.

Redwing
Uniform, large onions that mature quite late in the season with deep red color and a moderately pungent flavor. Can be stored for months. Long-day variety.

1 ONIONS AND SHALLOTS can be lifted as soon as you need them, although they store better if allowed to die back first.

2 PUSH A GARDEN FORK under the plants and lever the soil up as you pull the bulb out of the ground by its neck.

3 LEAVE BULBS to dry out in the sun or take them directly to the kitchen for immediate use.

Caring for the crop

Onions and shallots are shallow rooting, and they should be weeded regularly to avoid competition for water and food.

At harvest time

Both onions and shallots are ready to harvest when the leaves begin to yellow. Use a fork to loosen the bulbs from the soil, and then spread the bulbs out in

ONIONS CAN BE PICKED as scallions from the time they are about pencil size. They have a much milder flavor than fully grown bulbs and can be added raw to salads and soups.

the sun to dry, ideally on chicken wire or hardware cloth above the ground so that air can circulate around them. Separate shallots into individual bulbs.

Storing and cooking tips

Once onions and shallots are thoroughly dry, gently knock off any loose soil and leaves, and then keep in a cool, dry shed or garage. At this stage the skins are brown and papery, and the remnants of stems and leaves make a convenient tool for bunching or braiding onions, so they can be hung in a cool, dry place.

In the kitchen, shallots can be used raw, in salads, or as a garnish, thinly sliced with a very sharp knife. They should always be cut in this way, because if shallots are chopped roughly they can get bruised at the edges and lose some of their flavor. Shallots are delicious baked whole, glazed with balsamic vinegar and oil or butter with a pinch of sugar, and can be added to many sauces. The taste of shallots is unique—intense, sweet, and aromatic, making them especially popular for cooking in vegetable stews, but they are never acrid in the way that onions and stored garlic can be.

THE IDEAL WAY to dry bulbs is to lay them out in the sun, either on chicken wire or hardware cloth raised above the ground so that air can circulate while they dry.

BULBS SHOWING SIGNS of damage or disease must not be stored. Either put them aside for immediate use, or discard or destroy them if the damage is bad.

Pests and diseases

Birds or frost can lift the bulbs out of the soil. Floating row covers placed over newly planted onions can help protect them from pests such as onion maggots. Control thrips by encouraging beneficial, insects such as lacewings, and maintaining good cultural practices.

Diseases should be minimal given good growing conditions and crop rotation, but onion downy mildew or root rot can strike during wet weather. Picking off affected leaves can sometimes save the crop but they won't keep as long as uninfected bulbs. If the foliage turns yellow and wilts, look for the symptoms of rot on the bulbs. Destroy any infected ones, and avoid growing onions and garlic on the same site for several years. If problems persist, look for resistant varieties. Rotating the crop site each year also avoids the buildup of nematodes.

GROWING SCALLIONS

Scallions take only 10–12 weeks to grow, so you can make successive small sowings through spring and summer. In the mildest regions, you can also sow through fall and winter. Scatter the seeds directly in rows 6in. (15cm) apart, spacing the seeds ½in. (1cm) apart. As they grow, apply a nitrogen-rich fertilizer every few weeks. Aim to keep the soil evenly moist throughout the growing season; regular, shallow sprinkler irrigation is best. Control weeds by pulling them by hand. Harvest the scallions when the white shank is ¼–¾in. (0.5–2cm) in diameter. Both the shank and the green foliage can be eaten raw in salads or cooked in soups and stir-fries.

Selected varieties (shallots)

Longor
Robust flavor and long storage ability characterize this Jersey long-type shallot.

Ambition
A traditional, reddish, globe-shaped French shallot with large bulbs and a delicate flavor.

Cabbage family

Members of the cabbage family are commonly known to vegetable growers as cole crops, or brassicas. They are among the most useful and healthful of all vegetable crops, providing a fresh, nutritious harvest year-round, and they're particularly welcome in the colder months of the year, when there is little else available in the garden. This group includes favorite vegetables such as cabbage and Brussels sprouts along with traditional southern ones such as collard greens, as well as a host of new choices from Asia such as mizuna, bok choy, and spicy mustards.

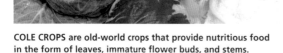

COLE CROPS are old-world crops that provide nutritious food in the form of leaves, immature flower buds, and stems.

Types of cole crops

Cabbage-family plants have been cultivated in North America since the time of the earliest explorers; in 1542, the French explorer Jacques Cartier planted cabbage in one of the first settlements in Quebec. In the United States, cabbage was a staple of colonial gardens from the 1660's. As cool-season crops, most are planted in early spring for harvest before the heat of summer, but in mild-winter zones, you can plant many cole crops in fall for a winter harvest. Because the time to maturity and heat-tolerance of these plants vary, you should check with your local Cooperative Extension Service for recommendations on planting times in your area.

If your impression of this family of vegetables is that they provide only boiled cabbage or coleslaw, think again. Cabbage exists in many guises, but all have their leaves formed into heads, whereas broccoli and cauliflower are grown for their immature flower buds—the Italian word *broccoli* means 'little sprouts.' Both the leaves and the loose flowerheads of broccoli raab, also called rapini, are edible. Other greens, such as kale and collards, have loose leaves much like lettuce. True cauliflower bear the characteristic, creamy white heads commonly known as curds. There are also varieties that bear purple, lime-green, and even orange heads. Asian greens are harvested when young, the leaves, stems, and immature flower shoots being eaten in salads, steamed, or stir-fried. Many have a spicy or mustardlike flavor that adds punch to soups and side dishes.

REGULARLY HOE and hand-weed to keep cole crops free of competing weeds. Take care not to damage the vulnerable stems or shallow roots.

Where to grow

Cole crops love a sunny spot and thrive on firm, rich soil improved with generous quantities of organic matter such as well-composted manure or garden compost. Whenever possible, prepare the soil in fall, giving it time to consolidate over winter. Before transplanting young seedlings onto the site, firm the soil by stepping along its entire surface on your heels, then rake it flat. Avoid digging at this stage. Inadequate soil anchorage is often the reason for poor development of the crop. As the plants develop, support any unstable stems with a 2 x 1in. (5 x 2.5cm) wooden stake.

Sowing and planting

Traditionally, cole crop plants were raised in seedbeds or cold frames for later transplanting to their final positions. This is because sowing each crop at its final spacing would take up a great deal of room early in the growing season when the ground could be used for fast-maturing crops such as lettuce. If you have the room, however, plants can be sown in place or grown from purchased transplants. Although many nurseries and garden centers offer young plants ready for planting in their final positions, cole crops are easily raised from seed. Sowing them indoors also protects the young seedlings from pests, such as slugs and snails, and allows the root systems to become extensive enough to resist diseases that can kill seedlings in the garden.

Fill a propagation tray or individual cell packs with good-quality potting mix and lightly firm down the surface of the soil. Then sow two or three seeds per cell, or sprinkle seed on the soil surface, and lightly cover with mix. Keep the seedlings moist and thin them to one plant per cell by nipping out the others with your fingertips. They can be transplanted into larger pots before being planted out.

Pests and diseases

A number of pests and diseases can affect cabbage-family plants, and they're often easier to prevent than cure. Crop rotation, good soil preparation, and keeping a watchful eye on growing plants will lessen the likelihood of many problems. Cole crops need good amounts of space between the individual plants to allow air to circulate around them, which helps to prevent diseases from taking hold. For the same reason, it is also important to remove weeds and any old, withered foliage as they appear.

Crop rotation reduces the buildup of soilborne diseases and disorders; cole crops shouldn't be grown in the same position within two or three years. A traditional crop rotation technique is to plant cole crops where beans and peas have recently been grown, as plants in the cabbage family like the nitrogen-rich soil left after a few season of legumes. Avoid acidic soil, which promotes the fungal disease clubroot. Liming the soil to raise its pH, providing good drainage, for instance, by using raised beds, and growing resistant varieties can help reduce clubroot.

A number of pests attack cabbage-family plants, including cabbage loopers, cabbageworms, cabbage maggots, and flea beetles. If your cabbage seem to be wilting and the cause is not drought-related, dig up a damaged plant and examine the roots. If they have been chewed and you see tunnels in the crown, the cause is probably cabbage maggots. Floating row covers set over young plants can prevent flying insects from laying eggs on or near the plants, thus reducing the number of caterpillars and maggots that hatch from those eggs. Row covers can also help to keep flea beetles off the crop. Individual collars around young plants can protect them from slugs, snails, and cutworms. Aster yellows is a disease spread by leafhoppers; controlling the pests and destroying affected plants can prevent recurrence.

PROTECTIVE COVERINGS of lightweight floating row covers keep many common pests at bay—such as flea beetles, or the butterflies that lay eggs that hatch into leaf-eating caterpillars such as cabbageworms.

BIRD-PROOF NETTING should be put in place if birds are a problem in your garden. Watering can be done in the usual way, but weeding is made more difficult as the nets will need to be removed.

Broccoli and cauliflower

Broccoli and cauliflower are valued for their heads of tightly gathered, immature flowers, which are harvested before they start opening into individual buds. Between them they offer a harvest that can last for months, although broccoli is a more useful and enduring crop, because it continues to produce shoots after the main head has been harvested.

Broccoli is a cool-season crop, and it will bolt if temperatures rise, so plant it to mature when temperatures are cool. Varieties of sprouting broccoli are typically very hardy and can stand for months right through the cold weather. Broccoli raab is a fast-growing crop with smaller florets. The leaves, stems, and florets are all edible.

Cauliflower is completely different. It has a reputation for being tricky to grow, but time spent on soil preparation and providing plenty of water throughout the growing season will reap rewards. It needs a long, cool season to grow and can be damaged by hard frost, hot sun, and rising temperatures. If it grows well, there is nothing

PLANTED IN THE SPRING or early summer, broccoli may stand in the ground for many months, so

more rewarding than folding back the fresh green leaves, to reveal tight, white curds, and carrying the cauliflower triumphantly back to the kitchen. Colored varieties of cauliflower make lively additions to the vegetable garden. 'Romanesco' cauliflower has flower buds that form peaked chartreuse spirals; it is sometimes listed as a broccoli or even a 'broccoflower' in seed catalogs.

Crop rotation probably benefits cole crops more than any other vegetable. If you can grow them where legumes, such as peas and beans, were growing the previous year, the cole crops will benefit considerably. When planting any cabbage-family plants, make sure that the ground is firm. Although walking on the soil destroys its structure, brassicas need firm planting, so don't be afraid to use your feet when planting, to press the soil around the base of the stems. If the plants work loose they will develop poor root systems and leaf structure so that they flower prematurely and produce small, poor-quality heads. Head production can also be affected by low temperatures or inconsistent watering.

Broccoli

Brassica oleracea

The large, green heads of broccoli are familiar vegetables in the kitchen, although the more ornamental, white, lime-green, and purple varieties are much less common. Broccoli raab enjoys similar conditions but is less prone to pests and is easier to grow than regular broccoli. Sprouting broccoli produces small, purple, green, or white florets as long as temperatures remain moderate.

Where to grow

Broccoli and broccoli raab (*Brassica rapa* subsp. *rapa*) like full sun and a rich soil amended with generous quantities of well-rotted organic matter. Check that the soil is firm and has a pH of 6.5–7.5 (see page 21).

Sowing and planting

Young broccoli plants are available in early spring from garden centers and nurseries and can be planted in the garden about two weeks before the last frost date. Broccoli is easily raised from seed, and you can sow it in place, or indoors in trays or cell packs 4–6 weeks before the last frost date for your area. For a fall crop, sow in midsummer. Broccoli raab is best sown directly where it is to grow. Thoroughly prepare the site by forking over the soil and raking the surface to produce a fine, crumbly texture.

Stretch a length of string as a guide, and draw out a straight, ½in. (1cm) deep furrow by dragging a hoe or broom handle along the line. If the bottom of the furrow is dry, lightly water first. Sprinkle the seed thinly along its length, and cover with soil, which should be gently firmed by lightly patting down. The seedlings should appear in 7–12 days.

Thin out seedlings so that they are 12–18in. (30–45cm) apart. Weed regularly, either by hand or by carefully hoeing between the lines. Slugs and snails will quickly devour seedlings, so lay traps or handpick the pests at dusk, when they are most active.

Leave 12–18in. (30–45cm) between plants and rows. The wide spacing will ensure good air circulation around the plants and help prevent diseases. When transplanting young plants, dig a hole big enough to accommodate the roots and deep enough for the lowest leaves to be near the soil surface. Cover the young crop with floating row covers to protect it from flying pests.

Caring for the crop

As the plants develop, make sure they never get dry. Water deeply and regularly, as broccoli needs consistent moisture to produce good flowering heads. If downy mildew is a problem in your garden, use drip irrigation or water so that the foliage does not get wet, thereby reducing the likelihood of disease.

Reduce competition for moisture and nutrients by carefully hoeing off the tops of weeds around the plants the moment they appear.

At harvest time

All types of broccoli should be picked when the flower shoots are well developed, but before the yellow flowers actually open. Picking regularly and early will encourage sideshoot formation for further harvests.

BROCCOLI HEADS are ready to cut when the buds are well developed but before the flowers actually open. Regular picking encourages more cropping.

Cut the florets from the plant using a sharp knife or pruners, cutting the central spear 6–8in. (15–20cm) below the head; when sideshoots grow, harvest them too, as regular picking can extend the cropping time for up to eight weeks. Cut broccoli raab shoots when they are 4–5in. (10–12cm) long, before the flower buds have opened.

Storing and cooking tips

Broccoli is virtually fat-free and packed with vitamins C and E, fiber, calcium, and iron—provided the florets are not overcooked. Florets will stay fresh in the refrigerator for about three days, and they also freeze well. Stir-fry or lightly steam them for maximum nutrients and flavor.

For sprouting broccoli, cook the thickest parts of the stems first to soften them, then cook the remaining florets. Broccoli raab can be chopped into pieces— stem, leaves, and flowers—and steamed or stir-fried.

Pests and diseases

Regularly check plants for signs of caterpillars and pick any off or use floating row covers to prevent butterflies from laying eggs. Remove any yellowing or fallen leaves, and dispose of them to prevent the spread of fungal diseases. Protect from slugs, snails, and cutworms by handpicking and by using individual plant collars. Resistant varieties can be planted if leaf spot, black rot, and downy mildew are persistent problems in the garden.

Selected varieties

Arcadia
Firm, small, dark green heads grow to 8in. (20cm) across. Large plants that have some disease resistance and some frost tolerance.

Belstar
Widely adapted broccoli with a large domed head and blue-green color.

Fiesta
High-yielding variety with bright green, domed heads of consistent quality. Tolerates both hot and cold temperatures; can be grown for spring and fall harvests.

Spring Raab
Large plants that can be grown in a range of climates and are suitable for overwintering in mild-winter areas.

Rudolph
A purple-sprouting variety that can be planted in summer for a good winter harvest. Produces lots of small purple heads.

Happy Rich
A green sprouting broccoli with jumbo-sized, green florets. Develops strong, uniform growth.

Brussels sprouts *Brassica oleracea*

Brussels sprouts are a sweet delicacy when cooked fresh from the garden. The sprouts stay ready to pick on their stems for some time and can be picked over a three-month period. By carefully selecting the right varieties, it is possible to enjoy fresh Brussels sprouts from early fall until spring, but frost—though not a hard freeze—really does bring out the best in them.

Where to grow

For a good crop of Brussels sprouts ideally you need a firm soil with a pH of 6–7.5, but they really aren't too fussy. Choose a sunny site with shelter from high winds to avoid the risk of this top-heavy crop being blown over. If in doubt, support plants with a bamboo or wooden stake to keep them upright.

Brussels sprouts are big plants, and they tend to be hungry and thirsty, so you need to have plenty of room if you are going to grow them. However, you can expect a fairly good harvest from just four or five plants.

Prepare the soil in fall by digging in generous quantities of organic matter such as well-composted manure or garden compost. This advance preparation helps ensure that the soil has consolidated by planting time. Avoid digging over the soil shortly before planting.

Sowing and planting

Brussels sprouts do not produce a crop for many months and their flavor is improved by light frosts. In cold-winter climates, plant transplants or sow in place in midsummer. In mild-winter climates, wait until late summer or fall. Young plants can be raised from seed started in spring. Sow seed in cell packs or trays about ½in. (1cm) deep. After three weeks, pick out the seedlings and put them into individual 3in. (7.5cm) pots. Let the roots fill the pots before planting them out in the garden. Large, healthy transplants are best able to resist clubroot disease.

Plant the seedlings so that the soil is level with the first set of true leaves. Allow 30in. (75cm) between the plants and the rows. Resist the temptation to

WHEN TRANSPLANTING the seedlings, make sure that you allow enough space around them for air to circulate over the leaves as this will help to prevent fungal diseases.

squeeze in more plants, because the distance makes picking easier and the improved air circulation will help to prevent fungal diseases.

Caring for the crop

Water the crop regularly while it is establishing and during dry spells. Also reduce competition for moisture and nutrients by regularly hoeing off weeds around the plants. Sprinkle nitrogen-rich fertilizer around plants that are not growing well. In hot weather, mulch around Brussels sprouts to keep the roots cool. Remove lower leaves as they dry out and start to turn yellow.

At harvest time

The first early varieties of Brussels sprouts are ready from early fall, although many gardeners wait until after the first hard frosts, which make sprouts taste sweeter. Select only firm sprouts, which should be about the size of a walnut, and snap them off or remove with a sharp knife. Start from the bottom and work up, removing a few from each plant at a time. Once the entire stem has been cleared, the leafy top can be harvested and cooked like cabbage.

Storing and cooking tips

Brussels sprouts are high in vitamin K, vitamin C, folate, vitamin A, and are a good source of fiber. They are also full of antioxidants. Freshly harvested sprouts should also be lightly cooked to obtain maximum crispness, flavor, and color. Brussels sprouts are usually boiled or steamed whole.

Because Brussels sprouts do not store well, unlike cabbage, it is best to leave them on the plant and pick as required. You can store sprouts, untrimmed and unwashed, in the fridge for a week or two at most. If there's a bumper crop, you can freeze some for later use. To freeze Brussels sprouts, first choose firm, healthy sprouts. Remove any brown or yellow leaves and wash them well. Heat a large pot of water to boiling and blanch the sprouts for 3–5 minutes. Cool off the sprouts immediately in icy water. Bag and put in the freezer. After freezing, sprouts require only a brief boiling or they can become mushy.

Pests and diseases

Protect Brussels sprouts from some of the more damaging insects with floating row covers—cabbage whitefly and caterpillars can be especially difficult to control. Blast aphids with a strong jet of water from the hose. Individual collars around the base of each

SUPPORT YOUNG BRUSSELS SPROUTS plants with a stake to ensure that they grow upright.

plant can protect from cabbage maggots and cutworms. Birds may feed on the plants; if so, cover with netting.

Like all cole crops, Brussels sprouts are subject to diseases, including clubroot, fusarium yellows, and stem and root rots. The best way to avoid infection is by rotating your crops and growing sprouts in a different bed every two or three years. Resistant varieties are available.

Selected varieties

Purple Red Bull
An unusual and attractive red variety with maroon leaves and dark red sprouts. The sprouts keep their color when cooked and are sweet, though plants are not as vigorous as green varieties.

Oliver
A dwarf cultivar with well-spaced sprouts. Grows to about 30in. (75cm) and is relatively trouble-free. Sprouts are small and bright green.

Cabbage

Brassica oleracea

Rather undeservedly, cabbage have a reputation for being uninteresting, but once you start to grow your own you will learn to love their diversity. The different sizes, shapes, and colors are a joy to behold, and they will feed you year-round. In the kitchen, you can use them raw in salads or coleslaw, as ingredients in soup, boiled or steamed in the traditional way, or lightly braised.

Types of cabbage

Many gardeners reject growing cabbage because they take up a lot of space—but a patch of cabbage can be both attractive and productive. Cabbage is totally hardy, and can face cold and exposure. It comes in every hue of green and purple, with textures ranging from smooth and tightly layered to open and crunchy with wonderfully puckered leaves. It can be spherical, pointed, or open and flat. And you can grow it for picking in every season. In the kitchen, cabbage can be double-cooked and fermented, as in sauerkraut, or thinly sliced and mixed with other raw vegetables for making coleslaw. It can be steamed briefly, or gently stewed with finely chopped garlic and onions, or used in stews and soups.

There are many varieties of cabbage. Red, white, and green ones have smooth textured leaves and colors range from creamy white to deep purple. Savoy cabbage has crinkled or ruffled leaves and colors may be shades of blue or bright green. Savoy types are usually milder in flavor and do not give off the characteristic cabbage cooking smell. Chinese cabbage is more elongated in shape than other cabbage, and sweeter tasting. It is excellent prepared raw in salads and coleslaws. Napa cabbage is a favorite type with a mild, sweet flavor with leaves that overlap at the top of the elongated head.

Cabbage is a cool-season crop that needs not only mild temperatures (55–65°F/13–18°C) but also sun to mature—the giant cabbage grown in Alaska is a result of the long summer day length that helps the cabbage to grow to enormous proportions. Planting times vary according to your region.

Seed catalogs list cabbage for sale according to season or the number of days required from transplanting to maturity. Early varieties are usually small and mature 60–75 days after planting out into

SOWING CABBAGE SEED

1 EVENLY SPRINKLE a good number of seeds across a whole tray of fresh planting mix. Allow a finger width between each seed when doing so.

2 COVER THE SEEDS with a thin layer of mix and then gently firm this down by hand or using the bottom of another tray.

3 WATER THE PLANTING MIX carefully so that it is evenly soaked. Leave the seeds to germinate in a sunny place. Keep the seedlings moist.

the garden. Late varieties grow into larger heads and are more suitable for storage. They can take well over 200 days to mature. Chinese varieties mature the quickest of all—sometimes in less than 60 days. In cool-summer areas, late varieties have time to mature over a longer period of mild temperatures. Elsewhere, plant early varieties that can mature more quickly and remain tender before hot temperatures arrive in your area.

Where to grow

To produce sound, large heads of crispy leaves, cabbage needs a sunny site and firm soil. It also requires constant moisture, which means that the soil should have good texture and be moisture-retentive. Dig in well-composted organic matter in fall to give the soil time to consolidate over winter, then add some balanced fertilizer. Also check the soil pH, as the ideal range is 6–7; if it is too low, you may need to apply lime, which will also help to deter clubroot.

Sowing and planting

Cabbage can either be sown indoors for transplanting into the garden or sown directly in place. Start seeds indoors 4–6 weeks before your planting date or the last expected frost for spring planting. In cold-winter areas, cabbage can be planted in both spring and fall as long as the heads can mature when temperatures are not too hot; in warm-winter areas further south, a late summer planting for fall harvest is typical. In climates where temperatures are fairly mild, cabbage can be planted through fall and winter. Thoroughly prepare the soil before sowing directly outdoors by raking the surface to create a fine, crumbly texture.

To sow cabbage in place, stretch a length of string as a guide, and draw out a straight, ½in. (1cm) deep drill by dragging a hoe or broom handle along the line. If the bottom of the drill is dry, lightly water first. Sprinkle the seed thinly along its length, and cover with soil, which should be gently firmed by lightly patting down. Seedlings usually appear after 7–12 days. Thin out to the strongest, and weed regularly. Protect cabbage seedlings from cabbage maggots and cutworms by placing collars around their stems. Cover seedbeds with floating row covers to exclude flying insects and egg-laying butterflies.

AVOIDING SPLIT HEADS

Cabbage hearts can be prone to splitting when watered irregularly, so it is essential to ensure that the plants have an adequate and regular supply. Frost can also cause splitting, so choose varieties that can withstand the typical low temperatures in your region. Overmaturity also leads to splitting. A folk remedy is to twist the plants when mature to stop growth and therefore prevent splitting.

For transplants or cabbage raised indoors, plant out the young cabbage into prepared, firmed soil. Allow 12–18in. (30–45cm) between the plants and rows, depending on the size of the variety—early varieties can be more closely spaced. Cabbage that is placed closely together can still grow well but it may produce smaller heads. Specific spacing advice should be provided on the seed packet. Alternate ones can be taken early for use in the kitchen as spring greens, which helps to thin the crop out. Any remaining cabbage should be left to mature in the ground for a later harvest.

Caring for the crop

Cabbage needs consistent water; changes in moisture levels can cause the heads to split. Drip irrigation is ideal for them. Keep an eye on the developing plants; when hearts begin to form, generous additional watering will greatly improve head size. Mulch will help conserve soil moisture. Side-dress plants with a high-nitrogen fertilizer once or twice during the growing season.

To provide additional protection from both wind and frost, you can pile up some soil around the base of each plant before the first heavy frosts. This protects the stem of the plant and is known as 'hilling up'.

To prevent any kind of rot, it is good practice to remove dead leaves when they appear. Remove weeds that compete for moisture and nutrients. For larger, later varieties that take a long time to mature, you can use the space between them by interplanting with fast-maturing crops like bok choy, radishes, or spinach. If temperatures suddenly rise, cabbage can bolt or send up a flower stalk and go to seed.

Selected varieties

Primavoy
A late-season Savoy with blue-green heads with lovely, crinkled texture. Stores well. Is resistant to yellows.

Jade Pagoda
A Chinese cabbage that produces tall heads up to 16in. (40cm) with creamy yellow hearts. Slow to bolt.

Hispi
Medium-sized, pointed heads that stay quite small; good for smaller gardens. Has a beautifully sweet flavor and stays in good condition without splitting.

Multikeeper
Keeps well for short periods and is resistant to diseases. Firm, light green heads resist splitting.

Ruby Dynasty
Midseason cabbage with red, 3–5lb. (1.5–2kg), oval to round heads and excellent color. Has some disease resistance.

Pixie
Small, early cabbage that reaches only 2lb. (1kg) at most. Sweet-flavored leaves arranged in a loose head. Is good for salads.

Tundra
Sweet, firm, tasty heads that can be picked right through winter, even after snowfall. High yielding.

January King
A favorite Savoy cabbage that can withstand severe winter weather and frosts. Produces crisp, crunchy leaves.

RED CABBAGE grows slowly, but is especially delicious. It is prone to damage by low winter temperatures, but some varieties can be lifted and stored over winter.

At harvest time

Cut off the whole head of cabbage plants close to the ground with a sharp knife, or remove young leaves when they are needed. After harvesting spring and early summer cabbage, cut a cross in the top of the stump, about ½in. (1cm) deep, and the plant will produce a cluster of smaller heads within about five weeks. Most cabbage can be harvested as required, with many winter varieties being tough enough to last outdoors through the whole winter.

Storing and cooking tips

Cabbage is extremely good for you, being full of antioxidants and a good source of vitamin C, beta carotene, and fiber. Many varieties can be used in stir-fries or turned into delicious home-made coleslaw. Red cabbage is also excellent for festive meals like Thanksgiving when combined with apples. To retain the red color when cooking, add vinegar to the water. White and Chinese cabbages are used in coleslaw and other salads. Napa cabbage is sweet enough to add to salads and makes wonderful coleslaw. It is also the main ingredient in *kimchi*, a spicy, pickled dish that is essential in Korean cuisine. Heads of cabbage and large leaves rolled up can be stuffed and baked.

Late varieties store best. Remove some of the outer leaves, and then store in straw-lined boxes in a cool, dry place where they will last until early spring. Inspect the heads periodically for signs of rotting and gently remove any withered leaves, taking care not to bruise the head. Alternatively, you could leave them in the ground and harvest them when needed.

Pests and disease

Like all cole crops, cabbage may need protection from caterpillars and flying pests by floating row covers. Gophers like to snack on young cabbages, so erect some fencing or other barrier. Clubroot can lead to swollen roots; practice crop rotation to avoid buildup of the disease in the soil. Increasing the soil pH by adding lime can also protect against clubroot. Varieties of cabbage with resistance to root rot, aster yellows, and thrips are all available. Your local Cooperative Extension Service can recommend resistant varieties for your area.

CABBAGE has immense value in the kitchen garden as it stands through the leanest months of the year, waiting to be picked for the table.

Cauliflower

Brassica oleracea

Cauliflower has a reputation for being tricky to grow but, for many gardeners, that's the challenge. It certainly needs attention, and is the most sensitive member of the cabbage family to the pH of the soil, but a little time spent on site preparation, followed by plenty of watering through the growing season, can achieve excellent results.

Types of cauliflower

True cauliflower has creamy white heads, or curds, but there are varieties with purple, lime-green, and even orange heads. They require a long, cool season to grow. Temperatures that are too hot or too cold can affect the development of the head, or prevent it from forming at all. Because cauliflower is so temperature-sensitive, check with your local Cooperative Extension Service for any recommendations they have for varieties that do well in your area. It's also a good idea to stagger your plantings of cauliflower, to minimize losses due to fluctuating weather conditions. For white varieties to develop snowy white heads, you'll need to blanch the heads by covering them with the plant's leaves, or choose self-blanching varieties whose uppermost leaves naturally grow to cover the head.

Where to grow

Cauliflower requires a sunny site with fertile, moisture-retentive soil. Amend the soil with plenty of compost to improve its moisture-holding capacity and firm it down well before planting time. Check that the soil has a pH of 6.5–7.5. Rotate your crops to reduce the likelihood of clubroot and other potential problems. Never grow cauliflower in the same position within two years.

Sowing and planting

Start cauliflower in early spring for a summer harvest or in midsummer to harvest in late fall or early winter. In cold-winter climates, a midsummer planting produces a fall crop. In mild-winter climates, you can plant cauliflower in early spring or late summer. For the best success, start with healthy transplants from the nursery or from seed started indoors. Water the ground well the day before planting. Set the young plants in the ground 18–24in. (45–60cm) apart and firm them with your feet. Water in well, adding a little diluted liquid fertilizer to the irrigation water.

Caring for the crop

Ensure that the soil is kept moist at all times through the growing season. To prevent the curds being discolored by direct sunlight or by a severe frost followed by a rapid thaw, bend the uppermost leaves over the developing curd to protect it. Sudden changes in temperature can also lead to bolting or poor head formation. Secure the leaves with rubber

HARVEST CAULIFLOWER while the heads are still firm and small, and before the curds have started to separate, to ensure that the crop lasts for a longer period.

bands, strips, or clips and continue to adjust as needed to keep the head covered as the plant grows. Cold weather may cause browning of the curds and leaves, although this can also be caused by boron deficiency, which is treated by regularly applying a liquid all-purpose fertilizer. Control weeds by hoeing carefully by hand. Mulch the soil to keep down weeds and maintain consistent soil moisture.

At harvest time

Begin cutting the heads while they are still small— before the curds start to separate—so that the crop can be enjoyed over a longer period as it gradually develops. It should be harvested by cutting through the stem with a sharp knife. Leave some of the leaves intact around the head to protect it from damage during handling and storage.

Storing and cooking tips

Cauliflower is best used right away but can be stored by being hung upside down by the stem in a cool, airy place. Spray the leaves regularly with water and it should keep for several weeks. It also freezes well,

after blanching, which might be a better way of maintaining supplies because cauliflower can be tricky to grow during the hot summer months or in the depths of winter. Cauliflower is low in calories and packed with vitamin C, and overcooking can easily destroy the nutritional value as well as the delicate taste.

The best way to appreciate cauliflower's flavor is to boil a shallow pan of water, add a squeeze of lemon juice, then carefully add the florets head-up and let them steam gently for about 10 minutes. Lemon juice also helps retain the hues of color varieties when they are cooked. Raw florets of colored varieties make an attractive addition to salads.

Pests and diseases

Like all cole crops, cauliflower may need protection from flying and crawling pests such as cabbage worms, harlequin bugs, flea beetles, and whiteflies. The best method is to cover plants with floating row covers and to handpick problem pests. Beneficial insects also help to control pests. Crop rotation can help prevent against soilborne diseases such as clubroot, black rot, and fusarium wilt.

Selected varieties

Gypsy
This vigorous variety produces large heads of clean, white curds, even on less fertile soils.

Romanesco
Unusual and much-photographed variety with pyramid-shaped whorls of chartreuse heads.

Igloo
An heirloom variety that can be closely spaced for a quick crop of small heads and dense, upright foliage.

Graffiti
Bright purple florets keep their color even after cooking. A large plant that produces big, solid curds.

Kale

A close relative of cabbage, kale shares a lot of its family's characteristics yet has a distinctive personality of its own. It's both hardier and more heat-tolerant than many other cole crops. And aesthetically it far surpasses its cabbage cousins. The leaves are so ornamental that many varieties are sold for purely decorative purposes. They are separated from each other, and often heavily serrated or fringed around their margins. Many, such as 'Lacinato', have deeply crinkled leaves

KALE is an excellent plant for the kitchen garden. Its tasty, nutritious leaves can be picked as needed through the winter.

of rich blue-green, held upright in a striking, architectural pose. Some, like 'Red Russian', are positively frilly and, when combined with such an opulent color, more attractive than almost any other vegetables and most ornamental plants. When the plant is full-grown the purple stems develop a velvety bloom. It's a small wonder that kale is one of the most photographed garden vegetables.

Kale is tasty and robust, full of vitamins A and C, and packed with minerals. And because of the extreme hardiness of most varieties, it is available when it is needed most—in late fall and winter. The flavor develops as the leaves mature, and frost improves it even further.

These winter leaves can be harvested from late fall to early spring, and an earlier harvest can be taken from plants sown in early spring. The tender young leaves from this earlier crop are delicious in salads or when cooked briefly with oil and garlic. A second sowing of kale in late spring or early summer will keep the harvest going for at least six months. Because only a few leaves are cut at a time, unlike cabbage or cauliflower where the whole head is harvested, kale really earns its keep.

With a little imagination the leaves can be turned into the most scrumptious dishes. Cut the mature leaves across the leaf in fine slices, deep fry for a maximum of one minute, and sprinkle with a mixture of salt and sugar to make Asian-style 'seaweed'. The older the leaves, the longer they may need cooking, but they retain their flavor and substance when combined in soups with white beans, potatoes, or meats like chorizo sausage. Young leaves can be picked and tossed into salads.

If space is limited, grow a few plants in your flower borders or in winter containers. If you are gardening in a cold part of the country, remember that kale is immensely tough. No wonder it has been a staple of kitchen gardens for centuries.

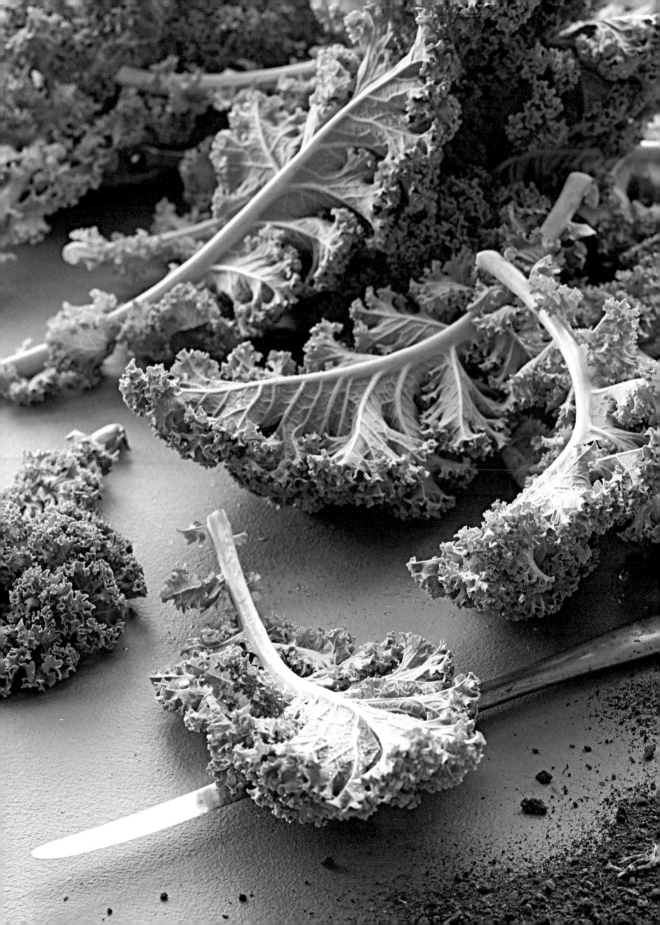

Kale

Brassica oleracea

Kale might not be familiar to every gardener, but it has been grown for centuries. It is tasty, nutritious, and a rich source of iron and vitamins A, C, and E. It is also very easy to grow. Some of the old-fashioned varieties had slightly bitter leaves, but new varieties—bred by crossing curly kale with its flat-leaved counterparts—are much more flavorful.

Types of kale

Edible kale is usually green, blue-green, or red, but maroon or nearly black varieties are available through seed catalogs. Scotch types have crinkled leaves and Siberian or Russian types have less texture and finely divided edges. Other varieties are grown in flower gardens and containers for their attractive leaves and used in winter as decorative 'ornamental cabbage'. These do not compare in flavor with edible kale. Dwarf and standard height varieties are available. The advantage of growing dwarf types is that you can cram more crops into the space, and they also work well as cut-and-come-again crops (see box, below).

Where to grow

Kale has many advantages over other cole crops. It tolerates a little shade (though full sun is best), is hardy, and is not so vulnerable to the pests and diseases that afflict the others. It can also be grown in virtually any soils, including impoverished, wet, soggy, and poor ones. Adding well-rotted organic matter, such as composted manure, leaf mold, or garden compost, or hoeing an organic fertilizer into the soil surface, will improve the crop, but heavy applications of fertilizer are not necessary.

Sowing and planting

You can sow kale directly in the garden or grow it from seed indoors. In mild-winter regions, a fall planting gives a winter harvest. Elsewhere, plant in summer for havesting in fall. For all types, thoroughly prepare the soil before sowing by raking the surface to create a fine crumbly texture. Use a length of string as a guide and make a ½in. (1cm) drill. The seedlings should appear within 7–12 days. If moving transplants to the garden, water them thoroughly before moving, and again generously once they are in their final position. The seedlings should be set 12–18in. (30–45cm) apart, depending on the varieties (dwarf varieties are planted closer together; check the seed packet for instructions). Plant to the depth of the first set of true leaves and firm in with your hands so the plant is well anchored.

Caring for the crop

Keep the plants watered during dry spells. Tall varieties may topple over; support stems firmly using a bamboo or wooden stake or pile up soil around the base of the plants to help support them as they get tall. Remove any yellowing leaves. Aphids are often a pest of kale. To control aphids, encourage beneficial insects such as ladybugs, and blast the pests off the plant leaves with a strong jet of water from the hose.

CUT AND COME AGAIN

Kale can also be grown as a ground-hugging, cut-and-come-again crop. This involves trimming off the tender young leaves to encourage more to form, so keeping the plants bushy and compact. This is an attractive, productive way to grow kale, particularly when using the purple-leaved varieties. Sow the seed where you want it to grow, either in blocks or in bands threaded through other plants, and harvest when the kale is about 2in. (5cm) high. It will soon grow more leaves, which can either be cut again or be allowed to mature into a shorter, bushier plant.

PLANTS WILL BE READY to harvest from late fall to midspring. Remove them when their leaves are still young and tender, and this will encourage more sideshoots to grow.

At harvest time

Kale is completely hardy, and young leaves can be picked and enjoyed for months. The flavor of kale improves after light frosts. Harvest all types while the leaves are still young and tender; older leaves quickly become tough and bitter. Start from the crown of the plant and work outwards, removing the tips of the stems with a sharp knife. This will encourage the plant to bush out and produce more sideshoots.

Storing and cooking tips

Harvest the crop as required, because it will stay fresh in the fridge for only a few days. When grown

KEEP PLANTS HEALTHY by hoeing weeds from underneath them and removing dead leaves from the lower stems. This helps to ensure good air circulation.

as a cut-and-come-again crop, kale is extremely tender and can be added to salads and stir-fries. It is usually boiled, but steaming or stir-frying retains more of the flavor and goodness. Wash the leaves thoroughly before cooking, to dislodge any aphids. You can freeze kale leaves, but blanch them first.

Selected varieties

Dwarf Green Curled
Grows to 24in. (60cm) high, unless grown as a cut-and-come-again crop, and has dark, tightly curled leaves all winter, keeping them well into spring.

Redbor
A beautiful, jewel-like purple that looks fabulous with the blue-green of leeks. A must for the kitchen garden and even ornamental beds and borders.

Lacitano
An Italian heirloom with leaves up to 24in. (60cm), slightly crinkled, deep blue-gray leaves. Heat- and cold-tolerant. Delicious flavor.

Blue Ridge
Dark green, very tightly curled leaves. Good heat resistance and so is slow to bolt in warm weather.

Asian greens

North American gardeners have welcomed a range of healthy, fast-growing, easy-to-grow leafy greens from Asia. Some of these greens taste like sweet cabbage, others are spicy, while yet others have a hearty flavor. Some—such as the mustards—are attractive enough for the ornamental garden. Experiment with different types to see what suits your garden—and your dinner table.

Types of Asian greens

The cool-season annuals sold as Asian greens or sometimes leafy greens are mostly members of the cabbage family. (A few, such as perilla, are herbs that belong to the mint family; these may tolerate higher temperatures and be grown as warm-season annuals.) The most familiar is probably bok choy (also spelled bok choi or pak choi), a mild-tasting cabbage that can be found in both dwarf and taller varieties.

A common way to grow Asian greens is to purchase a seed package of mixed types. These can be sown much like a mesclun mix and harvested as cut-and-come-again crops.

Many Asian greens, especially the red mustards, have striking leaves and interesting shapes that make them good options for ornamental plantings.

Where to grow

Most Asian greens grow best in cool temperatures. In cool regions, you can raise both spring and fall crops. In hot climates, sow in late summer or fall for a winter crop. In mild-summer coastal areas, you can grow them through the summer months, but they cannot tolerate high temperatures. Asian greens make good choices for raised beds and containers, as they prefer well-drained, fertile soil. Prepare the bed by digging in well-composted manure or garden compost and some organic fertilizer before planting. Like other cabbage-family plants, Asian greens suffer some of the same pests and diseases, so crop rotation should be practiced. This means you should plant them in the same spot for no more than two or three years. If planting in containers, use a well-drained planting mix and renew it each year.

A MIX OF ASIAN GREENS can be sown densely over some well-drained soil and then harvested when young in order to eat them like salad greens.

Sowing and planting

It's best to sow seeds of most Asian greens directly in the garden, but in cold areas you can also sow seeds indoors 4–6 weeks before the last frost date. Check the seed packet for specific planting times.

To sow directly in the garden, stretch a length of string as a guide, and draw out a straight, ½in. (1cm) deep drill by dragging a hoe or broom handle along the line. If the bottom of the drill is dry, lightly water it first. Sprinkle the seed thinly along its length, and cover with soil, which should be firmed by lightly patting down.

If you are planting a seed mix of Asian greens, mark out blocks in the soil and sow the seeds densely. Just make sure the blocks are no wider than you can comfortably reach into for harvesting.

Caring for the crop

Asian greens germinate and mature quickly, many in as little as 4–6 weeks after sowing. As the seedlings emerge, keep the soil moist but not soggy. Drip irrigation is a good choice for greens, as it keeps moisture off the leaves, which can encourage fungal diseases. As seedlings reach a few inches high, thin them to 4–6in. (10–15cm) apart. Weed carefully by hand around the plants, to prevent weeds competing for moisture.

At harvest time

Snip leaves as they grow, or remove entire plants, when flavors are stronger. Harvest plants before hot weather arrives, as most Asian greens will bolt in high temperatures.

Storing and cooking tips

Asian greens make great additions to a variety of dishes, especially stir-fries, salads, and side dishes.

Pests and diseases

If flea beetles or caterpillars are attacking the crops, use floating row covers to protect the plants. Control slugs and snails by handpicking.

Selected types

Komatsuna
A fast-growing leafy green with a taste that falls between mustard and spinach. Is somewhat drought-tolerant.

Mizuna and mibuna
Mizuna (left) has serrated leaves, where mibuna's are more rounded. Both have light-textured leaves with a mild mustard flavor.

Bok Choi
Also spelled bok choy or pak choi. Cabbage with tender leaves and edible, fleshy, white stems. Can be steamed, stir-fried, or added to stews.

Red Perilla
Also called Shiso, this is a member of the mint family and is a common ingredient in Japanese dishes. Grows as a warm-weather annual. Both green and red types are available.

Tatsoi
Forms a rosette of rounded, green leaves that have a mild, sweet flavor. Can be eaten raw or cooked.

Gai Lan
Also known as Chinese broccoli, these fast-growing greens have thick stems and glossy leaves. Flower shoots are edible, much like broccoli raab.

Collards

Brassica oleracea

Collards are a traditional staple in Southern vegetable patches, and in Southern kitchens. Mustard greens have similar growing needs but a more piquant flavor. Both collards and mustard greens have recently become more popular in Northern gardens because of their heat tolerance, hardiness, taste, and high nutritional value.

Types of collards

Although collards share a botanical name with kale, they don't look like the same plant. They have a main stem that can reach up to 3–4ft. (1–1.2m), with a

COLLARDS ARE A FAVORITE plant in Southern gardens but they can be grown anywhere as long as they have ample moisture. A good covering of mulch keeps the soil damp.

rosette of broad, uncrinkled leaves at the top. Several varieties are available. If your local garden center or nursery doesn't carry them, check the list of seed suppliers on page 219.

Where to grow

Collards like rich, well-drained soils with a pH of 6–6.5. If your soil is sandy, dig in plenty of well-rotted manure or compost. A few weeks before planting, dig in some all-purpose fertilizer to prepare the bed.

Sowing and planting

Collards can be planted in early spring for an early summer crop, or in fall for a winter crop. However, they will not germinate until soil temperatures rise above 70°F (21°C), so wait until the ground has warmed in your area before starting to sow. Sometimes, gardeners plant collards in spring, pick the younger leaves in late spring, then leave the plant in the ground until fall, when the entire plant can be harvested. You can start seeds indoors 4–6 weeks before the last spring frost, then move the young plants to the garden, spacing them 18–24in. (45–60cm) apart.

To sow collards directly in the garden, stretch a length of string as a guide, and draw out a straight, ½in. (1cm) deep drill by dragging a hoe or broom handle along the line. If the bottom of the drill is dry, lightly water first. Sprinkle the seed thinly along its length, and cover with soil, which should be firmed by lightly patting down. Collards usually sprout in 6–12 days. Let them grow to 4–6in. (10–15cm), then gradually thin to a spacing of 18–24in. (45–60cm). The thinnings can be thrown into a stir-fry or soup.

Growing mustard greens

Mustard greens (*Brassica juncea*), also known as leaf mustard, are not the same as the mustard that is grown primarily for its seeds, nor the yellow-flowered mustard cover crop. They are tall, leafy vegetables that are, like collards, Southern favorites. Curly leafed and flat-leafed types are available. Grow mustard greens like collards, direct-sowing in the ground as cool-season crops. Thin largest varieties to 8–12in. (20–30cm) apart. Keep the crop well watered. Mustard greens grow quickly—from 35 to 60 days after planting. Sow successively through the season. Start to harvest when leaves are 4–6in. (10–15cm) long; the larger the leaf, generally the hotter the taste. Steam the leaves, or add them to stir-fries, or serve as wilted greens with garlic and a bit of chopped bacon.

Selected varieties

Georgia Green
Frost- and heat-resistant collards that grow well on poor soil, including sandy soils. This variety grows to 3ft. (1m) tall.

Southern Giant Curled
Deeply frilled, bright yellow-green leaves that have an upright growth habit. An old Southern favorite, this variety of mustard greens has a pungent, full-bodied flavor.

Champion
Dark green, large, cabbagelike leaves stay tender for weeks. Produces very cold-hardy, compact collards.

Caring for the crop

Collards need regular moisture, so keep them well watered and control weeds that compete for water. Side-dress the plants with a high-nitrogen fertilizer once or twice during the growing season, or if they become pale and growth seems to slow. Collards need sufficient nitrogen to develop their good, deep green color.

At harvest time

Like other cole crops, the flavor of collards often sweetens after a light frost. Harvest collards from the lower leaves, which encourages the plant to produce more foliage further up.

Storing and cooking tips

Rinse the leaves thoroughly to remove any aphids. Collards must be cooked for some time to taste their best. They are rich in vitamin A, calcium, and iron.

Traditional ways of preparing collards include simmering them with salt pork or ham hocks or sautéing them with black-eyed peas.

You can also cook collards as wilted greens, or chop and stir them into bean or lentil soups. If you have a bumper crop of collards in your garden, you can freeze them, but they should be blanched before freezing. If not, the leaves will become tough and flavorless upon thawing and cooking. To blanch, chop and then cook the leaves in boiling water for a few minutes, then plunge into icy water. Then bag and freeze the collards

Pests and diseases

As with all cole crops, cabbage loopers, cabbageworms, flea beetles, and harlequin bugs like to feast on collard leaves. Diamondback moth larvae are also pests of collards. Floating row covers can keep them at bay. To control aphids, encourage beneficial insects such as ladybugs, and blast the pests off collard leaves with a jet of water from the hose. Downy mildew can infect collards. Control it by keeping the leaves of the plant dry. Water in the morning or use drip irrigation. Destroy affected plants to avoid spreading the disease and choose varieties that are resistant to downy mildew.

Beans and peas

Beans and peas, also known as legumes, are delicious and decorative as both pods and seed. The range of choices is astonishing—beans that can be eaten fresh or dried, in hues of purple, red, white, green, and black, and peas that may have edible pods, or must be shelled to reveal their embryonic treasures. Legumes make great plants for the small garden because most can be grown vertically, taking up little space. Beans and peas are invaluable in the sustainable vegetable garden, too, because bacteria in their roots 'fix' nitrogen in the soil, maintaining its fertility and preparing the bed for a new round of crops.

Fava beans

Fava beans are great plants for first-time vegetable gardeners. Anyone can grow them, their only requirements being decent soil, good light, and water. They are easy to sow directly in the ground or to start indoors. In the kitchen garden, they are frequently the first crop to be sown and, where the soil is well drained and stays reasonably warm over winter, such as zones 7 and 8, fava beans can be sown in fall and you may even be able to grow two crops a year. Unfortunately, fava beans are not as well known to North American gardeners as they should be. They are highly nutritious and full of protein, vitamin A and vitamin C. And the taste is hearty and robust.

If you are not yet familiar with fava beans, you are in for a treat. As with shelling peas, you get to eat the seeds inside the pod, which can be eaten raw or cooked, used fresh or dried, and can be stored over winter. Their texture is rich and thick, and their taste floury as well as satisfying.

Because of their 'storeability', fava beans were once highly prized and put to a number of uses. In the Roman senate, black fava beans denoted a 'No' vote,

FAVA BEAN PODS will be ready in late spring or early summer when the pods are full and fresh.

pale ones a 'Yes'. In China, they are recent arrivals, appearing there only from AD 1200, but the Chinese now grow more beans than anyone else.

Like other legumes, fava beans make handsome plants, although taller varieties may need some support to stop them looking ungainly. They are strong, eager plants with attractive foliage borne in whorls around the stems. The dense clusters of flowers, white with a chocolate-colored blotch, are sweetly scented to attract pollinators. A few heritage varieties have deep pink flowers. As they fade, the tiny pods begin to grow, eventually swelling to fat, waxy pods, shiny and robust.

Fava beans need cool conditions to grow. The young pods can be harvested and eaten whole, but you can also pick them for shelling just before they reach maturity, when the pod is tight with its cargo, but before it reaches bursting point. It's a little work to get at the beans as the hard, shiny exterior casing contains a furry interior that encloses the beans. For storing, place the picked beans in a warm place until they are completely dry, then put them in an airtight tin or paper bag. Like all beans, they are rich in protein and high in riboflavin and vitamin C.

Lima beans, also called butter beans, are grown for their edible, protein-rich seeds and are more suited than fava beans to the hotter conditions of the South. Except for the temperature difference, they are grown much like fava beans, preferring a soil with a pH around 6 and moist, well-drained conditions. However, some lima beans are grown like pole beans (see page 100).

Fava beans *Vicia faba*

Easy-to-grow fava beans can produce a huge crop, they are ~~fast to pick, and~~ they are absolutely delicious. They have large seeds that you can plunge directly into the soil. All you have to do is mind the weeds. In mild-winter areas, a fall sowing will give a winter harvest that can be cleared away immediately and planted with the next summer crop.

Where to grow

Fava beans need a sunny, sheltered site because mature plants, when bushy and weighted with pods, are susceptible to wind damage. They are less fussy about their soil requirements than peas or other beans, but still benefit from well-rotted organic matter being dug in the ground before planting.

Sowing and planting

In most areas, sow beans directly outdoors as soon as the soil has warmed up in spring. You could also sow the seeds indoors, one per cell pack, taking care to harden off the seedlings before planting them out.

Fava beans are prolific croppers once they get going, so aim for a series of small sowings of 8–12 seeds, with a few substitutes in case of failures. Using a trowel or dibble, sow seeds individually at a depth of 2in. (5cm). Seeds should be 9in. (23cm) apart, either in double rows or in small blocks, but in either case make sure that the rows are staggered to maximize the spaces between.

SOWING BEANS in cell packs is a little more high-maintenance than direct sowing, but it ensures successful early sowings.

Successive sowings

Fava beans take 80–100 days to mature, which means that between early and late spring you should be able to manage another one or two sowings to ensure a more prolonged, even harvest. There is no

Selected varieties

The Sutton
Dwarf variety and prolific cropper, excellent for containers, exposed sites, raised beds, and small gardens.

Sweet Lorane
Delicious, small-seeded, and productive fava bean that is hardy and disease resistant.

set time for a second or third sowing; just wait until the previous one has reached a height of 6–8in. (15–20cm) before sowing the next crop. Do not be tempted to sow more plants before this, however, or the second sowing will probably catch up with the first. Fava beans won't produce once summer temperatures rise above 70°F (21°C).

Caring for the crop

Plants in exposed sites will fall over in the wind or lose stems under the weight of the swelling pods unless they are staked. Old, long, strong, and twiggy tree and shrub prunings can be used to create an unobtrusive network of support; put these in place once the seedlings have emerged. Alternatively, plants can be tied, using a figure eight, to structures made from string roped around a series of stakes or strong bamboo canes.

Supporting the plants

When the young beans begin to appear at the base of the plant, it is time to pinch back the growing tips in order to concentrate the beans' energy on pod formation. Nip off the top of the stem with two pairs of leaves attached; these can be thrown into a salad or stir-fry, or can be lightly steamed. Pinching back the tips can also help deter the major pest of fava beans, which is black aphids (see right). Keep the ground moist, but not soggy.

At harvest time

Harvest beans when they are small, before the flesh becomes starchy and the skin bitter. Take pods from the base of the plant and work up. Because it can be easy to damage plants while picking pods, it is best to use scissors or pruners to snip them off.

Storing and cooking tips

Young beans can be cooked and eaten but mature fava beans need to be shelled twice to reveal the tender inner seeds. First snap off one end of the pod, then pull the string that runs along the inner curve of the pod. This opens up the pod so that you can easily remove the seeds. Cook them in boiling salted water for one or two minutes, then let them cool and peel them again, removing the pale, waxy outer skin that covers the darker fava bean inside.

HARVESTING FAVA BEANS

1 START TO PICK beans, using scissors or pruners, when the pods are full but still fresh.

2 REMOVE THE MORE MATURE pods from the bottom of the plant first. The beans should be a good size and firm to the touch.

Fava beans freeze well but they must be blanched first. Shell as above, then boil and place immediately in ice water to cool, before bagging and freezing.

Pests and diseases

Black aphids can be quite a pest. They often colonize the young shoots first, where they find it easy to suck the sap. Insecticidal soap or horticultural oils should be used only if infestations are severe, so they do minimal harm to helpful insects. If you do see aphids, immediately pinch back the tips with finger and thumb or remove them with a strong blast of water from the hose; take care not to damage growing stems or knock over the plants when spraying.

Sometimes flea beetles, mites, or other chewing beetles attack fava beans. Plants are unlikely to be seriously damaged by this, except in very poor weather when new leaf growth is slow. Covering with floating row covers is the best remedy.

Two common fungal diseases are chocolate spot and rust, visible as brown or orange spots on the leaves. Chocolate spot tends to occur in damp, humid weather early in the season, and rust during dry spells later on. Neither is usually severe, but improving ventilation by introducing wider plant spacing may help.

Pole and bush beans

There are broadly two types of common beans: bush types, which grow on compact stems; and pole beans, which have a climbing habit and are grown up teepees and trellises. But within these two categories are a huge range of possibilities for the kitchen gardener, both for vegetables to eat fresh from the garden, and for those that can be dried, frozen, or made into pickles and relish.

Snap beans are grown for the edible pods (the 'snap' is the sound the pod makes when you break the pod). They include: long, thin filet beans; purple types that turn green when cooked; flat-podded types with large, visible beans; and yellow wax beans.

Shelling beans, in contrast to snap beans, are removed from their pods before they are eaten fresh (as in kidney beans or soybeans), or are dried for later use in soups, stews, and a wide range of vegetarian dishes.

Finally, runner beans are easy-to-grow pole beans with brightly colored flowers and broad, flat edible pods. Although the term 'string bean' is still familiar, modern beans have been bred without a fibrous string along the pod, which used to make beans tough and hard.

POLE BEANS are an attractive vertical feature of both large and compact vegetable gardens.

Most gardeners are now familiar with growing snap beans, and the range of dry shelling beans is also worth exploring, as you can quite easily stock your cupboards with a wide range of protein-rich and versatile white, black, red, yellow, and multihued beans. Some favorites are adzuki, blackeye, cranberry, navy, and pinto beans.

Your climate will strongly influence the type of beans you choose for your vegetable garden. Most beans are warm-season vegetables that require warm temperatures in which to grow. Runner beans are an exception; like fava beans, they do best in cooler climates such as in the Pacific Northwest.

Beans, like all legumes, are beneficial in the vegetable garden because bacteria in their roots 'fix' nitrogen in the soil, which can nourish a subsequent planting of alternate vegetables. If you sow beans in a spot where no legumes have been grown, it can be useful to inoculate the seeds with a special *Rhizobia* bacteria to help with this process. You can either buy pre-treated seeds, or purchase the inoculant powder and apply it yourself before planting.

Beans are often grown with corn and squash in a triad sometimes called the 'three sisters.' If you have the room, growing corn and beans together is a good option, as you can plant lower-growing bush types at the base of the corn. Beans grow easily on most unimproved soils. If your soil is poor, however, regardless of whether you are growing pole or bush varieties, dig out a decent trench and enrich it with well-rotted organic matter.

Pole and bush beans *Phaseolus vulgaris*

Crunchy, fresh beans are wonderful ~~to eat. There are far more varieties~~ of pole and bush beans than most people realize, and many are highly ornamental. As well as green beans, some are yellow, purple, or cream— and sometimes flecked. The vining habit of pole beans means they must be grown over some kind of structure, making them ideal for compact spaces.

Types of beans

There are more similarities than differences between beans—all are frost-sensitive, heat-loving plants that are easy to start from seed. Your choice of what kind to grow will depend on how much room you have in the garden and what kind of beans you want to eat—whether fresh snap beans for summer eating, pinto or kidney beans to dry and add later to soups and stews, or soybeans that can be steamed in the pod and then opened with your fingers and enjoyed with a little soy sauce.

Some gardeners prefer to cultivate bush beans rather than pole beans because the former, shorter plants are more productive and have a faster cropping period. This quick growth means that plants are less likely to be bothered by pests and diseases, too. Although bush beans take up more room than their climbing cousins, they can also be grown successfully in containers—such as oak barrels—where space is tight. In addition, you can use bush beans to underplant taller crops, such as corn or sunflowers, with which they make excellent companions.

Where to grow

Like all legumes, beans need a warm, sunny site with light soil that's moisture-retentive without being wet. Fork in some well-rotted manure or garden compost in late fall or early winter so that it settles into the soil before planting in spring. If you are planting against a trellis, put it on the north side of the garden, so the tall-growing beans don't shade other plants.

Where beans are to be planted in a spot that has not previously been occupied by legumes, buy seeds that have been treated with an inoculant that will help the beans fix nitrogen in the soil, thereby increasing its fertility. If your preferred variety is not available pre-inoculated, you can purchase the inoculant separately and treat the seeds before planting.

Sowing and planting

Because beans are tender plants, they will quickly succumb to a late frost. But even without frost, seedlings grow slowly and erratically in cool temperatures. It is therefore far better to wait until late spring or early summer to sow outdoors

Selected varieties (pole beans)

Kentucky Blue
A favorite pole bean developed from popular varieties 'Kentucky Wonder' and 'Blue Lake'. Sweet pods, up to 7in. (18cm) long, are produced over a long period.

Purple Teepee
A variety with beautiful, purple pods. They turn green on cooking and have excellent flavor.

ALL POLE BEANS, such as 'Algarve' (above), must be grown up a sturdy support. They make good, fast-growing screens and are decorative when in flower.

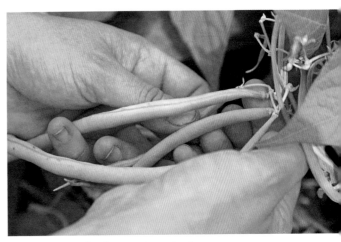

PICK BEANS once the plants start cropping in summer. The young pods will be sweetest, and regular picking will stimulate the growth of more beans.

—until the soil has warmed and there is no danger of frost. Beans need the soil temperature to be at least 50°F (10°C) otherwise the seeds will rot. Your local Cooperative Extension Service is a good source of advice for planting times in your area. Alternatively, start beans inside, with two seeds per cell or peat pot at 2in. (5cm) deep; plant out once they are 3in. (7.5cm) tall. In mild climates, you can also sow in midsummer for a fall crop.

Bush beans are best grown in small blocks, where neighboring plants provide support and some protection. Space the seeds 2in. (5cm) apart and 1in. (2.5cm) deep. Alternatively, sow in single or double rows using the same spacing. Continue to sow every few weeks throughout the growing season; plants grow quickly and you can have beans throughout summer and fall. When the young beans emerge and grow to several inches in height, thin seedlings to 6–8in. (15–20cm) apart.

For pole beans, the simplest structure is a bamboo teepee or a double row of supports (these are helpful in windy areas). Make sure the support is sturdy, with canes spaced 8in. (20cm) apart, and a minimum of 6ft. (1.8m) tall. Grow one plant per cane to avoid congestion. Pole beans can also be trained up a trellis, over arches, or along fences to make the most of their beautiful, red, white, lilac, purplish, or pink flowers and ornamental pods.

GROWING SOYBEANS

Soybeans are one of the most protein-rich beans you can grow, and they have a unique flavor whether eaten fresh, or dried and roasted. You can grow soybeans much like other bush beans but they prefer hot, humid conditions to produce a good crop; the South and Midwest are the best places to grow soybeans. Buy garden varieties; these are larger than those sold for agricultural use. Although there are not many available, most seed companies sell at least one or two kinds of soybean. Plant seeds 2–4in. (5–10cm) apart in rows 2–3ft. (0.6–1m) apart. Mulch plants to protect the roots and to retain moisture. Keep an eye out for red spider mites in dry weather; wetting the plants can help to deter them. Soybeans are tasty crops for rabbits and deer, so if either animal is a pest in your area you'll need to protect the crop with barriers or fences. Soybeans are ready to harvest when the seeds are fully enlarged, but before they have started to harden; at this point you can pick the beans and eat them steamed as edamame. For dry shelling beans, wait until the pods start to wither on the plants, then pick them and lay them out in a dry, well-ventilated place to dehydrate before shelling. You can also wait until the entire plant has browned and dried out, then pull it up by the roots and hang in a well-ventilated place. When fully dry, shell and store the dried beans.

Caring for the crop

Bush beans in blocks usually need no support, although staking with lightweight sticks or canes and string can lift the crop off the ground and improve air circulation. Help young pole bean plants to attach firmly to their supports by gently winding them around the uprights when they first start to grow. When the beans reach the top of their supports, pinch out the growing tips to prevent the plants becoming top-heavy.

Although bush beans are not as sensitive to water as pole beans, all beans need moisture when flowering, so water deeply and consistently. Drip irrigation is ideal, as it also keeps the foliage dry and discourages disease. After plants have flowered, you can ease up on the watering. Mulching around the plants helps to retain sufficient soil moisture and to minimize weeds.

SOYBEANS can be picked when young or be left to mature and harvested for dried beans.

Control weeds by hand—pull them or use a hoe but be extra careful when doing this as beans are shallow-rooted.

If there is a spell of unexpectedly cold weather after sowing, cover the plants with floating row covers until it is warmer. Windy weather is another problem, because it can desiccate or strip leaves, and damage any climbing stems that aren't tied in.

Beans in reasonably fertile soil need no extra feeding. If you do have to add fertilizer, use a balanced formula and apply once the plants are 1ft. (30cm) tall and then again when the pods start to form.

Growing in containers
Use a large container such as an oak barrel or a 24in. (60cm) pot and fill it with a growing mix specifically formulated for containers. Before sowing pole beans, insert a trellis or teepee firmly in the mix. Sow beans 1in. (2.5cm) deep and 6–12in. (15–30cm) apart, then cover the surface of the soil with a lightweight mulch like compost or wood chips. Water the young beans regularly, especially when the plants are flowering, and make sure moisture levels are maintained as soil in containers dries out quickly.

At harvest time

Pick snap beans as soon as they are large enough—this will depend on the variety so read the seed packet for specific instructions. Generally, pods that snap crisply in half are at their peak. Continue to pick beans regularly to prolong cropping. For dry shelling beans, you can wait until the individual pods become brown before picking them or until the whole plant has turned brown, after which you can pull it up, including the roots. Once the beans are fully dry, shell and store them in an airtight container

Storing and cooking tips

Beans can be steamed, sautéed, boiled, or eaten raw with dip. Young bean pods freeze well. Dry beans must be kept in airtight containers and then soaked before being cooked and eaten. You can either leave the dry beans to soak for up to 12 hours, or bring them to a boil first to speed up the process. Discard the soaking water and rinse the beans to reduce sugars in the beans that can cause digestive upset.

Pests and diseases

HARVESTING BUSH BEANS calls for lots of bending. As an alternative, pull the whole plant, pick off the beans, and put the remaining plant on the compost pile.

Japanese beetles and Mexican bean beetles can chew leaves to lacy remnants. Handpicking and floating row covers can control them, but bush beans mature so quickly that they can usually outgrow the pests. Aphids may cluster on plants; blast them off with strong jets of water from the hose, as soon as you spot them. Red spider mites can be a problem in hot weather; insecticidal soap sprayed on the underside of leaves can help this problem. If pest infestations persist, contact your local Cooperative Extension Service for advice. Several diseases, including viruses and rust, can be avoided by choosing resistant varieties of pole and bush beans, by using drip irrigation to keep foliage dry, and by avoiding working around the beans in wet weather.

Selected varieties (bush beans)

Derby
Tender, flavorful beans, up to 7in. (18cm) long, on upright plants. This disease-resistant variety has a long cropping season.

Tricolor Blend
Ideal for smaller gardens, this blend contains purple, yellow, and green beans for a heavy harvest of snap beans.

Runner beans
Phaseolus coccineus

Tall teepees of runner beans are a classic feature of summer vegetable gardens in milder regions, and with their fast, lush growth and bright red flowers, they are sometimes seen in the ornamental garden too. Runner beans also tolerate a little bit of shade. Like all peas and beans, bacteria in the root nodules fix nitrogen into the soil from the air, which helps to maintain fertility levels in the soil.

Types of runner beans

Although native to Mexico, runner beans have been much more popular in English gardens than North American ones, but where they grow well—particularly in the Northwest—they are easy and productive plants. The beans themselves are large, with a sweet but meaty flavor.

In many gardens, runner beans are grown decoratively, and varieties with white or bicolored flowers are available from specialty seed suppliers, although there is little difference in taste from the scarlet types. The fresh speckled seeds are small objects of beauty.

As a bonus, and unlike other beans, runner beans are pollinated by insects or birds and they are a good plant for attracting hummingbirds to the garden. They are also great plants for children, as the seeds are colorful, and the plants germinate quickly. You will have to go to a speciality seed supplier to find unusual varieties of runner bean, including dwarf varieties suitable for containers.

RUNNER BEANS should be grown in a warm, sheltered position in the garden.

Where to grow

Runner beans are not difficult to cultivate, but they are sensitive to frost, which is why they are grown as annuals and need a warm, sheltered position. They are best suited to mild climates, as high temperatures inhibit flower production. This also benefits pollinating insects, which are essential if the beans are to set their fruit.

It is best to position these tall plants so that they do not shade the other plants in the vegetable garden. Construct a strong, well-secured support at least 6ft. (1.8m) tall with canes 8in. (20cm) apart.

You need to improve the soil before growing runner beans. Therefore, a few months before planting, dig in plenty of well-rotted organic matter. Add a balanced fertilizer before sowing.

Sowing and planting

Wait until mid- or late spring before sowing these seeds in cell packs indoors or on a windowsill. Sow two seeds, 2in. (5cm) deep, per cell; they will soon germinate and can be planted out at the bottom of each upright support in early summer, 6in. (15cm) apart, once the danger of late spring frosts has passed. The seedlings will soon wind their way onto the supports if you can give them a little direction; they grow at quite a rate, although they benefit from being loosely tied in the initial stages. Watch out for slugs and snails. For a late crop in fall, sow a batch of seeds in midsummer.

Caring for the crop

Weed around the plants regularly, and water the plants in dry weather, particularly once the flowers

REMEMBER TO PINCH back the growing tips of stems when they reach the top of their support to prevent the beans becoming too top-heavy.

begin to form. This helps with the development of bean pods. A thick mulch around the base of the plants is a good way of keeping the soil moist as well as suppressing weeds.

Pollinators may fail to do their job if the weather is too cold or windy, and this as well as inefficient irrigation are usually the cause of poor yields. Wetting foliage on warm evenings may cool the plants, improving pollination.

To prevent the beans becoming too top-heavy, pinch back the growing tips when they reach the top of their support.

ASPARAGUS BEANS

The asparagus or 'yard long' bean (*Vigna unguiculata*) grows like a pole bean but it needs an especially sturdy, tall support, as the plants are very vigorous and have a long, trailing growth habit. They need long, hot summers and consistent moisture for best growth. Plant as for pole beans, and then thin plants to 8in. (20cm) apart. As with fava beans, black aphids may be a problem.

HARVEST ASPARAGUS beans when they are at maximum length, but before they develop a crinkled texture.

At harvest time

It can take up to 12 weeks before you get your first crop of runner beans, but once they start coming it is generally not easy to pick them fast enough. Harvest beans while young before there is any hint of the seeds swelling.

Pods that are too old become stringy and are not worth eating; remove these unless you intend to save the seed to use next year. By removing the old pods, you will stimulate the plant into further production.

Storing and cooking tips

Runner beans can have tough strings down both edges of the pod, and these need to be removed before the beans are sliced and then cooked. Beans picked young, however, will not have developed tough strings. Once sliced, the beans are ready to be frozen, or they can be boiled or steamed right away for the table. A handy device available from kitchen suppliers and some garden catalogs simplifies the task of slicing the beans lengthwise.

Peas

Some legumes are at their best before the seed starts to swell, but with peas you can eat not only the seeds but also, in some varieties, their pods.

Peas have been planted in America since the earliest colonists started growing food, but their history as garden plants stretches back thousands of years. Formerly, many of the most popular varieties were developed in England, but much breeding work in America has also led to types that are resistant to disease and suitable for a range of climates. Three types of peas are available to gardeners, although there are plenty of varieties within the following categories: Garden or shelling peas (sometimes called English peas) are thin-walled types that must have the peas removed from the pod before they are eaten; petit pois varieties have tiny seeds. Snap peas, or sugar snaps, can be eaten unshelled, pod and all. Snow peas are similar to snap peas in that the entire pod is eaten, but they have flat pods with undeveloped seeds.

RIPE PEAS in summer are irresistible. Pop them open between your fingers and eat the peas fresh.

These are especially popular for salads and for Asian dishes such as stir-fries.

Unlike beans, peas are cool-weather crops. They are among the first vegetables to be planted in spring and, in mild areas, they can be sown again in fall for a late winter or early spring crop. Dwarf types can be cultivated in containers, while taller varieties can be grown up wall trellises, or the plants can be supported by twiggy sticks for a no-fuss approach and a country-garden look.

Peas are favorites with children, as they are easy to grow, given the right conditions, and kids love to hunt for pods amid the leaves and tendrils. The large seeds are easy to handle and the bright green leaves and white or purple flowers are a pretty sight in the garden.

The sugar in peas begins to convert to starch right after harvesting, so nothing can compare to just-picked peas. Eat them raw, or possibly add a little butter and some mint.

Peas are not generally high-yield plants, so choosing the best variety for your area is important. You can sow them throughout the season to prolong the harvest. Experiment with different varieties in your own garden, while paying attention to the growing times given to harvest in seed catalogs. You may find that peas grow and ripen faster or more slowly depending on your climate and weather. When growing peas, try to avoid a glut, but if you do get a run of hot weather the peas will all ripen within a few days of each other. What do you do? Pick them all, make lots of soup, eat as many as you can, and freeze the rest.

Peas

Pisum sativum

If you grow your own peas, don't be surprised if they never get as far as the kitchen. One of the many pleasures of having a vegetable garden is eating sweet, tender peas straight from the plant. The whole pod and its contents are used when you grow snow peas and snap varieties, and they are delicious. Peas wilt in hot weather, so they must be grown in the cooler months.

Types of peas

Peas are vines with strong tendrils, and some varieties can reach heights of more than 6ft. (1.8m). Although tall varieties are an effective way of using vertical space in a small garden, they require strong support. The quest for a self-supporting pea has led to much shorter cultivars, including dwarf and semidwarf varieties suitable for containers. Semileafless peas were bred for commercial crop production, being particularly well adapted for mechanical harvesting.

As their name implies, they produce fewer leaves but more tendrils; grown in blocks, the plants can support one another without the crop becoming smothered by too much foliage.

Like potatoes, peas are grouped by the time taken to mature. Earlies take 52–62 days and main crops are ready after 62 days, but you may find that growing times vary depending on your garden conditions. In cool-summer areas, earlies can be sown successively throughout the summer.

PLANTING OUT SEEDLINGS

1 SOW EARLY PLANTS under cover in cell packs. This provides essential protection and is useful where pests such as rabbits are a problem to young seedlings.

2 PLANT PEA SEEDLINGS into the ground, when they are about 4in. (10cm) tall. Handle carefully, as the young peas have delicate roots. Remember to harden off the seedlings first.

When sowing different varieties of peas, you will notice that some seeds are wrinkled, whereas others are rounded. Generally, the latter are hardier and are used for very early sowings, but they lack the sweetness of wrinkled varieties, which are better for later sowings.

Flat-podded snow peas are eaten pod and all, as are snap peas, which have a sweet and crunchy pod even when the peas have swelled. Many of these varieties can also be used as shelling peas when left to develop. Peas described as petit pois remain small even when mature.

Where to grow

Peas like rich, moisture-retentive soil that has had additions of well-rotted compost or manure. Good soil preparation helps them through hot, dry weather (which they dislike), as does watering and then mulching around the base of the plant. If your garden soil is heavy clay, grow peas in raised beds in the sunniest spot in the garden. In hottest zones in the South and West, plant peas in semishaded spots.

If you are planting peas where no legumes have been grown, the plants may benefit from an inoculant that contains beneficial bacteria to fix nitrogen in the soil. Buy inoculated seeds or inoculate them yourself.

Sowing and planting

First sowing times outside vary according to location and weather. They are normally between early and midspring, but check with a local nursery or your Cooperative Extension Service if you need more advice. For late spring peas, sow 6–8 weeks before the last frost date. For fall crops in areas with a long, mild fall, sow in late summer. In mild-winter zones, you can often sow through fall for winter and early spring harvests.

If spring is slow to arrive, warm the soil by covering it with plastic mulch before sowing, and then protect the seedlings with floating row cover. Do not be tempted to sow into cold, wet soil because germination will be poor.

A traditional method of sowing peas, which works well with shorter varieties, is to make a flat trench, 2in. (5cm) deep and about 10in. (25cm) wide, with a hoe. Water the trench first, then sow the seeds 2–2 1/2in. (5–7cm) apart in three rows along the bottom of the trench. Press the seed in a little so that it does not become displaced when the trench is backfilled with soil. Firm the ground lightly.

Dwarf and semidwarf pea varieties can also be sown in small blocks. Lay seed on the soil in a staggered pattern so that each is 6in. (15cm) apart. If the soil is loose, simply push in the seed to a depth of 2in. (5cm); otherwise use a trowel.

For taller varieties, sowing seed in a single row, or pair of rows, works best because the plants are easier to support. This method also provides increased air ventilation around the plants, helping to prevent powdery mildew as well as making weeding easier. It's best to put your trellis or support in place before you sow or transplant taller varieties, to avoid disturbing the growing plants. Build a support of bamboo canes or stakes, with string, pea netting, or chicken wire secured between the stakes. It is easy to underestimate just how sturdy such supports need

Selected varieties (garden)

Mr. Big
Named for its huge pods, up to 6in. (15cm) long, this 2000 AAS winner is resistant to wilt and powdery mildew.

Mrs. Van's
An heirloom shelling pea from the Pacific Northwest. Abundant, plump pods grow on vines to 6ft. (1.8m) tall.

Selected varieties (sugar snap)

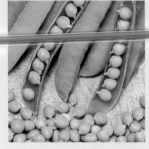

Sugar Ann
The medium size of this sugar snap pea (about 2ft./60cm tall) will not need support. It bears a very early crop of succulent, sweet pods; older ones can be shelled.

Sugar Snap
variety yields well in hot and cold weather. Tall vines grow to 6ft. (1.8m) or more; pods are 3in. (7.5cm) long and sweet.

Selected varieties (snow peas)

Oregon Giant
Produces large pods with exceptionally sweet flavor. Plants grow 2-3ft. (0.6-1m) tall and their pods are 4-5in. (10-12.5cm) long.

Oregon Sugarpod
A superb snow pea with flushes of broad, flat pods over an extended season. Must be picked while young and stringless and be cooked whole.

THE BEAUTIFUL SIGHT of nine perfect peas in a pod. These must be eaten fresh, or be cooked or frozen immediately if they are to be enjoyed at their best.

to be, especially in windy weather. The foliage of fully grown plants acts like a sail, and everything could go flying, so make sure that the supports are strongly tethered. Make a single V-shaped furrow, 2in. (5cm) deep, water the base of the furrow, and sow the peas 2–4in. (5–10cm) apart. You can add a second row, providing it is 12in. (30cm) away, and insert the supports between the two rows.

Caring for the crop

For dwarf and semidwarf varieties, put supports in place before the young plants become top-heavy and flop over; use twiggy sticks, chicken wire attached to stakes, or string and stakes.

Once flowering has begun, plants must have enough water for the pods to swell properly. During dry spells, check the soil moisture (dig under the surface near the plants to see if the soil is damp at root level) and if necessary give the crops a good soaking once

UNUSUAL VARIETIES of peas, such as this purple-podded type, can be found through specialty nurseries or seed catalogs. They add ornament to the garden but vary in yield and taste.

or twice a week. Apply a thick organic mulch after watering to lock in the moisture, and weed regularly.

At harvest time

Pick peas frequently to ensure they are at the peak of freshness. Even if some pods are clearly past their prime, take them off anyway to leave more resources for the remaining pods and thus prolong the harvest. Pick from the bottom of the plant and work upwards. Eat or freeze the peas as soon as possible after picking, to retain maximum flavor and nutrients. After the harvest, cut off the stems at ground level; do not pull up the spent crops because the much-needed clusters of small, white nodules found at the roots are full of nitrogen-fixing bacteria. If left in the ground these nodules will rot down, releasing their nitrogen back into the soil for the next crop to use.

Storing and cooking tips

The shoots and sideshoots of pea plants taste remarkably like a fresh pea and make excellent additions to a salad. Use these shoots before the leaves have opened out.

Peas are good candidates for freezing. Blanch them first for just a few minutes, cool them immediately in ice water, then seal the peas in plastic freezer bags, and pop in the freezer. They make great treats for the kids' lunchboxes.

Pests and diseases

Rabbits and birds can devour seeds and seedlings. To keep birds off, protect young plants with chicken wire, floating row covers, or plastic netting. Once plants are growing strongly, bird attacks usually cease to be a problem. Alternatively, start plants off indoors and plant out when the seedlings have grown to 4in. (10cm) tall. The tiny caterpillars of the pea moth can develop inside the pods, where they feed on the peas. Attacks can be very severe; in extreme cases, they can wipe out entire crops. Aphids can be removed from growing plants by a spray of water from the hose and with the help of beneficial insects. Peas are also susceptible to powdery mildew in dry conditions in late summer. Bacterial and fungal blights can be problematic. Grow resistant varieties to avoid disease problems.

PESTS SUCH AS PEA MOTH can ruin crops and lead to dismay as you open seemingly healthy pods. Avoid them by growing early or late crops, or protecting with floating row covers.

Perennial vegetables

Perennial vegetables, like herbaceous perennials, die down at the end of the year and re-sprout the following spring. Although they take some work to get going, they are are ideal for beginners, because they don't need replanting every year and they provide excellent value, cropping for many years. Some have extra benefits: Artichokes, for example, provide dramatic architectural foliage and have striking blue or purple flowerheads; asparagus foliage can be used in cut-flower arrangements so they, and other larger vegetables such as rhubarb, can be grown in the ornamental garden, freeing up valuable space in the vegetable garden.

Asparagus

Asparagus officinalis

Asparagus spears are harvested each spring. Cutting then stops, to allow the young shoots to develop foliage – essential for building up the plant's food reserves. Asparagus has a harvest period of up to eight weeks, and it can be two or three years after first planting before the first crop. But the delay is worth it for a delicious crop that can last up to 20 years, or even more.

Where to grow

Asparagus is a cool-season perennial that can be grown in zones 4–9. Choose a sunny, sheltered site free of perennial weeds such as Bermuda grass (grassy weeds can be difficult to remove from a growing asparagus patch). Avoid frost pockets because they can damage emerging spears early in the season, and windy sites, which can snap off the mature fern, reducing the amount of food being stored in the crown. The fleshy crowns are likely to rot on waterlogged sites, so choose well-drained soil and dig in plenty of organic matter before planting to improve soil structure. Asparagus needs fertile soil, so don't skimp on the soil amendments. The pH should be 6.5–7; add lime if needed to raise it to this level. If the soil drains poorly, consider building a raised bed for your asparagus. It's worth the investment in time and money, as the plants will produce for many years.

TO PLANT one- or two-year-old asparagus crowns, dig a trench for each row, 6in. (15cm) deep, and carefully spread out the fragile crowns. Cover with 3in. (7.5cm) of soil and water well.

Sowing and planting

It is better to grow male hybrid asparagus, because the male plants are generally more productive, with larger and more abundant spears. Female plants are less so because they produce seeds. Asparagus is usually planted from crowns, although it is possible to grow it from seed, and more varieties may be available. You can also buy container-grown plants, but they are expensive. Crowns are more expensive than seed, but they can be cropped one year earlier.

Buy one- or two-year-old crowns to plant in late winter or early spring, though some suppliers also send out crowns for fall planting. It is important that the ground is ready on delivery because the fleshy crowns mustn't dry out. If planting is delayed, wrap up the roots in wet newspaper.

The bed system gives high yields in a relatively small space, with one bed consisting of three rows of crowns, spaced 12in. (30cm) apart each way. Even if you don't have a true raised bed, the soil can be mounded up to improve drainage. Then dig a trench for each row, 6in. (15cm) deep, and carefully spread out the fragile crowns. Cover with 3in. (7.5cm) of soil and water well. Do not cut any emerging spears, and keep well watered during this first summer. Top up the trench to soil level in fall.

Caring for the crop

Apply a balanced fertilizer and a 2in. (5cm) thick mulch of organic matter in fall or in early spring before the spears emerge to help suppress weeds, retain moisture, protect the early spears from frost, and help prevent the soil from forming a crust (called 'capping'), which causes bent spears. Side-dress with the same fertilizer at the end of the harvest period each year. As the foliage turns completely yellow in fall, cut it down to within an inch or two of the base. To protect the roots further and to control weeds, hoe up the soil to form a mound over the crowns. Remove any weeds as they appear.

At harvest time

It is essential not to over-crop asparagus: If you do, future yields will be severely reduced. For the second and third years, cut lightly for a few weeks. Starting with the fourth year, you can harvest the bed fully.

Spears usually begin emerging around midspring. Using a small, sharp knife, cut off each spear just below soil level when it's roughly 8in. (20cm) tall. It is essential to cut every spear, even those that are thin or bent, because this stimulates the dormant buds in the crown to grow. Be careful not to damage shoots that are just emerging nearby. If they are damaged, they will not form full spears. Stop cutting in early summer.

Storing and cooking tips

Asparagus will keep for up to a week in the fridge, if stored upright in a small amount of water (replace the water daily). One of the best ways to cook asparagus is to boil it in salted water for six or seven minutes, drain, and add butter, salt, and ground black pepper. Steamers can be used to hold the spears upright. Alternatively, brush with oil and fry on a griddle for 6–8 minutes, turning frequently. You can also wrap the spears in foil with a pat of butter, pepper, and salt, and cook on the barbecue.

If you are freezing asparagus, first blanch the chopped spears for two or three minutes.

HARVEST ASPARAGUS SPEARS when they are about 8in. (20cm) tall. Cut every spear, just below soil level, and this will ensure that dormant buds in the crown will begin to grow.

Pests and diseases

Occasionally slugs and snails can nibble at emerging spears, but they don't pose a significant problem. The main pest is the asparagus beetle, because both adults and larvae graze on the emerging spears and foliage. Adult beetles are ¼in. (6mm) long, with black-and-white wing cases and a red under-body; larvae are dark gray, caterpillarlike, and twice as long. Look for adults emerging in late spring, and pick off larvae and adults by hand. Discard—do not compost—old foliage in the fall in case any beetles are tucked in amongst it. Asparagus rust is less of a problem than it once was, thanks to the development of resistant varieties.

Selected varieties

Jersey Knight
Widley adapted and dependable male plants with medium-sized spears ready for harvest at 7-8in. (18-20cm) tall. Is resistant to crown rot and rust.

Purple Passion
Fat spears that are a lovely, deep purple color at harvest; the color fades when cooking. This variety is fairly disease resistant and has a sweet, mildly nutty flavor when cooked.

Artichokes

So many vegetables are such beautiful plants they are worth including in any garden for their looks. Two of the most statuesque perennial plants, the artichoke and the cardoon, are also mouth-watering vegetables. They are closely

related—almost twins—and share the same stature and appearance. In spring, their jagged, gray leaves push through the middle of the desiccated clump of last year's plant. Within a matter of weeks, they have put on good growth, and they continue to grow through summer, providing real drama in the kitchen garden.

Although the plants hail from the Mediterranean, almost all of the artichokes grown commerically in the United States are grown on California's Central Coast, where they thrive in the region's typically frost-free winters and cool, moist summers. The deep, fertile, well-drained coastal soils encourage artichokes' optimum root development.

Although artichokes are perennial, it is best to renew them every 3–5 years. The best way to do this is by taking offsets from existing plants in spring. These can be planted in fresh ground amended with lots of organic material.

With cardoons, the base of the stem is eaten when young, but with artichokes it's the flowers or, more precisely, the calyx. The flowerheads are severed before the flowers show and can be cooked in several ways. Each sepal, thick and fleshy, is dipped in butter and pulled off with your teeth or, when really young, the small heads can be stewed in olive oil and white wine. Big plants, small eating; but the flavor justifies their space, and they are such magnificent plants, how could you not grow them?

ARTICHOKES are regal-looking plants, and every ornamental vegetable garden should have at least one.

Artichokes Cynara scolymus

Artichokes are cool-season perennial vegetables that can be grown in zones 6–9. In zone 5, they will need protection with mulches and cloches, or you can grow them as annuals. The plants look terrific both in the flower border and vegetable garden. The edible part of the huge plants—the base of the mature flower bud—is small. Juvenile flower buds can also be eaten whole.

Where to grow

You need plenty of room to grow artichokes as the foliage can reach up to 4ft. (1.2m) in diameter and flowerheads can reach 5–6ft. (1.5–1.8m) high. Artichokes need a sunny, sheltered site with well-drained, moisture-retentive soil to which plenty of organic matter has been added. Dig deeply or rototill the soil to help mix in the amendments. Avoid growing artichokes in shade or a frost pocket. Also avoid clay soil that gets waterlogged in winter. The best yields are obtained in cool, moist summers that allow plants to build up plenty of foliage.

Sowing and planting

Buy artichokes as container-grown plants, or you can grow from seed. Position plants 4–6ft. (1.2–1.8m) apart, or space them out in a big perennial border. Remove any flowerheads produced in the first year. Plant at any time, but ideally during spring or fall.

In cold-winter areas, sow seed 8–12 weeks before the last spring frost, sowing one seed per 3½in. (9cm) pot filled with potting mix. Seeds will germinate best at 75°F (24°C), so use bottom heat if necessary. Harden off seedlings gradually, and plant out in early summer. If growing artichokes as annuals, you can space them 2–3ft. (0.6–1m) apart. Because plants are very vulnerable to frost, mulch them well or cover young plants if late frosts are forecast.

Caring for the crop

Weed and water plants well, especially during the period when flower buds are forming. Mulch plants well to conserve moisture and keep down weeds. Feed perennial plants monthly during the growing season with a balanced fertilizer.

In spring, mulch with well-composted manure or compost, keeping it away from the stems. In fall, cut off the old flower stems and tired foliage. If growing as annuals, dig up the entire plant and add to the compost; chop up thick stems and roots to speed the composting process. In exposed

GROW ARTICHOKES in a sunny and sheltered site in well-drained, moisture-retaining soil. Ensure they have plenty of room in which to grow without hindrance.

WHEN HARVESTING your artichokes, make sure that you cut the immature flowerheads with pruners just above a leaf junction.

areas likely to experience prolonged frosts, cover the crowns with mulch in late fall.

At harvest time

Large terminal heads are produced in early summer followed by a smaller, secondary flush. Harvest the artichokes with pruners before the scales start to open. Because heat and drought can cause the heads to open rapidly and toughen, check plants regularly in such conditions. If you don't intend to eat the head straight away, leave a length of stalk attached and stand in a glass of water in the refrigerator.

Storing and cooking tips

Soak newly harvested heads in water with 2 tsp. (10ml) salt and 2 tsp. (10ml) vinegar to dislodge any hidden insects. Simmer whole heads for 40 minutes in stock flavored with wine, herbs, diced bacon, mushrooms, and onion, and baste regularly. The tender sepals (like overlapping, fleshy leaves) of small heads, sepal bases of large heads, and the basal disk can be then torn off and eaten. Alternatively snap or cut off the sepals, remove the 'choke' or immature flower, and pare the base with a sharp knife, to leave the artichoke heart. Plunge in water and lemon juice if not cooking immediately, to avoid discoloration. Or steam the entire head, stuffed with a breadcrumb and Parmesan cheese mix, then bake in the oven.

Pests and diseases

Aphids may cluster on stems and heads of artichoke; dislodge them with strong jets of water from the hose. Earwigs like to hide in the tightly balled heads, but they don't usually cause damage to the plant.

Selected varieties

Green Globe
The standard, green-headed variety with large, good-quality heads. If allowed to flower, it bears attractive, thistlelike, blue flowerheads.

Imperial Star
Very high-producing plants with rounded, thornless flower buds that are easy to harvest. Mild flavor; harvest heads when 4½in. (11cm) across, for best quality.

Sunchokes

Sunchokes, also called Jerusalem artichokes, are perennial sunflowers grown for their potatolike tubers. They are extremely hardy and can be grown in zones 3-9. The tubers have a nutty, sweet flavor and can be eaten raw or cooked. They store well, providing invaluable food right through winter. Use them as the basis of warming soups, deep fry to make chips, and bake or combine the tubers with sweet, dried fruits and spices in pies and other desserts.

In a good year, a sunchoke's monumental stems–they can be up to 6-7ft. (1.8-2.1m) high–are decked in yellow, daisylike flowers that smell to some gardeners like chocolate. There's also lots of strong branching growth making an effective summer windbreak for an exposed site. When the foliage collapses after the frost, the knobbly tubers can be left in the ground and harvested as required. Sunchokes are hardy but shoveling a few inches of earth or mulch over the bed provides adequate insulation if conditions are severe. This is by far the best way of storing them. And any tubers left in the soil will grow again, so if the ground is needed for different crops every trace of them must be removed. In this way the sunchoke resembles horseradish, another perennial grown from tubers that are capable of producing new plants from even a tiny piece of root.

All that is needed for a new planting is a few healthy tubers. They can be bought commercially but most gardeners who are already growing sunchokes will pass on a few. Although plants will grow well if compost is added to the planting trench, this might well promote vegetative growth at the expense of tuber production. Pinching out the growing tips, and therefore the flower buds, is sometimes recommended to help the plant concentrate its energies on tuber production– as if it needed any help!

BY LATE SUMMER, your sunchokes will look like this (left), with small, yellow sunflowers soon appearing at the growing tips.

Sunchokes *Helianthus tuberosus*

A member of the sunflower family, this plant is native to the eastern seaboard of North America. Sunchokes were grown by Native Americans and adopted by colonial settlers. The plant is sometimes called Jerusalem artichoke; 'Jerusalem' is a corruption of *girasole* (Italian for sunflower), and the misnomer 'artichoke' was given to them by the French explorer Samuel de Champlain.

Where to grow

Ideally, provide a sunny position with well-drained, moisture-retentive soil. However, because the plant tolerates heavy, shady, and dry sites, it can be raised in areas where other crops won't grow (such as under trees and next to hedges), although the yield will be lower. Sunchokes do need careful positioning because of the shade they cast. They are a useful crop on new sites, because their roots help break up the soil, and they can also be grown as a windbreak because they grow to 10ft. (3m) high when planted in two or three rows, but they will need support on open sites.

Sowing and planting

You can plant sunchokes in spring or fall. Tubers can be bought from specialist suppliers or, more economically, can be donated by a fellow gardener. You can even try planting tubers purchased at the supermarket, but don't let them dry out before planting. Larger tubers can be cut into egg-sized

REMOVING AND SAVING THE TUBERS

If you don't want any sunchokes next year, make sure that you dig them all—even the smallest—out of the ground or they'll regrow. Have a good look around, especially on sandy soil where they might be quite deep. If you are aiming to grow them again, save a few of the healthiest ones for replanting later.

portions provided they have two or three buds. Amend the planting bed with organic matter and plant clean, healthy tubers, each one 6in. (15cm) deep and 12–24in. (30–60cm) apart. Space rows 3ft. (90cm) apart.

Caring for the crop

Once stems are 12in. (30cm) tall, pile up the soil around the roots to make plants more stable.

Selected varieties

Fuseau
The long, relatively smooth tubers make this variety quick to prepare in the kitchen as they are easy to peel. The taste is said to be slightly smoky.

Stampede
An early-maturing variety with large tubers that have a very good texture and flavor.

ONCE THE PLANTS are mature in fall, you can begin to dig out the sunchoke tubers when you need them, as they don't store well out of the ground.

Weeding should be minimal because the quick-growing foliage smothers out other plants. There is also no need to fertilize.

You may need to stake plants on windy sites to prevent the plants from rocking, which can cause the stems and the tubers to rot, reducing the yield. An alternative is to cut back any stems more than 6½ft. (2m) tall by about one-third, but don't be tempted to cut off any more, or the yield will suffer.

Plants initially produce foliage but, in midsummer, they bulk up their tubers, most of which have developed by midfall. When the stems get frosted and die back in late fall or winter, cut back the plants to 6in. (15cm) above the soil. The tubers will survive perfectly well in the ground, but over winter it is best to provide a mulch to protect them. You can pile up a mulch of straw or hay, or use some well-rotted manure or compost to keep the tubers protected.

WHEN HARVESTING the plants, you can pull them out in whole clumps at a time. Each plant will provide about a dozen tubers.

At harvest time

Harvest tubers when they are needed, but they do store fairly well out of the ground with their thick skins. The flavor is said to improve after a frost. Expect at least a dozen tubers from each plant.

Storage and cooking tips

The fleshy, knobby tubers of this very hardy perennial contain the carbohydrate inulin as its storage material, rather than starch. This means that fresh sunchokes are a good starch substitute for diabetics, as the inulin does not covert to glucose but rather to fructose.

Store tubers in the ground or, if it is likely to be frozen solid, waterlogged, or colonized by slugs and snails, store them in moist sand in a cool, frost-free place such as a shed or basement. Sunchokes can also be stored in a perforated plastic bag in the fridge for a couple of weeks. The tubers can be scrubbed and roasted, or sliced thinly and fried like crisps. Once peeled, they can be made into soup or mixed with butter, seasoned, and mashed. Peeled and chopped, they make an excellent ingredient for salsa or salads.

Pests and diseases

Slugs and snails can hollow out tubers, and they like to eat the young shoots. Aphids may cover the stems and leaves; remove them with blasts of water from the hose. Voles and mice can sometimes eat the tubers. If they are persistent pests, plant tubers in raised beds lined with chicken wire or hardware cloth, or in baskets.

Rhubarb

Rheum x cultorum

Although the edible stems of rhubarb are treated like a fruit in desserts, it is truly a vegetable. Related species can be found in the flower garden, but this is a plant best confined to the vegetable garden. The plants can be forced to produce an early crop with longer stems; placing forcing jars over the crowns is the traditional method.

Where to grow

Rhubarb is a herbaceous perennial that does best in areas with winter chill, in zones 3–8. Provide a sunny position and well-drained, moisture-retentive, fertile soil. In warmest areas, rhubarb needs partial shade as the leaves can scorch in hot sun. Before establishing a new bed, amend the soil with plenty of organic matter and remove all perennial weeds. Rhubarb needs a cold period to break winter dormancy before spring growth starts, but it shouldn't be planted in a frost pocket. Also avoid heavy clay soil, which can rot the fleshy crowns. Cool, moist summers and dry winters provide optimum growing conditions, but you can grow rhubarb in a range of climates. In mild-winter areas, some gardeners grow it as a cool-season annual.

GROW RHUBARB in a sunny position and in well-drained, moisture-retentive, fertile soil that has been prepared with lots of organic matter.

Planting rhubarb

Rhubarb can be bought as dormant crowns or container-grown plants, or you can get offset plants from another gardener. It is not usually started from seed. One or two plants should be enough for most people, but if more are required space plants 3ft. (1m) apart. Whichever method you choose, don't harvest until the second

CREATING VIGOROUS NEW PLANTS

Although a single rhubarb crown can be productive for up to five years, plants should be divided every three to four years otherwise they can become congested and weak. If clumps of rhubarb start to die in the center after a few years, dig out the clump and divide the healthy sections from the old crown. Each division should have a few buds and plenty of roots. Replant the divisions immediately and discard the older, less productive center portion.

year. To grow rhubarb as an annual in mild-winter climates, plant crowns or container-grown plants in fall for a late winter and spring harvest.

Dormant crowns Buy crowns from reputable suppliers, who are known to sell reliable stock. Plant in winter or early spring with the dormant buds just above the soil, and keep well watered for the first growing season.

Container-grown plants These can be more expensive than crowns, but can be planted at any time of year, ideally in spring or fall. There's a more limited choice of varieties than with crowns.

Caring for rhubarb

Rhubarb responds well to feeding, especially with nitrogen. A spring side-dressing of general or high-nitrogen fertilizer can be scattered around the plant in spring. Water plants well in their first season. Mulch around the plants to keep the soil moist and to deter weeds, but keep the mulch just away from the stems.

RHUBARB FORCERS are specially designed to encourage the growth of early, tender stems. In winter, check that the emerging crowns are slug- and snail-free and cover them.

TO PULL RHUBARB, grab the stem at its base, close to the crown of the plant, and pull it down with a slight twist. Stems come away easily.

Forcing This is a technique for obtaining earlier, more tender stems. Three-year-old plants with large crowns are most suitable; crops can be forced in the ground or lifted. For forcing in the ground, cover healthy crowns with a rhubarb forcer or large, tall pot in midwinter. Forcing can be hastened by mounding compost or mulch around the forcer to heat it. Once shoots appear, check them daily and harvest in 2–4 weeks.

At harvest time

Stems can be harvested until midsummer, after which they become rather tough and green. Stopping then also allows the plant to produce sufficient foliage to build up food reserves for next year. Remove no more than half the stalks at one time, harvesting as soon as the leaves open fully. To remove a stalk, hold it at the base, pull down, and twist. Cut the stalks from the leaves and put the leaves in the compost. Do not eat the foliage, as it is poisonous!

Storing and cooking tips

Store washed and dried stems in a clear plastic bag in the fridge for two weeks. Rhubarb also freezes well, and there is no need to blanch it first. Rhubarb stems can be stewed in a little water and sugar for crisps, tarts, and pies; it is also used to make preserves and a medium-sweet wine.

Pests and diseases

Slugs and snails will eat young shoots, especially those being forced. Curculios—½in. (1cm) long, yellow-gray weevils—may feast on rhubarb and their alternate host, dock. Handpick these pests and destroy any nearby dock plants. Crowns can be infected with crown rot, in which case dispose of affected and surrounding plants—but do not compost them. Improving drainage can help prevent crown rot. If plants are weak or the foliage is mottled or distorted, dig them up and discard them. Replace with healthy, virus-free stock obtained from a reputable supplier.

Selected varieties

Canada Red
Extra sweet variety that is good for pies and preserves. Produces long, thick, deep red stalks that are very juicy.

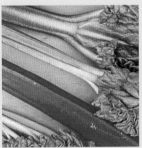

Victoria
Prolific, long-favored variety that produces delicious, juicy, medium-sized, green stems with a red blush. It forces well.

Root and stem vegetables

You must make room for at least a few of these wonderfully productive crops. Although their bounty is mostly hidden from view, either buried in the ground or concealed below foliage, this secret harvest includes valued vegetables, such as potatoes, carrots, and beets. Although you may think of many root vegetables as traditional crops for Northern gardeners, those in warmer climates can successfully grow them during the cooler months of early spring and fall, and even through the winter.

Beets *Beta vulgaris*

Beets are grown primarily for their edible roots, which are usually blood-red but may also be white, yellow, or striped different colors. The colors intensify when the roots are left in the ground as the weather cools. But beets are also grown for their edible, ornamental leaves, which look good in the garden and can be harvested as greens.

Where to grow

Beets are easy to start from seed, and they grow so quickly that they can be used to fill in between other longer-term crops of the kitchen garden. They are compact crops that can be grown in even the smallest home garden. Choose an open, sunny site in well-drained, very light, fertile soil that has been deeply amended with well-rotted organic matter. Beet roots need to grow deeply into the soil, so remove any sticks or trash that may impede their growth. About one week before sowing, apply a balanced fertilizer to the soil and rake the soil smooth. Sandy, free-draining soil produces the best early crops because it warms up more quickly than heavier soil, and beets need good soil temperatures to germinate. If you have very heavy clay soil, start seeds indoors for planting out as seedlings or grow them on ridges or in raised beds.

THE BEST WAY to make beet seeds germinate is to soak them overnight. Sow extra short rows every 14 days to provide a continuous crop.

> ### THINNING
>
> Beet seeds may actually contain as many as four seeds in a single fruit. That's why several seedlings may emerge even if you have been extra-careful with spacing. Thin the excess seedlings so you leave the strongest one in each clump.

Sowing and planting

Most beet varieties produce rounded or globe-shaped roots, while there are also long and cylindrical or stump-rooted types that are best for winter storage. The large, corky-textured seed is easy to handle but can be slow to germinate. You can plant beets in early spring or midsummer in most areas; in mild regions, you can do so through the winter. In order to have a regular supply of tender roots, sow a short row every couple of weeks. Mark out straight rows using a string line or bamboo cane, water the drill if the soil is dry, and sow the seed thinly, 1in. (2.5cm) deep, in rows 12in. (30cm) apart. Space beet seeds with about ¾in. (2cm) between them. Seedlings should appear in 10–14 days. Thin to 4in. (10cm) between seedlings when four or five leaves have grown.

If starting beets indoors for planting out in colder areas, sow or thin to one plant per cell pack. Plant as soon as possible after the last frost date and protect with floating row covers to keep the seedlings warm.

Caring for the crop

Beets are generally trouble-free. Water thoroughly every 10 days during dry spells: Lack of water causes woody roots; a fluctuation in water supply can cause splitting; and an excess means leaves at the expense of roots. Regularly hand-weed close to the plants and hoe the soil between the rows, keeping the blade well away from the roots because they will 'bleed' if damaged. Leaf miners may sometimes tunnel through beet leaves; dispose of any damaged foliage. Blast aphids off the crop with a strong jet of water from the hose. Beets require adequate boron for good growth; if your beets show signs of nutrient deficiency, a soil test or your Cooperative Extension Service can tell you if your soil requires amendment to increase the boron level.

At harvest time

For the best flavor and texture, harvest when the roots are tennis ball-sized—any larger and they develop an unpleasant, woody texture. Succulent and tender baby beets can be harvested as soon as they're large enough to eat, usually around golf-ball size. Before lifting, use a garden fork to loosen the soil beneath, but take care not to damage the roots, particularly if they're intended for storage.

Storing and cooking tips

Beets store well and will keep through winter. Lift the roots in fall and select only sound ones for storage. Gently knock off any extra soil and twist off the leaves a few inches from the top of the root, wearing rubber gloves to avoid staining your hands. Then carefully place the roots, not touching each other, in boxes of dry sand or coir. Store in a cool shed or garage. Small, succulent beets are delicious eaten raw, but boil or roast larger ones until tender. Leave the skin on for cooking to prevent the color from bleeding. Once cooked, the skins separate easily.

HARVEST A CROP OF BEETS by loosening each swollen root with a fork or trowel under the soil, which enables you to lift the beets gently out of the ground.

Selected varieties

Detroit Dark Red
A round, red, quick-maturing variety that can be harvested young as baby beets.

Burpee's Golden
With its golden skin and flesh, this non-staining beet has been a favorite since the 1940's. Sweet, mild flavor.

Carrots

Along with tomatoes and peas, carrots are a favorite in the children's garden. They are so easy—pull them young, wash them, and eat raw. The taste is much sweeter than the 'manufactured' carrots of supermarket shelves. Home-grown baby carrots are a delicacy in the early season, but pull them in the middle of winter when something earthy and comforting is required and the same roots, grown to maturity, are instantly warming and filling.

Carrots love sandy soil and their ancestor, a wild member of the parsley family, flourishes in light, well-drained soil. On heavy clay, the roots struggle to push themselves down into the soil and expand into anything approaching a respectable root. That's why it's important to prepare the soil well and to choose the right variety. If your soil is shallow, rocky, or heavy clay, then opt for round or half-long carrots rather than long-rooted types that are likely to develop stunted or forked roots in difficult soil. Use only well-rotted organic soil amendments; don't plant carrots in soil that has recently been amended with fresh compost or even composted manure. To find the best varieties for your growing conditions and region, consult a seed catalog, a knowledgeable nursery, or your local Cooperative Extension Service.

TO MATCH THIS healthy, prolific crop, you'll need protection against carrot rust fly and, ideally, light, free-draining soil.

In addition to different lengths and shapes, newer carrot varieties boast purple, white, or yellow flesh. Some types are called 'finger' carrots. These produce early roots and should be harvested before they become tough and thick. Those varieties that take longer to mature, producing a later-season crop, are better for storing.

Carrot seeds are tiny and may be available 'pelleted'—coated with a compound that makes them easier to handle and sow. Carrots do well in containers and raised beds and make good crops for roof gardens and balconies, where they will be out of the reach of the crop's main pest, the carrot root fly.

Although they are thought of as savory vegetables, carrots bridge the gap between savory and sweet. Thus they are one of the few vegetables that can make wonderful soup and are also a popular ingredient in muffins and cakes. Try cooking your carrots with a little butter and a splash of marsala or white wine and a drop of water. Keep the lid on the pan and shake fairly often. The melting flesh of the carrots is imbued with all the taste of the wine and will gradually become glazed to an amber color. Carrots can also be tossed in olive oil and roasted in the oven with other root vegetables, such as turnips, parsnips, and potatoes, along with grated ginger.

Carrots

Daucus carota

Choose the right varieties and you can harvest carrots over a long season. They will have excellent flavor and texture—and a load of healthy vitamin A. Carrots store well over winter and come in a range of shapes and colors—not just orange, but also red to yellow to purple and are grouped into categories that include Nantes, Chantenays, Danvers, and Imperators.

Where to grow

All carrots require an open, sunny site and deep, well-drained, fertile soil, but you need to find out exactly what type of soil you have and choose varieties to suit. To grow long-rooted carrots, you require a good loam or sandy soil that can be cultivated to a depth of 12in. (30cm).

No matter what your soil is like, remove all rocks, trash, and weeds from the bed. If the soil is completely unsuitable or space is limited, sow carrots in raised beds filled with all-purpose planting mix.

Sowing and planting

Carrots are grown from seed, and can be sown over a long season, depending on your climate. In cold-winter climates, sow in early spring for a summer harvest and then again in late summer for a fall crop. In mild-winter ones, start sowing in spring for summer harvest, and continue to sow in fall and winter for cool-season crops.

Before sowing carrots, deeply dig the ground and break up clumps and remove stones. Dig in compost and rake to a fine tilth. Don't try to work wet soil; wait until it dries out and doesn't clump. Avoid walking on the soil, which compacts it. About a week before sowing, apply a balanced fertilizer and rake it into the soil.

Some gardeners plant carrots on raised mounds or in trenches. To make a trench, dig along the length of a row about 12in. (30cm) down in a V shape. Fill the trench with planting mix and sifted compost, or a good commercial soil mix.

In the garden or in a raised bed, use a string line or bamboo cane to mark out lines, then make shallow drills using a hoe or trowel ½in. (1cm) deep with 6–12in. (15–30cm) between the rows, depending on the variety. If the soil is dry, water the drill and allow it to drain before sowing. Sprinkle the fine seed along the drill, cover with a thin layer of soil and firm down. It's essential to keep the soil moist while the seeds germinate, which can take several weeks. Carrots still produce a good crop even when interplanted with other crops, such as radishes and lettuce.

Caring for the crop

Control weeds while the young carrots grow, using a trowel or hand weeder to remove weeds between the rows, taking care not to damage the developing carrot roots. Keep the soil evenly moist by using drip irrigation, or by watering deeply once a week.

Thin to around 2in. (5cm) between plants, using the thinnings as baby carrots as soon as possible. Thinning or weeding is best done in the evening to reduce the smell from the foliage, which attracts carrot rust fly, and it is easier if you water the crop several hours beforehand. You can pull out the young seedlings, or snip off the foliage with scissors. Cover the bitter-tasting green 'shoulders' on the root tops by mulching or piling soil on them as the carrots grow.

At harvest time

Carrots are ready for harvesting about 12–16 weeks after sowing, although the timing depends on whether you prefer tender baby carrots or larger roots. Young carrots can be pulled up carefully by hand, while larger ones and those intended for storage are best lifted by gently easing them up with a fork, to avoid damaging or breaking the roots.

Storing and cooking tips

Carrots keep best in the soil. Remove the foliage and cover with 6in. (15cm) of a lightweight organic mulch such as straw or leaves. Where soils become waterlogged in winter, carrots can be lifted and stored in boxes of sand or sawdust, but their flavor and texture suffer as a result. The sweet taste and vitamin content are highest in roots that are scrubbed and eaten raw. If you prefer carrots cooked, however, then steaming them gives the best results.

Pests and diseases

Carrot rust fly is the main pest of carrots. The insects lay their eggs at the base of the young carrots and

SURROUND CARROTS with a 3ft. (1m) barrier to exclude the carrot rust fly, which flies close the ground.

the larvae chew tunnels through the root. Protect carrot seedlings with floating row covers or surround the crop with a barrier 3ft. (1m) high; the carrot rust fly is not actually a very good flyer. Wireworms can also attack carrots; draw the pests away from the growing crop by placing fully grown potatoes or carrots in the bed. Every few days, discard the bait vegetable, along with the wireworms that have been attracted to it.

Selected varieties

Purple Haze
Deep purple skin and bright orange inside, this 2006 AAS award winner has slender roots to 12in. (30cm) long.

Flyaway
This variety has the sweet, crisp flavor of a Nantes carrot. Roots are of medium length and may resist carrot rust fly.

Parmex
A round-rooted carrot, ideal for shallow soils and growing in containers. It has good uniformity and core color.

Rainbow Blend
A mix of red, yellow, orange, and purple carrots that retain their colors; all have a slightly different taste. Fun in the kid's garden.

Celeriac

Apium graveolens

Celeriac is much easier to grow than its cousin, celery, and easily slots into spare gaps in the garden, forming neat clumps of celerylike leaves. Beneath its stout, gnarled appearance lies delicious, creamy flesh with a texture that resembles potato but with a subtle flavor that hints of celery. The similarity to celery stops at the taste, because you grow it for its root, not the stalks.

Where to grow

Choose ground in full sun or partial shade. In the wild, celeriac grows in moist soils, so well-drained, moisture-retentive soil is ideal. Before planting, improve the soil's water-holding capacity by digging in generous amounts of organic matter such as garden compost or well-rotted manure.

Sowing and planting

Sow the tiny seed about 10 weeks before the last spring frost to give the crop plenty of time to grow to a good size. You can also start celeriac in summer for a fall crop in warm areas.

Sow thinly in cell packs filled with well-drained potting mix. Then cover the seed with vermiculite; they need light to germinate so don't cover them too much. Bottom heat from a propagating unit or heating mat may hasten germination. Gradually thin plants to one per cell and keep the seedlings moist.

Transfer the seedlings into peat pots filled with growing mix once the first true leaves have formed, with one plant per pot. Grow the seedlings in a warm, light place. The seedlings should be acclimated to outdoor conditions before being planted out at the end of spring or early summer. Space the seedlings 12in. (30cm) apart in rows 18in. (45cm) apart, and water in. Protect the young seedlings from slugs and snails.

Caring for the crop

Keep the soil moist and hoe regularly to keep down weeds. In midsummer, cut off the lower leaves to expose more of the crown. Also remove any leaves that show signs of white tunnels, which may be a sign of attack by leaf miners. In fall, draw soil around the swollen stem bases to keep the flesh white. Mulch plants to keep soil cool and moist in summer, and to protect from frosts in fall.

At harvest time

You can leave celeriac in the ground until needed, as long as the stems are well covered with mulch. Or lift

A WELL-GROWN, well-tended celeriac is quite a sight, and can easily rival a coconut in size. Make sure that seedlings have enough room to expand.

TO ENCOURAGE GOOD GROWTH such as this, water emerging celeriac every 5–10 days during dry spells, adding a high-nitrogen fertilizer if growth is poor.

ALLOW 3–6 MONTHS for celeriac to mature. Ease the stem out of the ground with a fork and trim off foliage and fine roots.

in fall before the soil freezes and store as described below. Harvest when the stem is between the size of an apple and a coconut—4–5 in. (10–12.5cm).

Storing and cooking tips

To store celeriac, twist off the leafy tops and place the vegetable in boxes of barely damp peat or sand in a cool shed. It can also be diced and lightly blanched for storage in the freezer. Celeriac is a hugely versatile vegetable and can be used in soups and salads. You can boil strips or cubes for a few minutes, then cool and add to salads. It can also be fried, roasted, and mashed with potatoes.

Selected varieties

Ibis
Produces fairly smooth, white roots with a flavor somewhere between celery and parsley. A fast-growing variety.

Brilliant
This European variety has large, round, fleshy, nearly fiberless stems of good quality and excellent taste. It stores well.

Celery

Apium graveolens

Celery can be a challenge for impatient gardeners to grow, yet it is a wonderful treat fresh from the garden, without the stringiness and bitterness of some supermarket celery. Like its cousin celeriac, celery needs a long, cool growing season and so does best in areas with cool summers. The reward for your patience is a crunchy, pale green, delicious vegetable with many uses in the kitchen.

Types of celery

Older varieties of celery require blanching—the exclusion of light from the stems—in order to produce pale stems. Newer varieties are self-blanching so naturally develop pale stems. The self-blanching types should be grown fairly close together so they provide shade for each other.

Where to grow

Celery needs moist, rich soil, recently amended with well-rotted manure or compost. It prefers temperatures that are warm but not hot. A few weeks before planting, dig in some balanced fertilizer. In warmest regions, celery needs light shade.

Sowing and planting

Grow celery as an early spring crop in cool regions, or plant in late summer for a fall crop. In mild-winter regions, you can plant in fall for a winter crop. Just remember that celery requires 90–120 days to mature after transplanting, so heed the time given on the seed packet and time your planting accordingly. If you are sowing seeds indoors, you need to start them up to 12 weeks before the last expected frost in your area. Soak the seeds overnight before sowing into cell packs or a propagation tray filled with good-quality potting mix. Seeds need temperatures of 70°F (21°C) to germinate, so use bottom heat until the seedlings emerge. Gradually thin plants to one per cell and keep the seedlings moist. Because raising celery from seed can be difficult, you may prefer to purchase young plants from the nursery. Either way, plant the young seedlings after all danger of frost has passed, hardening them off gradually to outdoor conditions if you have grown them from seed.

Position the young plants in blocks, about 8in. (20cm) apart each way for self-blanching varieties so that they will shade each other. Light must be able to reach the leaves, though, so don't plant near taller crops that will completely shade the plants. Other types can be planted 10in. (25cm) apart in rows 18in. (45cm) apart.

Caring for the crop

Celery needs consistent moisture as the plants must not dry out. Keep the soil moist with frequent soakings, or use drip irrigation. Apply a high-nitrogen liquid fertilizer regularly during the growing season. Plants may bolt if the soil dries out, or if the temperatures fall below 50°F (10°C), so surround the plants with an organic mulch such as straw to help keep the soil moist and protected.

Self-blanching varieties will develop whitened stalks naturally. To blanch other celery types, tie the tops of the stalks together 3–4 weeks before harvest time. Then either mound soil or mulch over the stalks, or cover them with some kind of sleeve—clay pipes if you have them, but cardboard works well, as do old plastic or paper milk cartons with both ends removed. Make sure the leaves are exposed but light is excluded from the developing stalks.

At harvest time

Remove the collars, if any, and cut off individual stalks from the outside of the plant as desired, or wait until the entire plant has matured and then dig up the crop. Use a sharp knife to snip off the stalks just at the soil line. Celery plants won't last long after the first hard frosts of fall or winter, so harvest before the first frost dates for your area.

CELERY IS A VEGETABLE for patient gardeners, as it needs a long, cool, growing season to produce tasty stems.

Storing and cooking tips

Celery is a great snack for children's lunchboxes and can be enjoyed raw with spreads such as peanut butter, cream cheese, or dip. But it's also an essential ingredient for soups, stock, and stir-fries. Tear off the leaves, rinse, and add them to soups, where they impart a more delicate flavor than the stalks. You can also throw celery in the juicer with other vegetables and fruit to make healthy juice drinks and smoothies. Store celery in plastic bags in the refrigerator.

Pests and diseases

Aphids, cabbage loopers, and leafhoppers may attack celery. Leaf miners can burrow through the foliage, leaving telltale, white tracks. Use floating row covers to help control these insects. If fusarium wilt or viral diseases are a problem, buy resistant varieties, amend the soil, or grow celery in raised beds filled with good growing mix. In soils with calcium deficiency, inner stalks may turn brown; you will need to amend the soil with lime or gypsum, depending on your soil type.

Selected varieties

Tango
A self-blanching type with apple-green, smooth stems and crunchy texture. Can tolerate some drought and heat without bolting.

Victoria
A bolt-resistant, upright, self-blanching type. Stalks are crispy and juicy.

Fennel

There are some vegetables that combine good looks, marvelous texture, and delectable taste in one package, and, fennel—sometimes called Florence fennel—is a prime example. It is not grown as often as many other crops, but it deserves wider use, as the taste is like no other vegetable. Fennel that is grown in the herb garden has the same feathery, anise-flavored foliage as vegetable fennel, but not the large, flat or round, edible bulb.

Fennel is a Mediterranean crop and if it experiences periods of cold temperatures after

THREE MONTHS FROM SEED to the table, fennel makes a swollen, crunchy, white, aniseed-tasting bulb. Water well, not letting the soil bake dry in summer.

it has started to grow, or if experiences warm weather, it attempts to flower and set seed. Because of this, it can be a difficult crop unless you know your local climate conditions well and can plant accordingly. The trick is to sow or plant it out after the threat of plummeting temperatures has passed, say in late spring or early summer. In climates that don't have a mild winter or a long, cool spring, you should sow seeds in summer and let the plants mature in fall.

Being a fast-growing plant there should be plenty of time for it to develop its big, white, swollen stems, unchecked by fluctuating temperatures. In California, where it was probably introduced by the Spanish centuries ago, it has made itself at home both in cultivation and in the kitchen. The Mediterranean-type climate there means it can be sown in late winter and early spring and can be harvested about 10 weeks later.

Fennel hates root disturbance. It is a member of the umbel family and, without exception, they all resent being transplanted. There is no reason, however, not to plant one or two seeds in cell packs or peat pots, taking out the weakest if both germinate, and setting out the young plant when it is fairly sturdy. This is a good way of stealing a march on the season: Plants suffer no check to their growth since their roots remain intact.

Because timing is so important when growing fennel, successive sowing isn't realistic, but it can be harvested for several weeks from the same sowing, and it will provide anything from a slender adolescent to a full-blown, mature vegetable.

Fennel
Foeniculum vulgare

Well known as a garden herb, the swollen, edible bulb of the fennel plant—known also as finocchio or Florence fennel—is a popular vegetable in Italy, from where it was introduced to northern Europe and eventually to North America. Unfortunately, it flowers rapidly if conditions aren't quite as Mediterranean as it would like, and if this happens the bulb will not swell.

Where to plant

Fennel is fussy and you may want to get some advice from a local gardener who has grown it successfully in your area before growing it for the first time. It thrives in a sunny, sheltered site with rich, moisture-retentive soil, ideally well drained and with lots of organic matter. Avoid heavy clay, stony, or poorly drained ground. If you can't meet its exacting requirements, don't try growing fennel because the plants will bolt if they become stressed.

Sowing and planting

Because fennel is frost-tender, you can either start seed indoors about eight weeks before the last frost date for your area, or sow it directly in the garden in spring or summer for a later harvest. The plants should mature 12–16 weeks after sowing.

When raising plants from seed, it's important to keep root disturbance to a minimum and avoid bolting. Seed should therefore be sown in individual pots or cell packs, to allow transplanting with the minimum of stress to the young plants. Fill containers with growing mix, firm gently, water well, and allow to drain. In each pot, sow several seeds ½in. (1cm) deep, spaced a little apart from each other, then cover with a little more growing mix. Place in a greenhouse or

HERB AND VEGETABLE FENNEL are both prolific flowerers, attracting bees and other beneficial insects to the garden.

FEATHERY SHOOTS

When harvesting fennel, cut each bulb off just above ground level and leave the stump in the ground. Young, feathery shoots will soon start to appear from the stump, and they can be used in the kitchen.

on a sunny windowsill and, once the seed has germinated, thin to leave one seedling per pot. Keep plants evenly moist, and plant out in 4–5 weeks; don't leave them in their pots for too long or they're likely to bolt.

When sowing seed in the garden from late spring to midsummer, mark out straight lines and make a shallow drill ½in. (1cm) deep. Water if dry, and allow to drain before sowing the seed thinly. Space rows 18in. (45cm) apart. It's a good idea to make several sowings over a period of several weeks as insurance against poor germination or bolting caused by low or fluctuating temperatures.

Container-grown plants can be planted out from late spring to very early summer, depending on whether you live in a mild or cold area. Acclimate plants to outdoor conditions for a couple of weeks, then plant out at 8in. (20cm) spacings and water well. The direct-sown seedlings need to be thinned once they have germinated and are growing strongly, leaving around 8in. (20cm) between each plant.

Caring for the crop

Keep well watered during dry spells. Weed the crop regularly, hoeing between the rows and hand-weeding close to the plants. As the bulbs start to swell, use a hoe or trowel to pile up the soil around the roots to make them whiter and sweeter.

At harvest time

Harvest once the bulbs are sufficiently large, using a fork to loosen the roots carefully before lifting. When harvesting, cut the bulb off just above ground level and leave the stump in the ground. Young, feathery shoots will soon appear, and these can also be used in the kitchen.

Storing and cooking tips

The succulent, aniseed-flavored stems are rich in potassium and folic acid, while the attractive,

FLATTISH BULBS are nearly as rewarding as rounded ones and can be harvested for the table as soon as they are ready. The foliage can be blended with other herbs for a salad dressing.

feathery foliage can be used in the same way as the herb, although the flavour is stronger. Florence fennel is superb with fish and in casseroles. The raw root can also be thinly sliced, grated, or shredded for salads—toss it with vinaigrette and citrus fruit for a refreshing summer appetizer. Cut the bulb in half, brush with olive oil, and grill on the barbecue for a tasty side dish. The bulb will keep for several weeks if stored in a cool, dry place.

Selected varieties

Selma Fino
Large, flat, white bulbs that mature in 80 days. Will not bolt from a spring sowing.

Victorio
This variety produces round, smooth, pure white bulbs with neat, feathery foliage and good resistance to bolting.

Sweet potatoes *Ipomoea batatas*

Although they share a name and are both edible tuberous roots, sweet potatoes and potatoes are quite different crops for the kitchen garden. Sweet potatoes are perennials grown as warm-season annuals, they love the heat, and they produce sprawling vines that can cover a lot of ground. If you live in an area where you can guarantee 100 days of heat, you can grow sweet potatoes.

Where to grow

You'll need a sunny site and well-drained soil to grow sweet potatoes. You'll also need plenty of room, though you can get bush varieties that occupy less space than the vines that can take over half the vegetable garden. Plant in a sheltered spot; sweet potatoes can be killed by even a light frost. Choose

SWEET POTATOES can be started off by placing them in a cup of water until they develop rooted shoots, or slips. When doing this, use only disease- and insect-free tubers.

a variety suited to your climate; short-season varieties are now available, which means even gardeners in northern states and Canada can grow this South American native.

Planting sweet potatoes

Sweet potatoes are grown from rooted cuttings called 'slips,' and not from seed. You can purchase disease-free slips from a supplier or you can grow your own quite easily. Do not use store-bought sweet potatoes; tubers from a fellow gardener or a community garden are a good source. To get slips started, place a healthy sweet potato upright in a container of water so that the bottom third of the tuber is immersed. Set it on a sunny windowsill and soon the tuber will sprout. Snap off the sprout and place it in water or damp compost until roots have grown, then plant the rooted slip in a pot filled with potting soil. Harden off slips before planting them out in the garden.

Whether you have purchased slips or grown your own, prepare the soil by digging and incorporating some well-rotted compost. Space the slips 15–18 in. (38–45cm) apart in rows 3ft. (1m) apart.

Many gardeners find it's best to grow sweet potatoes on ridges or hills 12in. (30cm) high. If your climate is marginal, try growing sweet potatoes in raised beds. Raised beds have the advantage of warming up quickly and staying warmer longer than regular garden beds. You can also fill the bed with the kind of light, free-draining soil that sweet potatoes prefer. Warm the soil by covering it with black plastic sheeting, then plant the slips through cross-shaped cuts in the plastic. You can further warm the crop and the soil by covering the newly planted slips with floating row covers.

Caring for the crop

Sweet potato vines root when in contact with the ground, so you lift them up on supports or mulch the ground with straw. Water sparingly—the vines are drought-tolerant. If you allow the plants to root, they will divert energy away from the initial roots, which is where the tubers for harvesting are developing. There is no need to fertilize them.

Keep the ground free of weeds while the plants first start to grow, although the vines will soon begin 'running' off the beds or planting mounds, smothering most weeds.

Cover the crop early and late in the growing season with floating row covers to protect from frosts.

At harvest time

The foliage will start to die down once the cooler weather appears. Before hard frost strikes, dig up the tubers, using a fork to loosen the soil. Be extremely careful not to slice or otherwise damage the tubers, in order to prevent bruising or tearing the skin.

Uncured sweet potatoes have a musty taste, so they must be first dried in the sun for a day or two, then cured in a warm, humid place for about two weeks. Curing increases the sugar content of the tubers. They need a place at least 85°F, with high humidity, in order to cure well. A potting shed or a warm kitchen is ideal.

CURE SWEET POTATOES to prevent them from developing an unpleasant taste. Don't wash or bruise the tubers before curing them in a warm place.

Storing and cooking tips

Once cured, sweet potatoes can keep in a cool, dry place for several months, but check them regularly for signs of rot. Sweet potatoes are a good source of vitamins A and C, as well as potassium. Like carrots, sweet potatoes can be served in both savory main dishes and in desserts. Roast or bake them in the oven like potatoes, or mash them to use in a pudding or pie. Or add them to casseroles and stews.

Pests and diseases

Minimize problems by planting only disease- and insect-free slips. In the South, sweet potato weevils can chew through the tubers; control them by rotating crops and cleaning up all plant remnants at the end of the season. Wireworms sometimes leave small, round holes in the tubers. Use deep tilling, crop rotations, and raised beds to help keep down populations of wireworms. Flea beetles can chew foliage; floating row covers will keep them at bay as well as heating up the crop. Sweet potato whitefly can be a problem that is difficult to control; try sticky traps and encourage biological controls in the garden.

SWEET POTATOES look like potatoes but the taste is completely different. They have a sweet flavor that is intensified when the tubers are roasted in the oven.

Parsnips

Pastinaca sativa

Parsnips are biennial, completing their life cycle of flowering and setting seed over two years. They are extremely hardy and can be left in the ground over winter and harvested when needed. It is well worth leaving a few roots unharvested to develop their pretty spring flowers, which attract many beneficial predatory insects, including flower flies, to the garden.

Where to grow

Although it takes time and skill to produce perfectly tapered, supermarket-worthy roots, growing parsnips for the supper table requires no special skill, and they will taste delicious. Parsnips like a sunny position and grow well in most well-drained soils, ideally one that is light and sandy. The soil should be free of clumps and stones—parsnips, like carrots, will fork and split if the soil is rocky or too rich. Add well-rotted compost or manure the previous year, and a few weeks before sowing rake the soil over thoroughly, adding a general fertilizer, then rake the surface to a fine, crumbly texture to prepare a seedbed. If your soil is shallow, or heavy and rocky and cannot be amended,

THE KEY to getting a good crop is to select the strongest seedling from each sowing, and to make sure that the crops are well spaced and the rows are well weeded.

then choose a bulbous variety or grow parsnips in a raised bed filled with good planting mix. Or dig a V-shaped trench 12–18in. (30–45cm) deep and fill it with good planting mix and well-rotted compost, then sow along the trench.

Sowing and planting

Parsnips do need a long growing season—up to 130 days after sowing—and are not ready for harvest until after the first fall frosts. For that reason, they are grown mainly in cooler regions or are sown in fall in milder regions for a winter crop. They are not a suitable crop for the warmest regions.

The seed of parsnips is notoriously slow to germinate, taking a few weeks before the first signs appear. For this reason, it is possible to sow fast-maturing vegetables, such as radishes, around them so that you are able to make good use of the available space. Some gardeners sow radishes along with the parsnip seed so the row is marked. You can harvest the radishes before the parsnips are ready.

Always sow resistant varieties to avoid canker, which results in rough, reddish brown areas around the top of the root. Parsnip seed stores badly, so use a fresh batch each year.

Make a drill ½in. (1cm) deep in the prepared seedbed or trench with a hoe. If the bottom of the drill is dry, dampen it first. Sow three seeds every 6in. (15cm), and then lightly cover them with fine soil. The rows should be spaced 12–24in. (30–60cm) apart.

Caring for the crop

When the seedlings appear, thin out so the young plants are spaced 4in. (10cm) apart, and hoe regularly to keep competing weeds down. Large, easy-to-peel roots are obtained by giving the crop plenty of space and ensuring an absence of weeds. Parsnips are highly drought-resistant plants that need watering only every 10–14 days if the foliage begins to wilt. Mulch around the plants to keep down weeds and maintain soil moisture.

At harvest time

Start lifting parsnips in late summer as baby vegetables, digging them up carefully with a fork. Most gardeners, however, wait until the foliage has died back and the first frosts have arrived, which is a sign that the roots have begun to sweeten. A hard frost will turn the starch content of parsnips into sugars, which is why parsnips make a popular winter vegetable, and they are at their sweetest during the coldest winters. The roots can be left in the ground until they are needed, but during hard frosts it may be impossible to dig them out of the soil.

Pests and diseases

Like carrots, parsnips suffer from carrot rust fly. If the crop is peppered with tiny holes on harvest, cover or surround future crops with low barriers or by using

GARDEN-GROWN parsnips may not be as pristine as those you find in the supermarket but the flavor is unbeatable.

floating row covers to stop the fly from laying its eggs. Row covers will also help to keep leafhoppers, flea beetles, and cabbage root maggots off the soil. Discard any leaves with visible tunneling or brown, dried-up patches, as they may be caused by leaf miners.

Storing and cooking tips

Although parsnips are winter hardy, you can lift some for storage so that you always have some in case the ground is too hard to dig. Arrange the roots in boxes so that they are not touching, in layers of sand or sawdust, and place in a dry shed. To use, cut the roots into 'fingers', removing any central woody parts, and roast or fry with garlic to bring out the rich, sweet flavor and unusual fibrous texture.

Selected varieties

Javelin
A wedge-shaped, canker-resistant parsnip with good yield. This variety has long, slender roots and a good flavor.

Gladiator
Germinates quickly and grows well, producing cream-colored, sweet, smooth-skinned, 7in. (18cm) roots.

Potatoes

Although potatoes are long associated with countries like Ireland or Poland, they are actually South American plants, with wild ancestors that grew in the high, cool Andes. They were introduced to Europeans in the 16th century and then spread back to the Americas and beyond. The plants are bushy, with dark green foliage and small white, pink, red, or blue flowers that sometimes form small, green tomatolike fruits. But don't eat these; the foliage and fruit are toxic.

Is it worth growing your own potatoes? They are the most readily available of all vegetables, and you can pick up a 10lb. (4.5kg) bag of Idaho or Prince Edward Island potatoes for under five dollars from any grocery store on the way home from work. But one very good reason for growing potatoes in the garden is that you can choose exactly the variety you want—for its flavor or specific culinary use—and harvest it when you need it or store it over winter. And once you start experimenting with different types of potatoes, you may never go back to the limited supermarket selection. The flavor of home-grown

potatoes is so concentrated, so earthy, it is almost like eating another vegetable. Another reason to grow potatoes is that you can be sure they contain only what you have put on the soil in your garden. Like all root vegetables, potatoes absorb and retain the chemicals, such as fungicides and pesticides, found in the earth around them. Home growers are much less likely to have to resort to chemical pest and disease control than commercial growers. So you can be sure your potatoes are organic and free of fungicides. And although it is true that potatoes take up lots of room, you can grow a few plants on even the smallest balcony or in a tiny backyard in containers.

Digging potatoes is everyone's favorite job. The number of tubers you find is a revelation. Although children enjoy digging potatoes, you must warn them that the foliage, flowers, and fruit of the plant are poisonous—their purple or white flowers being a reminder that potato plants belong to the deadly nightshade family.

Dig them up on a dry, sunny day and leave them on the surface of the soil until their skins are quite dry. Before the sun starts to go down, drop them into paper or burlap bags for storing.

COLORFUL POTATOES with red and white skins are a treat to dig up at harvest time.

Potatoes *Solanum tuberosum*

Where would you be without the humble potato? New potatoes are eaten with butter and mint in late spring and mashed ones are essential at Thanksgiving and Christmas dinners, when it is cold and dark outside; few weeks pass by without potatoes appearing in a meal in one form or another. And they're nutritious—full of vitamin C, iron, potassium, and fiber.

Types of potatoes

Potatoes come in a great diversity of sizes, shapes, and colors, but they are usually classified as either early, midseason, or long-season types. Early types are ready to harvest much sooner than the other two categories, which are the ones that can be stored over winter. You will also come across 'fingerlings': These are long, narrow, flavorful potatoes. New potatoes are not a type, but are simply harvested before full maturity.

There are a dizzying number of potato varieties sold through specialty suppliers and even from local

YOU CAN PLANT seed potatoes whole, or cut them into sections, each with two or three eye buds.

POTATO BLIGHT

Late blight is a fungal disease that first appears as brown blotches on the leaves and stems, and then affects the tubers, which soften, blacken, and smell awful. It can spread rapidly, so you must act quickly. Cut off the foliage to prevent the fungus from spreading down to the tubers. To prevent it in the future, choose disease-resistant varieties and ask your local Cooperative Extension Service about using copper fungicides.

nurseries and farm-supply outlets. You can find types described as having smooth or rough skin, or with dry or moist flesh, in colors that range from white to yellow, blue, red, and brown. They may also be classified as good for frying, baking, boiling, or storing. Your local Cooperative Extension Service can provide information on which varieties are best and available in your area, but it's worth experimenting with different types. After a few seasons you'll discover which ones you and your family enjoy both in the garden and at the supper table.

Where to grow

Potatoes can be grown on almost any deep soil in a sunny site, but sandy, well-drained soil is best. It certainly helps if the ground is fertile and moisture-retentive, so add plenty of well-rotted organic matter such as compost in the fall of the year before. Just ahead of planting, you can dig in some balanced fertilizer, and be sure to rake the soil well to break up any large clods. Avoid waterlogged ground, low-lying spots where frosty air could collect, and alkaline soil (which can result in a disease called 'scab' unless you choose scab-tolerant varieties). A soil pH of 5.5–6 is a good range for potatoes. Practice crop rotation with potatoes, leaving a break of about three years before growing them in the same spot, to avoid the accumulation of soilborne pests and diseases.

Small crops of potatoes can be grown in large containers such as tubs or old wine barrels. Placed in a warm, sunny place under cover, this is a good way of getting an early batch of new potatoes. You could even have new potatoes in the middle of winter.

Sowing and planting

Planting times for potatoes vary by climate. In most areas, planting is in spring, a few weeks before the last frost, but in mild-winter climates you can plant again in late summer or fall for a winter crop. Again, your Cooperative Extension Service can advise on times for your region.

Getting potatoes started couldn't be easier. Just like in the supermarket, you buy potatoes off the shelf, but the difference is that the ones you need are special 'seed' potatoes—certifiably free from viruses. Usually they are available from late winter, and your order may contain more seed potatoes than you need or have room to plant. In this case, share the purchase with a friend or the local community garden. It is worth trying a range of potato varieties in order to discover which ones you prefer to eat and which ones grow best in your soil.

You can plant seed potatoes right away or get a jump start on their growth by presprouting them. Set the tubers on end, with their 'eyes' uppermost, in egg cartons or seed flats, and place in good light in a cool room. You can either plant seed potatoes whole or you can cut them into chunks, each about 2in. (5cm) square, with at least two eyes or sprouts. Potatoes or pieces with more eyes or sprouts will produce larger quantities of potatoes, but they will be smaller. If you do cut the seed potatoes into pieces, let the cut sections dry for a day or two, which helps the skin to callus and protects the tuber from rot. Each potato will develop short, green shoots, and after about 10 days they are ready for planting.

There are several methods of growing potatoes: in hills, in trenches, or in individual holes on flat ground. When planting, handle each sprouted potato or section carefully, so that you do not knock off any of

WHEN PLANTING OUT sprouted potatoes, take care not to damage any of the delicate, new shoots.

the shoots, and plant 6–8in. (15–20cm) deep. Space according to the length of the plant's growing season—generally 12in. (30cm) apart, with 24in. (60cm) between rows for early varieties, and 18–30in. (45–75cm) for mid- and late-season types. Closer planting may result in smaller potatoes at harvest time.

You may want to get your early varieties in the ground first so that they crop sooner; in areas with warm summers, it is better to harvest them before the hot weather arrives. To increase the soil temperature and so accelerate growth, cover the planting area with black plastic mulch several weeks before planting. You can insert the sprouted tubers through holes made in the plastic.

To plant in tubs or large containers (of at least 2 gal./8l), first fill the container with a good potting mix. Plant one potato for this size container. Cover with 4in. (10cm) of potting mix and continue to keep covering the tops with soil as the plant grows. When the tops start to yellow, you can harvest the container-grown potatoes.

Caring for the crop

Outside, as soon as the first shoots emerge, start the process of hilling up by drawing up soil around and over the plants to produce a rounded ridge, repeating at one- to two-week intervals until the ridge is around 8–12in. (20–30cm) high. This kills weeds, helps keep

MOUNDING THE SOIL around developing potato plant prevents the tubers from turning green.

the soil moist, and prevents the tubers from being exposed to the light and turning green and poisonous. (You do not need to earth up potatoes growing under black plastic mulch.) During dry spells, give the plants an occasional but thorough watering to increase the yield. Consistent water early on in the

plants' development will lead to initiation of many tubers and a heavy crop later on. Mulch with an organic material such as straw or compost to help retain even soil moisture.

At harvest time

You can start to harvest early varieties when the flowers open or the buds drop, but choose a dry day and first scrape away a little soil to check that the tubers are large enough. Lifting the first potatoes of the year is like digging up buried treasure. Feel through the ground with your fingers and lift any egg-sized tubers without uprooting the entire plant. Or dig them up with a garden fork, taking care not to spear the tubers, and throw out any that are too small or excessively damaged or diseased, or have gone green through exposure to light—these are potentially harmful.

Start lifting mid- and late-season in late summer, for immediate use. They are ready for harvest when the foliage starts to yellow and die. Leaving the potatoes in the ground for a few weeks can allow the skins to harden. You can leave late-season potatoes in the ground, digging as you need them, but be aware that

Selected varieties

Mixed Fingerling
Popular types with long, thin tubers and waxy, buttery flesh. Wonderful flavor that varies along with color.

Sieglinde
Early season, slightly flattened tubers with firm, yellow flesh and smooth skin. Scab resistant and good for storage.

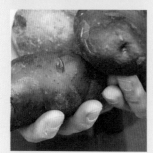

Russian Blue
Heirloom variety with dark blue to purple skin and flesh. This variety keeps its color if not overcooked and can be used to make colorful French fries.

Chieftan
Midseason, oval to oblong potatoes with red skin and white flesh. Good for making French fries.

NEW POTATOES can be lifted by hand. Feel around under the ground for those at least the size of a chicken's egg.

WHEN DIGGING UP potatoes, try to avoid piercing the tubers with your garden fork.

the longer they are there, the greater the chance of slug damage. Always let the potatoes air dry for a few days before storing them.

Storing and cooking tips

Store your potatoes in burlap or paper sacks and keep in a cool, dry, frost-free place until they are needed. Store only undamaged potatoes with any

loose soil removed, and check the sacks regularly for signs of rot. Depending on how large your harvest, and how often you eat potatoes, the store may last you right through until early spring.

With experience, you will find that different varieties of potato suit different types of cooking, and that others are not to your taste at all. Keep the largest potatoes for baking, and the smallest ones for boiling. Some varieties are great multipurpose potatoes, and they are just as good baked as they are roasted, fried, mashed, or blended into soup.

Pests and diseases

Potato scab causes raised, scablike lesions, but they are just superficial and are easily removed on peeling. If the whole crop is affected, select a resistant variety to grow the following year. A more serious problem is late blight, which is especially prevalent during warm, wet summers, although early crops are not usually affected as they are harvested before blight can strike.

Colorado potato beetles are probably the greatest threat; handpick or trap the insects or treat with a recommended form of *Bacillus thuringiensis* (Bt) or with pyrethrins. Plants that yellow, dry up, and die from the bottom up may be showing signs of nematode damage. These are quite common pests, and the best way to avoid them is to rotate your potato crop around the vegetable garden year after year and choose resistant varieties. Use certified disease-free seed potatoes to avoid viral diseases.

Yukon Gold
Early to midseason, with yellow skin and light yellow flesh. Produces large, versatile potatoes— good for storing, boiling, baking, and frying.

Dark Red Norland
A heavy cropping, early potato with dark red skin and pure white flesh. It has a good flavor for boiling and roasting.

Turnips
Brassica rapa

Turnips are an old-fashioned crop but they are a useful member of the vegetable garden, as they are quick growing and the entire plant is edible. The bonus of digging turnips when they are young is that you can also enjoy the fresh, green leaves, or 'turnip tops', which have a peppery taste and can be added to salads or steamed. Some varieties are sold for the turnip greens alone.

Where to grow

Turnips are members of the cabbage family and perform best in cool climates with plenty of rainfall or irrigation in an open, nonshaded site. The soil should be reasonably fertile and enriched with plenty of well-rotted organic matter before seeds are sown. Turnips may develop clubroot if grown on acidic soil, so check the pH of the soil and add a dressing of lime before sowing, if necessary, to increase the alkalinity. A moderate dressing of a balanced fertilizer prior to sowing and planting is also a good idea.

THIN OUT TURNIP SEEDLINGS to prevent overcrowding. They will need plenty of room to expand.

Sowing and planting

Like most root crops, turnips must be directly sown outdoors where they are to grow, as they do not transplant well. It is best to sow the crop in gradual succession, so that gluts are avoided and you can continually harvest the emerging young plants. Depending on your climate, you can begin sowing turnips a few weeks before the last frost date and continue right through to the end of summer, with at least two weeks between each sowing.

Seed should be sown thinly in ½in. (1cm) deep rows; thin the emerging seedlings in stages until the plants

are 4–8in. (10–20cm) apart. If growing the plant for the leaves only, the remaining plants can be spaced more closely together. Very early sowings may need to be protected from frost with floating row covers. The seedlings are especially vulnerable to slugs and snails at this stage.

Cultivating the crop

Water the developing plants every 5–10 days in dry spells to avoid irregular growth and splitting roots. Hoe or hand-weed around the plants on a regular basis. Mulching around the plants will help control weeds and keep the soil moist.

At harvest time

Harvest greens for cooking when they are around 6in. (15cm) long, snipping them off with scissors. New leaves will grow until the plant begins to set seed. Do not harvest all the leaves if you are growing turnips for the roots.

The roots will be ready in 6–10 weeks, depending on the variety grown, which means that the season for turnips runs from midspring well into fall. A useful guide is to start pulling turnips when they reach the size of a golf ball, and do not let them develop any larger than a small orange, beyond which they become woody and much less tasty—check first by pulling back the foliage.

Remember that turnips are not winter hardy, so they will need to be lifted before the ground freezes, although they can stay in the ground before then, especially if protected with a mulch of straw or other organic material.

HARVEST TURNIPS before the winter frosts and store them in a shallow box in a cool, frost-free place.

Storing and cooking tips

Like most vegetables, turnips are best fresh. The late summer or fall harvest can be stored in a cool, frost-free place; turnips last longer if placed in a shallow box and covered with moist peat, sawdust, or sand.

Pests and diseases

In summer, flea beetles can pepper the foliage with tiny holes, and this can be devastating. It will also mean that you won't be eating any of the turnip tops. If flea beetles or other cabbage family pests such as cabbage root maggots or caterpillars are likely to be a problem, cover the entire crop with floating row covers after sowing.

Selected varieties

Tokyo Cross
An AAS winner with smooth, white, globe-shaped roots up to 6in. (15cm) in diameter. Harvest when young to eat raw.

Oasis
A good, early crop of conical, white turnips. It has very sweet flesh, which tastes of melon.

Rutabagas

Brassica napus

Also known as the Swedish turnip, because it is a close relation of the less hardy turnip, rutabagas are a winter staple. The crop can be left in the ground until midwinter. Although they are often confused with turnips, the purple- or green-skinned roots are allowed to grow to a much larger size than turnips and have a yellow flesh that tastes milder and sweeter.

Where to grow

Like turnips, rutabagas are members of the cabbage family grown for their edible root. Grow in full sun and well-drained, moisture-retentive soil that has been enriched with plenty of organic matter, such as compost or well-rotted manure. This encourages strong growth and reduces the chances of the roots rotting over winter. Because rutabagas are prone to clubroot if grown on acidic soil, check the pH of your soil and add a dressing of lime before sowing, if necessary, to increase the alkalinity. A moderate dressing of a balanced fertilizer prior to sowing and planting is a good idea. When digging the planting area, clear away rocks, roots, and clumps of dirt so the soil texture is relatively fine.

Sowing

Rutabagas can take up to 90 days to reach maturity and should do so before temperatures reach above 75°F (24°C), so start them in late spring for a fall harvest, or in midsummer for a fall harvest. In warm-winter regions, a late summer sowing will give a winter harvest. Sow the seed directly into the prepared soil in rows ½in. (1cm) deep and spaced 15in. (38cm) apart. Thin the seedlings in stages until the plants are 9in. (23cm) apart.

Cultivating the crop

Like turnips, rutabagas share their cultivation needs and many of the pests and diseases of the cabbage family. Keep the crop well weeded so that the plants do not have to compete with other plants, and take precautions against pests like cabbage root maggots, caterpillars, and flea beetles, by covering with floating row covers. Slugs and snails may attack the young

GROWING KOHLRABI

The sweet, crunchy roots of this cabbage-family vegetable may be white or purple and can be eaten fresh or cooked like turnips and rutabagas. It's a cool-season plant, but grows quickly and can be used to fill in gaps in the garden or in raised beds. As with all cole crops, it appreciates rich, moisture-retentive but well-drained soil. In most areas, sow seeds indoors about four weeks before the last frost date for spring planting. For a fall crop, sow in the ground four weeks before the first fall frost date. The plant is quite hardy, and you can continue to sow seeds until temperatures regularly drop below 40°F (5°C). Protect from pests with floating row covers and give regular waterings during the growing season to prevent the flesh from becoming woody. Harvest when roots are about 2in. (5cm) in diameter.

'Elder', 'Kolibri', and 'Winner' are all fast-maturing varieties of kohlrabi that mature in less than 45 days.

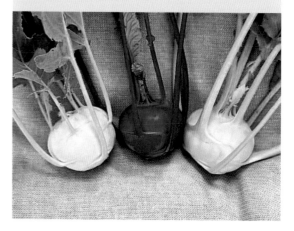

crops and you will have to control these by hand. Water the developing plants every 5–10 days in dry spells, to avoid irregular growth and splitting roots and to prevent powdery mildew on the leaves.

If rutabagas have soft brown flesh, this can indicate boron deficiency—something that can affect a few other vegetables, such as beets. This isn't usually a problem for home-grown rutabagas, but a soil test done through your local Cooperative Extension Service can tell you if you have a boron deficiency in the soil and advise how to correct it.

At harvest time

Rutabagas can be harvested as soon as they are large enough to use—the larger the better. This may be as early as late summer, but since the plants take quite a long season to mature much depends on growing conditions, variety grown, and time of sowing.

Harvest the roots as required over fall and winter and into early spring; carefully pull or lift them from the soil, with a fork if necessary, and cut off the top growth. If you still have rutabagas in the ground in early spring, you can harvest the fresh young growth and serve it like cabbage.

Storing and cooking tips

For most varieties of rutabaga, storage is straightforward. Up until early spring, simply leave the roots where they are growing in the ground

RUTABAGAS CAN BE USED to perk up all kinds of winter recipes, from casseroles to roasts. They can be stored in the ground or in cool, frost-free conditions.

until they are needed. Some varieties, however, can become woody if left in the ground beyond early winter, and these should be lifted for storage before then. It's a good idea to check the storage potential before you choose the variety.

All types are an excellent source of vitamins, calcium, and magnesium. The buttery yellow flesh of rutabagas (some are white) darkens to orange on cooking. Use the mild flavor in casseroles, or mash with garlic and butter as part of a roast dinner. It also mashes or roasts well with other root crops, particularly carrots.

To roast rutabagas, peel the thick skin with a knife and dice the flesh into cubes. Boil the cubes for several minutes, then coat with butter or olive oil and cook in the oven until the cubes turn brown. Serve with mustard greens; the flavors complement each other beautifully.

Selected varieties

Laurentien
This rutabaga has round, evenly shaped roots with a sweet mild flavor. The flesh is pale yellow and the skin is yellow with purple tops.

Helenor
A round bulb with light orange, sweet-tasting flesh. Good for storage.

Salad vegetables

For many gardeners, an assortment of lettuce, a few herbs such as basil, and tomatoes are all that is needed for a kitchen garden. Add some cucumbers, radishes, and a few edible flowers and you have a complete salad bar in your backyard. In fact, in some parts of the country, you can pick fresh leaves for salads every day of the year. As a bonus, some salad veggies are decorative enough to grow in borders and containers, so sow or buy a few for filling in gaps as they appear.

Leafy greens

Leafy greens have reached a high level of popularity with gardeners and cooks alike. From farmer's markets to grocery stores, from gourmet restaurants to burger stands, the idea of what should be tossed into your salad bowl and garnish your sandwiches has moved far beyond tasteless iceberg lettuce into a range of colorful, flavorful greens, flowers, and fresh vegetables.

In fact, the tradition of eating salad greens dates back to colonial days. Thomas Jefferson grew a variety of lettuce, cress, corn salad, and endive in his garden at Monticello, including numerous varieties of lettuce. Now, even the smallest balcony, rooftop, or urban garden has room for a bed of lettuce, which is one of the easiest and most rewarding plants to grow. Many varieties are ready for picking within weeks of sowing, and can be repeatedly sown as long as temperatures do not rise too high or fall too low.

Decorative pots or containers make excellent 'gardens' for cut-and-come-again crops, but lettuce

YOU CAN'T BEAT a trip to the salad garden, picking your own fresh ingredients and garnishes, and mixing the colors, tastes, and textures.

is just the start of it. There are a host of other salad leaves—chicory, endive, chervil, sorrel, and spinach—that can be used in this way. Arugula has become a regular item on supermarket shelves, but leaves straight from the garden with a drizzle of olive oil and shaved Parmesan are another experience. And of course eating fresh leaves full of vitamins and minerals is the best possible diet.

Unlike the Asian greens that can be cooked in stir-fries and soups as well as used in salads, most lettuce and leafy greens must be enjoyed raw and fresh. One of the best salads is a good mesclun mix. Mesclun has no essential ingredients but is an elegant mixture of young leaves, according to what is available, but always perfectly balanced so that no one ingredient dominates. The contents may be any or all of the following: baby lettuce, arugula, corn salad, endive, and chervil. Keeping to the spirit of mesclun, a modern mix might include Chinese and Japanese mustards, mizuna, and mibuna (described in Asian greens on pages 90-1). All are fast-growing and have various degrees of spiciness.

Lettuce  *Lactuca sativa*

Although many grocery stores and markets carry a range of lettuce types, these represent just a fraction of the many delicious salad greens available to home gardeners, each with its own flavor, texture, and color. Some are even decorative enough to grow with grasses and other cheerful annuals.

Types of lettuce

Lettuce can be divided into two main kinds: hearting lettuce, which produces a dense center; and looseleaf types with a more open arrangement of leaves. Within those two categories are several other subtypes. In general, though, the big advantage of growing looseleaf lettuce is that you can just cut a few leaves at a time, whereas hearting lettuce is generally harvested whole.

Hearting Crisphead, or iceberg, lettuce has wavy outer leaves and a crisp, pale heart. Although crispheads add a refreshing crunch to salads, they can be low on flavor. Romaine, or cos, lettuce is distinguished by its upright leaves. A dwarf romaine is smaller, denser, and sweet-tasting, the best-known being 'Little Gem'. Butterhead lettuce, as the name implies, has soft, tender leaves (it is also called Boston lettuce). Butterhead types quickly wilt after cutting unless they are plunged into water, but the hearts have excellent flavor.

PLANTS LEFT TOO LONG after maturing will go to seed or 'bolt', and go on to flower.

Looseleaf This kind has a highly decorative leaf shape and includes curled and frilly-leaved 'lollo' or 'salad bowl' types as well as striking 'oak leaf' varieties. There are many beautiful, red-leaved varieties, some of which can have a slightly bitter taste.

Where to grow

Lettuce is easy to grow, but needs conditions that allow it to develop quickly so the leaves do not develop a bitter taste. Sow in full sun on moisture-retentive, reasonably fertile soil. In warm areas, summer crops may need light shade. Early and late sowings may need protecting against the cold. Lettuce is well suited to raised beds and containers.

Sowing and planting

In most areas, lettuce can be sown in the garden in early spring for a summer crop and again in late summer for a fall crop. Sow the seeds thinly, in drills ½in. (1cm) deep. Because germination can be erratic in hot weather, sow seed in the afternoon so that it

---

BOLTING LETTUCE

Lettuce is an annual that matures in weeks and then goes on to flower. The time between reaching maturity and bolting is partly governed by the environmental conditions; hot, dry weather encourages bolting, but all varieties react differently. Looseleaf, romaine, and many crisphead kinds usually take the longest time; the butterheads bolt more quickly. To help prevent flowering, mulch around plants and water during dry weather. Lettuce that has gone to seed is often bitter and will produce a cascade of foliage and flowers if left alone.

SOWING LETTUCE IN SMALL SPACES

1 YOU CAN GROW different varieties of lettuce or mesclun mixes in raised beds or containers. Make drills for the seed.

2 SOW THE SEED successively throughout the season. Thinnings from the crop as it germinates can be eaten as baby leaves.

3 WATER WELL and ensure the seedlings get plenty of sunlight. Regularly water —in hot, dry weather—and weed.

will germinate in the cool of the night. Gardeners in cold-winter areas often start lettuce and other salad greens in cold frames in late winter, where they can be protected against frost. You can also sow lettuce indoors in flats or cell packs in a good potting mix. Warm but not hot conditions are needed for lettuce seeds to germinate and grow on—keep the soil temperature below 75°F (24°C). Harden off seedlings before planting out in the garden.

Make final spacings in the row 6–12in. (15–30cm), depending on the variety; see the seed packet for individual instructions. Thinned seedlings can usually be transplanted, provided this is done in cool weather and plants are well watered afterwards; replanting the seedlings amongst slow-maturing crops such as cabbage or broccoli is an effective use of space. Thinnings can also be eaten. Alternatively, rows of seeds can be sown more densely as cut-and-come-again crops. In regions with reasonably cool summers, sow successively throughout summer. In mild-winter areas, you can often sow throughout the winter months.

Selected varieties

Little Gem
A favorite dwarf variety of romaine lettuce with a small, solid head of midgreen leaves. It has a sweet, crisp heart.

Green Towers
Mild flavored romaine, with a crisp, gray-green head. Suitable for a wide range of conditions.

Sangria
A butterhead variety for summer with soft, pale green, pink-tipped leaves. It is slow to mature and resistant to bolting and mildew.

Tom Thumb
A small and solid butterhead lettuce, with soft leaves and a mild taste. It crops early and is suitable for growing in containers.

THE MORE YOU PICK, the more the plants grow tasty replacement leaves.

Caring for the crop

Keep lettuce well watered. Feed only if growth is poor, using a nitrogen-rich fertilizer. If frost threatens, cover the crop with floating row covers or cloches.

At harvest time

Harvest lettuce by cutting rather than pulling; looseleaf kinds will often sprout fresh leaves. Snip off cut-and-come-again crops like meslun with scissors. In hot weather, pick lettuce in the morning, to prevent wilting. Many varieties will store well in the refrigerator for a couple of days at least in a plastic bag, if wetted first, but wash again before use.

Pests and diseases

Slugs, snails, and caterpillars can demolish seedlings. Trap or handpick the pests, especially in the evening, when slugs and snails tend to feed. If young plants seem to wilt overnight, it's probably because they've had their roots attacked by cutworms, root aphids, or chafer grubs in the soil. Fork through the soil to expose and get rid of any pests. Other chewing pests such as aphids, flea beetles, and leafhoppers may be problematic. Try to use barriers rather than pesticides. Gray mold or downy mildew may be a problem in cold, damp weather. To prevent these attacks, increase the spacing between the plants, avoid getting water on the leaves, and remove any infected material immediately.

Cimmaron

A gorgeous, red romaine with bronze-red leaves, 10–12in. (25–30cm) long, with a green heart. Slow to bolt; an old American favorite.

Mesclun

A mix of sweet lettuce and tangy greens, with colorful leaves and stems. Snip off the fresh leaves with scissors.

Merlot and Salad Bowl mixture

Merlot has deep red, frilled leaves with a firm, crunchy texture, while Salad Bowl is fairly heat resistant, with mid-green, deeply notched leaves and a tender flavor.

Lollo Rosso

A hardy, slow-to-bolt looseleaf lettuce with attractive, pale green, red-tipped leaves. It has a distinctive, peppery taste.

Sorrel

A perennial herb that is hardy in zones 4–9, sorrel (*Rumex acetosa*) can be grown as an annual elsewhere, and will often survive into early winter. Bright green, arrow-shaped leaves have a sharp, lemony, astringent flavor. Use sparingly to perk up a salad, or use for sauces or soups. Sorrel self-seeds quite readily.

Red Orach

Also known as mountain spinach, this fast-growing, hardy annual has arrowhead-shaped leaves of deep maroon-red. It forms bushy plants with tall, attractive seedheads, and bolts quickly. Make successive sowings because the young leaves are the most tender and have the best color. Initially sow seed in shallow drills, and thereafter allow to self-seed or collect seed for reuse.

Corn Salad

Corn salad, also called lamb's lettuce or mache, forms rosettes of small, bright green, succulent leaves. It is very hardy and can withstand frost. Although it will stop putting on new growth in very cold weather, it is a good source of salad over winter and in early spring, before it goes to seed. Sow seed of corn salad in shallow drills in late summer for a winter crop, and then sow again in early spring for a second crop.

Arugula

The leaves have a distinctive peppery taste. Sow in early spring and again in late summer, in shallow drills. Harvest as a cut-and-come-again crop, snipping off the leaves with scissors when the plant is about 6in. (15cm) high. In summer, arugula will bolt rapidly, the leaves becoming tough and coarse. Arugula can be made into pesto, steamed briefly and added to pasta dishes, or enjoyed raw in salads.

Edible flowers and herbs

Some flowers simply look exquisite, and are therefore fun to use as garnish for your serving platters. But the petals of other flowers are edible—with a strong peppery or fruity taste; others impart more subtle aromas and flavors. They can be scattered in salads, frozen in ice cubes, crystallized, or used to flavor cookies, crackers, and ice creams.

Preparing and collecting flowers

Growing a few edible flowers in your kitchen garden often reaps other rewards. Many of the flowering plants that are suitable for culinary use also make excellent companion plants or attract pollinating insects. Some of the more vigorous annuals such as nasturtiums grow like ground covers, suppressing weeds and reducing evaporation of moisture from the soil's surface.

Blossoms wilt quickly, especially in hot weather, so pick in the morning where possible. Take care not to get stung by bees or wasps, particularly when picking borage, lavender, and chives. Pick whole flowerheads rather than petals, then go indoors where it is cooler to prepare them. Spread the flowers out on a piece of paper towel as you work; this will allow any small

black flower beetles or earwigs to be easily removed as they move between flowers.

In most species, the flowers are too tough to consume whole and the petals should be removed from the flowerhead or calyx by gently pulling them away. Put the prepared petals or flowerheads into a small plastic bag and seal it with a little air inside to stop the contents from getting squashed. The flowers should keep in good condition in the refrigerator for several hours.

Avoid washing flowers as most are easily damaged, but if they are wilting put the heads in a bowl of water to revive them.

Never eat any part of a plant unless you are certain that it is edible. If in doubt about the identity of a flower in your garden, double-check with a knowledgeable source.

A FLOWERY SALAD

1 TREAT THE FLOWERS with care. First, remove them whole, letting any insects escape. Then nip off the petals and add to a salad, or briefly store in a plastic bag in a refrigerator.

2 A LIVELY MIX of edible blossoms and leaves gives a salad an extra peppery, fruity, or nutty taste. Possible ingredients include nasturtiums, violas, and signet marigolds.

Calendula (*Calendula officinalis*) – An annual with double and single varieties in shades of orange. Deadhead to prolong flowering or sow repeatedly through the season. Petals add color to salads.

Nasturtium (*Tropaeolum majus*) – Both the leaves and petals have a strong peppery taste, which takes a few seconds to develop on the tongue. Flower color can vary from deep red to buttery yellow. The fresh seedheads can be collected and pickled to use like capers.

Annual flowers

Annual flowers such as borage and nasturtiums are the easiest to include in the kitchen garden because they are short-lived and they self-seed readily, so you have to buy only one packet of seed to get started.

Herbs

The flowers of many herbs retain the flavor of the leaves but with less intensity, making them perfect for adding to salads. Dill, cilantro, and basil are annuals that can be used in this way when they go to seed, using whole flowers. The flowerheads of chives, garlic chives, and lavender are composed of lots of smaller individual flowers which can be eaten whole. Lavender and mint flowers can be used to flavor cookies, cakes, and ice cream. The intensity of flavor can vary significantly from plant to plant, so it is worth experimenting with quantities and varieties.

Perennial flowers

If you get the taste for edible flowers, there are numerous garden perennials that can supplement your harvest. Try roses, daylilies, and pinks for flavor, and primulas and scented geraniums (*Pelargonium*) for decoration.

Squash blossoms

The large flowers of many different types of squash are edible. A favorite method of preparation is to stuff them with cheese and herbs, then fry them in batter. Pick the flowers in the morning; select male flowers if you can as they last a little longer after picking. (You can tell the male flowers from the female ones as they have longer stalks and no bulge at the base of the blossom.)

PICK LARGE BATCHES of lavender flowers just as they open, and the leaves at any time, to use in a wide range of recipes including biscuits and ice cream.

Signet marigold *(Tagetes tenuifolia)* – The best varieties ('Lemon Gem', 'Tangerine Gem') do not self-seed very reliably, but are very easy to raise from seed or grow from transplants. The petals have a distinctive, zesty flavor, but do not eat the center disk of the flower.

Johnny-jump-up *(Viola tricolor)* – This delicate wild flower is small enough to use whole. Just snip as much of the calyx off as is possible without causing it to fall apart. It is particularly pretty frozen in ice cubes and used in summer drinks. Cultivated violas and pansies are widely available as bedding plants at the garden center or nursery. Winter-flowering pansies will provide a useful supply of flowers when little else is available.

Clary sage *(Salvia sclarea)* – Strictly speaking, it is not the flowers that are of interest here but the purple and pink bracts. Select the younger ones as these are brighter and will not yet have become papery. They can be used to flavor wines and liqueurs and make a decorative garnish. Clary sage is also used for medicinal purposes. Other sages that can be used in the kitchen include pineapple sage *(S. elegans)*, which is often made into tea, and common sage *(S. officinalis)*, whose flowers make good garnishes for roasts and soups.

Borage *(Borago officinalis)* – This is a tall bushy plant up to 3ft. (1m) high and apt to flop without some support, so make sure you have allowed enough room for it. The blue, starry flowers are easily detached from the hairy calyx by gently pulling at the center of the flower. They look particularly beautiful in ice cubes or mixed with dark-leaved lettuce. The young leaves have a refreshing, cucumberlike flavor and can be added chopped to summer drinks.

Endive and chicory *Cichorium* spp.

In addition to lettuce and other salad leaves, this group of leafy greens is grown mostly for adding to salads. They are similar to lettuce, but call for some special tweaking in the garden, depending on their degree of frost hardiness and heat tolerance. There are several different kinds of endive and chicory, and common names vary and can be somewhat confusing.

Types of endive and chicory

Curly endive, also known as frisée, has narrow, ruffled leaves. Escarole is a broad-leafed version of endive with a creamy white heart. It is hardy and can be grown through winter in some areas. Sugarloaf chicory is a leafy green with a somewhat bitter flavor—it resembles romaine lettuce but the leaves are much tougher. Radicchio is a red-leafed chicory that forms tight hearts—it resembles a small, red cabbage but the taste is very different. Witloof chicory, or Belgian endive, is also a hearting chicory with blanched leaves known as chicons.

Where to grow

All types of endive and chicory grow best in a light soil with a reasonable amount of organic matter.

CHICORY CAN be grown along with other cool-season, leafy crops such as lettuce and kale. There are several different kinds that are worth trying in the garden.

They can be intercropped between taller plants and, with their decorative leaves, make a nice addition to window boxes, containers, and ornamental borders.

Sowing and planting

Endive and chicory are cool-season plants, though they can tolerate higher temperatures than other salad greens. Sow seeds outdoors from midspring to summer, depending on your climate. In a very warm climate, radicchio may be best grown as a fall crop; heat can make the plants bolt.

Sow seeds directly into the ground ½in. (1cm) deep in drills 12in. (30cm) apart. Thin the young seedlings as they appear, to a spacing of 6–12in. (15–30cm) depending on type and variety.

Caring for the crop

Water plants during dry weather and apply a nitrogen-rich fertilizer if growth begins to flag. Drip irrigation is a good option for these leafy greens; avoid overhead watering, as it may cause the interior to rot. Endive, escarole, and sugarloaf chicory can develop a bitter flavor in hot weather. To moderate the bitterness, blanch the leaves by drawing up the leaves and tying them together loosely. It should take about 10 days for blanching to take place.

Forcing chicons
When forced, the deep roots of witloof chicory produce chicons. To grow these outdoors without having to dig up the roots, cut off the leafy head to leave a 2in. (5cm) stub. Use a hoe to draw soil over these stubs, and within a few weeks chicons will form under the soil, particularly if you cover the plants with a cloche to warm them. Better results are often achieved by forcing indoors, where plants

TO GET A GRADATION of colors from green at the leaf tips to white at the base of sugarloaf chicory, grow a self-blanching type. Tie the leaves together, to increase the effect.

TO BLANCH an entire plant, cover it with a bucket to exclude light. This should take approximately 10 days, after which the plant will be pale, with a mild flavor.

are lifted and planted in a box of moist peat or peat substitute, with the leaves trimmed to ½in. (1cm) from the roots. Cover the roots with 9in. (23cm) more peat and put the box in a warm, dark place. Modern witloof varieties may need darkness only to form chicons. Chicons will be ready for eating about one month after being covered.

Harvesting and cooking tips

You can harvest leaf chicory, escarole, and frisée as cut-and-come again crops. Cut blanched plants immediately, as once the cover is removed the plants will start to revert to their dark green coloring and bitter taste. Radicchio is ready to harvest when the head is firm and growth stops. In addition to making a great addition to salads, radicchio leaves can be grilled or added to pasta dishes and stir-fries. To grill, drizzle the leaves with olive oil and balsamic vinegar, place on the barbecue or in the oven for about five minutes, then sprinkle with Parmesan cheese.

Pests and diseases

Leaf endive and chicory grow quickly, so they are not troubled by many pests and diseases, apart from the usual suspects: slugs, snails, and the occasional caterpillar. The plants do have a habit of bolting, however, particularly if the soil dries out or if they were started too early in spring. Curly-leafed frisée and radicchio can hold water inside, so they may be prone to fungal diseases or rot. Earwigs may also hide in the tightly curled leaves.

Selected varieties

Radicchio
This has dark red leaves and forms a tight head with firm, crisp leaves that are good for colorful salads. May bolt in the hottest weather.

Frisée
A frizzy mass of crinkled leaves that have a slightly bitter taste. It has stiff, white stems where the flavor is most concentrated.

Cucumbers *Cucumis sativus*

Cucumbers have tremendous versatility in the kitchen, as they range from immature gherkins, which can be picked and pickled when just a few inches in length, to long slicers suitable for salads and sandwiches. There are even types bred to be 'burpless', without the bitterness that causes some people indigestion. Pickling types are perhaps the most useful.

Types of cucumber

Most cucumbers are self-pollinating, that is, they have both male and female flowers. Seed packages containing female-flowering only, or gynoecious, cucumbers usually contain a few male seeds so that the females will be pollinated.

Where to grow

Cucumbers need plenty of sun, moisture, and good soil, with a helping of balanced fertilizer. They are deep-rooted plants and should not have to compete with nearby trees or shrubs. Vining cucumbers need plenty of room to sprawl, or you can grow them up

SUPPORTING CUCUMBERS

In cool climates, some gardeners grow cucumbers in greenhouses, in which case you'll need some kind of support in the form of canes or netting. Put it up before you plant. Tie in shoots regularly, pinch out the growing tip once the plant reaches the top of its support, and pinch out lateral shoots when there are two leaves. Outdoor varieties can be allowed to trail without support; the main shoot should be pinched at five to six leaves to encourage branching, and black plastic can be spread beneath to protect the crop.

a trellis or other support. For smaller spaces, choose compact bush varieties. Fill containers with rich, fresh potting soil, and beds with plenty of well-rotted organic matter. To avoid a buildup of pests and diseases, grow cucumbers in a different site every year.

Sowing and planting

In cold climates, you can start cucumbers indoors four weeks before the last spring frost, but they should not be planted outside before soil temperatures have warmed; sow three seeds in a small pot or cell packs. Thin seedlings to one plant when they are big enough to handle. As soon as each rootball holds together, harden off seedlings and plant outside.

In warm areas, sow three seeds ¾in. (2cm) deep where the cucumbers are to grow; this can be on mounds or hills of soil, to help drainage. The use of cloches or floating row covers increases soil temperatures, boosts growth and yield, and protects plants from insects. Just be sure that pollinating insects can reach the flowers when they bloom.

CONTAINER-GROWN CUCUMBERS can be grown on a deck or patio. Choose a compact bush variety and set up a trellis to keep the fruit off the ground and maximize the growing space.

Caring for the crop

Water regularly to prevent bitterness in the crop, and mulch the soil to help keep it cool and retain moisture. You can also tie sprawling plants to supports to help keep the fruit off the ground and improve air circulation around the plant. Cucumbers require regular feeding with a balanced liquid fertilizer or a high-potassium fertilizer.

At harvest time

Once the cucumbers are sufficiently large, cut them off using a sharp knife. Harvest regularly, because leaving mature cucumbers on the plant will stop the development of new ones.

Pests and diseases

Troublesome pests include striped and spotted cucumber beetles, aphids, squash bugs, and flea beetles; floating row covers can help keep them at bay. Squash vine borers can enter the plants at soil level; introduce parasitic nematodes to help keep them in check. Choose disease-resistant varieties to combat bacterial wilt, viruses, powdery mildew, anthracnose, downy mildew, and leaf spots.

HARVEST when fruit tips are rounded with parallel sides and no longer pointed.

Selected varieties

Fancipak
Produces heavy crops of medium, dark green pickling cucumbers. Harvest when the fruit is about 4in. (10cm) long. Disease resistant.

Lemon
An hierloom cucumber, 3-4in. (7.5-10cm) round with lemon-colored skin and crunchy texture. Suitable for a container.

Carmen
A heavy-cropping variety with excellent disease resistance. The fruit are of average length, dark green and slightly ribbed.

Suyo Long
Heat-tolerant, burpless Chinese cucumber with fruit 16in. (40cm) long, which can be eaten fresh or pickled.

Radishes *Raphanus sativus*

Summer radish is an easily grown vegetable that adds crunch and spiciness to salads. It is fast-growing, usually maturing in about four weeks. The roots may be red, pink, or white, and pointed, cylindrical, or round. A small number of varieties are grown for their crunchy seedpods, eaten raw. Winter, or Oriental, radishes are excellent winter vegetables.

Where to grow

Radishes need fertile, moisture-retentive soil. Avoid dry conditions when they might well go to seed or produce tough, pithy, or hot, peppery-tasting roots. In the height of summer, radishes may grow better in the partial shade of other crops. They make good crops for interplanting with more slow-growing vegetables or to fill gaps left by lettuce or beets. Radishes can also be grown as a cut-and-come-again crop for its spicy leaves.

Sowing and planting

Summer radishes can be sown in the garden from late winter to late summer in many regions, though in hot-summer areas they will not grow well during the hottest months of summer. For early and late sowings, use early varieties and keep warm with a floating row cover.

Prepare the soil well by removing roots, stones, trash, and weeds from the planting bed. Incorporate some balanced fertilizer and rake the soil smooth. Sow seed thinly, in drills 1/2in. (1cm) deep that have been

SOWING SMALL SEED means you'll inevitably end up with rows of tightly packed seedlings, but they can easily be thinned.

MARKING OUT OTHER CROPS

Radishes can be used as a 'marker' for slow-to-germinate crops such as parsnips, to prevent the slower-growing seed rows from being accidentally disturbed while weeding. Sow alternate pinches of seed so that the radishes can be pulled up without disturbing the parsnips.

watered beforehand. Thin the seedlings to at least 1in. (2.5cm) apart, or the overcrowding makes them spindly and may delay or prevent the roots from developing fully.

Caring for the crop

Water regularly in dry weather to prevent plants from bolting or becoming woody. Irregular watering can result in splitting, while lush, leafy growth may be caused by overwatering, so consistent water, such as provided by drip irrigation, is best. Keep the ground free of weeds, which can draw moisture and nutrients away from the growing radishes. Mulch will help keep the ground moist and prevent weeds. Don't make it too thick—just 2in. (5cm) will do.

At harvest time

Pull up radishes as soon as they are mature. Summer radishes are best harvested when they are still small and tender. They do not last well in the ground, but will store for several days in the refrigerator if they are first rinsed, patted dry, and placed in a plastic bag. Use sliced or grated in salads and sandwiches.

Long-podded varieties (also called rat-tail varieties) are grown for the edible seedpods that develop, which happens in warm weather. Allow the flowers to bloom; they will be followed by shiny, pointed, green or purple pods, which can be gathered and eaten raw.

Pests and diseases

Protect radishes from flea beetles with floating row covers. When aphids cluster on the leaves, use a strong jet of water from the hose to wash them off. Seedlings are also at risk from slugs and snails, and from the cabbage root fly whose larvae feed on the roots. Any damage is more likely to occur the longer radishes are in the ground.

Alternative radishes

Winter Radish A hardy, black-skinned form, winter radish can be harvested in late fall or winter. It generally forms larger roots than summer radish, but can be used in the same way. Direct sowing is restricted to mid- to late summer. Sow as for summer radish, but thin to 4–12in. (10–30cm) apart, depending on variety, in rows 10in. (25cm) apart. Harvest from the late fall through the winter, before the soil freezes.

HARVEST RADISHES by taking hold of the top growth and easing them out with a fork, trowel or even a plastic plant label. Don't leave them in the ground for too long when mature.

Daikon Also known as Oriental radish, or mooli, daikon have larger, longer roots than other radishes and are harvested in late fall or winter. Seed catalogs list different varieties, some red, green, or white flesh; many have a strongly pungent flavor, while others are milder. They can be eaten raw, stir-fried, or cooked. Some daikon, such as 'Long White Icicle', can be eaten when immature, as summer radishes.

Selected varieties

Black Spanish
A spicy variety of winter radish with black skin and white flesh. Grate into salads or cook like turnips.

French Breakfast
Cylindrical variety; 3-4in. (7.5-10cm) long, scarlet with a white tip. Initially has a mild taste but will become hot if left in the ground.

Sparkler
Its medium-sized roots are slightly flattened with a white base. It grows reliably and easily, and matures quickly.

Scarlet Globe
Attractive, uniformly round, bright red heirloom radish that matures early.

Tomatoes

Imagine the banks of a Peruvian river, swathed in mist, the temperature warm and even. Perfect conditions for tomatoes. This is where most of the tomato species come from, including their direct descendants, which we grow and eat today.

Surprisingly, the tomato hasn't always been popular. It was largely ignored in Peru where it grew wild, but traveled one way and another to New Mexico, where it's believed to have become a food crop from around AD 400. The Aztecs grew it and, in the 16th century, it was brought to Spain along with the potato, eggplant, and maize. When the kingdom of Naples fell under Spanish rule a few years later, it made its debut in what was to become the country of Italy, where it has become an essential ingredient in many dishes.

TOMATO PLANTS are vigorous and sprawling plants that need the help of some kind of stake or cage to keep them in check.

Gradually tomatoes found their way around Europe and to North America, and were recorded in a 17th-century herbal as 'love apples'. The tomato was commonly regarded as an aphrodisiac, which is why it was also called pomme d'amour and pomum amoris, now pomodoro. It was also viewed in some circles with suspicion and disdain because of its similarity to the highly toxic nightshade, and to mandrake which, legend has it, screams if you pull it out of the ground.

Eventually taste overcame doubt, and tomatoes are now the most widely grown vegetable in America. They are good for you and, although they can be very acidic, they are packed with vitamins A and C. Because of their high acid content, tomatoes have been traditional vegetables for canning. They can also be served fresh, cooked in numerous ways, dried, frozen, and juiced.

Most gardeners have their favorite varieties, many of them heirloom types that have become very popular in recent years. When you're growing your own fruit and vegetables, taste is what counts. You can choose tomatoes that are less perfectly round and uniform in appearance but that are infinitely more delicious than supermarket-bought fruit. For the longest harvest period and the greatest selection, it's worth growing several varieties of tomatoes even if you have just a small garden or raised bed.

Children love tomatoes, especially the sweet cherry tomatoes. Grow them in baskets or containers on the deck so that kids can pick and eat them like fruit.

Tomatoes
Lycopersicon esculentum

Tomatoes need heat and sunshine to grow, and gardeners in many marginal regions employ a variety of techniques to ensure the vegetable's conditions are met—from grow bags in greenhouses to planting through black plastic mulch. If you get it right, you are likely to be picking tomatoes into the dying days of summer, relishing those last fruity drops of sunshine before fall kicks in.

Types of tomatoes

As an indicator of their popularity, hundreds of tomato varieties are available to gardeners, which can make for a lifetime of experimentation. The fruits vary from tiny cherry tomatoes to the giant beefsteaks, from yellow to red to purple, and they may be round, flattened, or elongated. Taste can range from fairly insipid to sweet or richly flavored.

Seed catalogs and nurseries categorize tomatoes according to their growth habit. Determinate tomatoes are bushy, with short vines that stop growing once the fruit forms. They crop for about six weeks and are ideal for container growth or small gardens. Indeterminate types keep growing and cropping until frost knocks them back. They have a vinelike growth and so they need to be trained and restrained using stakes or tomato cages to prevent completely unruly growth. Semideterminate tomatoes have the short vines of determinate kinds, but produce for longer periods.

Where to grow

Tomatoes can be grown in greenhouses, out in the garden, and even in hanging baskets and window boxes. In cool areas with short summers, tomatoes that are growing in a greenhouse will fruit earlier and for longer, but even a hoop house or an individual insulating teepee that can be filled with water will help keep your tomatoes snug and speed up ripening.

Tomatoes can also be planted through slits in black plastic mulch, which warms the soil and hastens

CHERRY TOMATOES are favorites for children's gardens and containers. The fruit is so sweet that it can be picked and eaten just like berries.

GROWING MARIGOLDS together with tomatoes is a traditional remedy for attempting to control whitefly and soilborne pests such as nematodes.

PLANTING TOMATOES IN GROW BAGS

1 PLACE THE BAG in a sunny position and cut two slits to form a cross in the plastic, peeling it back to expose the potting soil.

2 SPACE THE SLITS about 18in. (45cm) apart. Don't try to pack the plants any closer together or they'll shade each other.

3 MAKE HOLES in the soil and gently ease in each seedling (they should usually be sturdier than shown and beginning to form their first flowers).

4 CONTINUE PLANTING, taking care not to damage any roots and stems, and then water. Fix strong supports above the plants to which the new growth can be attached.

growth. Floating row covers will help raise the temperature and provide the bonus of pest control.

When growing plants in the open, choose a sunny, sheltered site, such as against a south- or west-facing wall. Fertile soil is also vital, and greenhouse plants can be set in grow bags (see above) or in large containers of fresh potting soil.

Plants in the ground will thrive provided the soil has been enriched with plenty of well-rotted organic matter and tomato fertilizer.

Tomatoes benefit from crop rotation as they can suffer from soilborne diseases such as cyst nematode. Rotate them along with potatoes, peppers, and eggplants, which can suffer from the same pests and diseases as tomatoes.

Sowing and planting

Tomato transplants are widely available in late spring at garden centers and nurseries. For the widest selection, you can also grow tomatoes from seed, getting them started 6–8 weeks before the last frost date. Sow seeds thinly in a tray or cell packs of moist potting mix. Cover lightly with a layer of mix and put the tray in a warm place. Wait several days and then check daily for signs of germination. Once shoots emerge, move the container to a warm, well-lit spot and let the seedlings grow. Pot them individually into 3in. (7.5cm) pots as soon as they are large enough to handle, and keep the potting soil evenly moist. Feed with a liquid fertilizer if growth is poor. Tomatoes usually germinate easily and you are likely to have plenty of seedlings, so keep a few as spares in case

GROWING TOMATILLOS

These green or purple tomato relatives can be eaten raw, with the outer husk removed, or be cooked to make salsa verde and other Mexican specialties. Grow them much like tomatoes, but because they set fruit and ripen quickly they can be sown directly in the ground soon after the last frost date. There is also no need to stake them, but space 2–3ft. (0.6–1m) apart, as plants are bushy.

TOMATILLOS are easy to grow and attractive, with papery husks that change color as the fruit ripens.

of emergencies, such as seedlings failing to thrive, and throw out or give away the rest of them.

When the time comes to plant out, be sure your stakes, trellis, or cages are in place. Commercial tomato cages are widely available, but most gardeners soon develop a preference for a particular supporting system.

Space tomatoes so the leaves do not touch—typically 18–24in. (45–60cm), but the seed packet will give information on proper spacing for different varieties. Tomatoes are traditionally planted deeply, so that much of the lower stem is covered. Water deeply and mulch around the base of the plant.

Caring for the crop

As the plants grow, tie them to the support. Use foam or velcro plant ties and check these regularly to ensure that they have not become overtight.

Tomatoes are thirsty and hungry plants, and the soil should be kept evenly moist; drip irrigation is an ideal method of watering, as it avoids fluctuations between wet and dry, which results in the fruit

Selected varieties

Sungold
An exceptionally sweet, orange-red cherry tomato of indeterminate type, with fruity flavor. Requires hot weather to ripen fully.

Big Beef
An extra large, globe-shaped indeterminate beefsteak. Disease resistant and widely adapted for many areas.

Gold Nugget
A very tasty cherry tomato of determinate type. The fruits are a shade of golden-yellow and are early to crop with good yields.

Jolly
Indeterminate tomato with small, pink fruits in heavy clusters. Sweet but with a meaty texture.

PICK TOMATOES when fully ripe and evenly colored, but don't leave them too long or they will split. You can ripen green fruit on a windowsill.

splitting, and dry conditions can cause blossom end rot when part of the fruit becomes blackened. Once plants are in flower, apply tomato fertilizer regularly, according to the manufacturer's instructions.

Bush or determinate varieties need little attention, but indeterminate types need to be tied in regularly and their sideshoots need snapping or cutting off, which concentrates the plants' energy on the fruit that grow from the main stem. Remove any yellowing lower leaves as they appear.

At harvest time

Pick the fruit when fully ripe and evenly colored, but don't leave mature fruit on the plant for long or it'll soften and split. At the end of the season, outdoor and unheated greenhouse plants are likely to be left with lots of green fruit. This can be picked and ripened on a sunny windowsill or in a drawer along with a couple of ripe apples or bananas, which give off the ripening gas ethylene.

Storing and cooking tips

If tomatoes are stored in the refrigerator, take them out early and serve at room temperature for the best flavor. Surplus fruit can be made into sauces, dried, canned, or frozen. Mail-order nursery catalogs often sell supplies for canning and drying tomatoes.

Green Zebra
A medium-sized, indeterminate tomato that ripens to a green color with creamy yellow stripes. Slightly acidic but still sweet flavor.

Yellow Pear
Sweet, pear-shaped fruit up to 2in. (5cm) long. Tall, indeterminat plants suited to large containers.

Gardener's Delight
Indeterminate, cherry tomatoes with an exceptionally sweet flavor. The plants bear long trusses of fruit and will grow either under glass or outside in a warm spot.

Heirloom
Open-pollinated varieties that may be determinate or indeterminate and have been handed down for many years rather than bred commercially. Look for varieties suited to your region.

Spinach and chard

Spinach and chard are stalwarts of the vegetable garden and will keep you in green, leafy vegetables almost year-round. They are highly adaptable, and the leaves can be harvested when small as a cut-and-come-again crop for salads, or be allowed to grow larger for cooking. They are particularly rich in iron and a good source of folic acid. Both are most useful in winter when other leafy vegetables may be scarce. The only time of year when they will not grow well is in the heat of midsummer, when they are likely to bolt.

Spinach and Swiss chard

So many people have strong feelings about spinach. You love it or hate it, and it has a reputation for being a chore rather than a pleasure to eat. But fresh spinach from the garden is a world away from the overcooked greens of yore, and it lives up to its reputation as a nutritional powerhouse.

Spinach is full of calcium, folic acid, vitamin K, and iron. It is a fast-growing crop, delicious when young and eaten raw in salads. The mature leaves can be blanched and creamed or used plain in soups and stir-fries or wilted over a gentle heat for a minute at most. As a cool-season crop, spinach has only one drawback: It bolts quickly in hot weather. Fortunately, there are several alternatives that have greater heat tolerance. Perpetual spinach is one of them. It's closely related to Swiss chard and beets, but its leaves are slightly coarser and more substantial than those of annual spinach. Although botanically unrelated, New Zealand spinach and Malabar spinach are often sold as warm-weather substitutes for traditional spinach.

BOTH SPINACH AND CHARD are grown for their tasty leaves, which can be harvested when young or left to mature before harvesting and cooking.

Swiss chard has become a favorite edible plant for its decorative qualities, although the striking, crimson-leafed variety with its luminous, red veins is not as tasty as the straightforward, green-leafed, white-ribbed plant. But whichever color you choose, its aesthetic qualities are always a delight. There are several seed mixes, including 'Rainbow' and 'Bright Lights', with superbly colored midribs and veins in bright yellow, shocking pink, and hot vermillion.

It is difficult not to get on your hands and knees on a September evening as the sun sits low in the sky to gaze at your Swiss chard as its stems light up. Use it in containers mixed with tropical cannas, purple and red peppers, and tomato-red dahlias. So full marks for its flamboyant looks, but what about its taste? Well, Swiss chard is a delicacy. Because the leafy part cooks more quickly than the midribs, cook the two separately for different lengths of time (that also applies to perpetual spinach). Serve hot with butter, or cold with a dash of olive oil and balsamic vinegar.

Spinach
Spinacia oleracea

Spinach leaves are among the very best raw in salads. If they're allowed to grow larger, they're delicious lightly cooked. Spinach suffers in summer and is not as good as perpetual spinach or chard for a year-round crop. If you give the plant the right conditions, choose the right varieties for your region, and make successive sowings, you can have fresh leaves year-round.

Types of spinach

Smooth-leaf spinach has light to dark green leaves that are roughly oblong in shape. Savoyed-leaf spinach produces thicker, rounder leaves and the leaf texture ranges from slightly creased to deeply crinkled. Some varieties that are slightly crinkled are known as semisavoyed. You can also find varieties with attractive, red leaf veins and stems, though these may be quicker to bolt than solid green spinaches. The smooth-leaf varieties are easy to clean, while the savoyed types have a crisper, crunchy texture.

Where to grow

Some gardeners think that spinach is a prima donna, refusing to perform if conditions are not right. This is only partly correct. Breeders have worked for years to hybridize varieties that are slow to bolt in hot weather and that are resistant to disease. Still, it's true that spinach does need plenty of moisture at the roots and lots of nutrients, so apply a general fertilizer and do not attempt to grow it in dry soil with low fertility. Add plenty of well-rotted manure or compost to the soil before sowing. Providing a little shade in summer will help, as this will keep the ground cool and moist. Also consider intercropping with taller vegetables that will cast a dappled shade over the spinach during the midday heat. Spinach suffers from few soilborne problems and can be grown anywhere in your crop rotation. However, downy mildew can be troublesome in warm, humid weather. Avoid congested plants and use resistant varieties where possible.

Sowing and planting

If you like spinach, be generous with your sowing so that you can gather great handfuls. Sow the seed directly where it is to grow in drills about ½in. (1cm) deep in rows 12in. (30cm) apart. Because spinach will not easily germinate in hot weather, and tends to bolt if sown too early, make sowings from midspring to early summer for summer leaves, and then in fall for a supply of leaves into winter. Despite this, it is possible, if you are determined, to get leaves year-round if you give plants the right conditions and choose suitable varieties. Make successive sowings of small amounts of seed every few weeks for a continuous supply of fresh leaves.

Selected varieties

Scenic
A high-yielding, semisavoyed variety with large, bright green leaves, which is particularly suitable as a cut-and-come-again crop. Resistant to mildew.

Bordeaux
Very attractive, dark green leaves with contrasting, red leaf veins and stems make this a good baby spinach for salads.

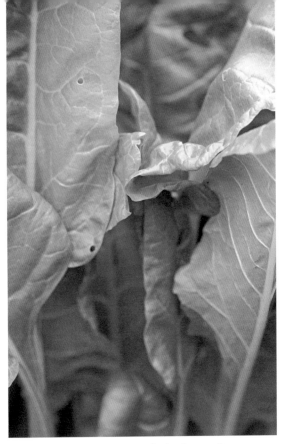

TO GET THE YEAR'S FIRST CROP of spinach, sow after midspring but no later than the start of summer because the seed won't germinate once there's hot weather.

To grow large plants, sow small clumps of a few seeds at least 6in. (15cm) apart. Thin to one seedling in each group once all have germinated. To grow small salad leaves, make a wide drill and scatter the seed thinly across it. You should not need to thin the seedlings.

Caring for the crop

Keep well watered at all times to stop the plants from bolting to seed at the expense of the leaves. Once a plant has bolted, there's not much you can do except pull it up and put it in the compost.

Remove weeds regularly, and apply a mulch to lock moisture in the ground. If the vigor of the plants seems to be failing, then apply a nitrogen-rich fertilizer following the manufacturer's instructions.

At harvest time

Pick individual leaves as required, or cut the whole plant 2in. (5cm) above ground level and leave it to resprout from the base.

EVERY SPINACH LOVER'S NIGHTMARE. A spinach bed sown too early in the year, right at the start of spring, resulting in wasted, bolted plants, which quickly flower.

Storage and cooking tips

Wash spinach leaves well to remove grit and any insects, which may like to hide in savoyed-leaf types. The soft-textured leaves of smooth-leaf spinach are particularly good raw; combine them with green and red lettuce to add extra texture to salads.

Whatever size of leaves you harvest, put them straight into a plastic bag to keep them fresh and succulent. Store in the fridge as soon as possible until you need them. Spinach can be successfully frozen either cooked or raw.

Leaves can be steamed before being eaten or stir-fried. Because spinach has such a high water content, you don't need to add water to sauté or stir-fry them. If you enjoy cooked spinach, remember that the leaves collapse down to almost nothing once heated, so be generous with your sowing so that you can gather great handfuls when the time comes for the steamer or wok. For every pound of raw leaves, you can expect to get a cup of cooked spinach.

Pests and diseases

Apart from the usual preventative measures against slugs and snails, which will devour emerging seedlings, other chewing insects such as earwigs, flea beetles, and caterpillars can attack spinach, along with aphids and leaf miners. Spinach is also vulnerable to downy mildew. Either give extra space to your crops to improve ventilation or grow a resistant variety.

Swiss chard

Beta vulgaris subsp. *cicla* var. *flavescens*

Swiss chard's colorful stems—yellow, pink, red, white, and orange—are its big attraction in a salad or cooking pot. And that color means it can be used to edge a vegetable bed or perk up a mixed border. It is more tolerant of heat than spinach, and will grow well through summer, but is more likely to make it to the kitchen table in winter when its color is most welcome.

Where to grow

Swiss chard is ideally grown in an open site, on fertile, moist soil. It can keep producing for a long time, so it's particularly important that you improve the soil before planting if you are planning to leave the plants in the ground over a long period instead of making successive sowings through the year.

Sowing and planting

When growing single plants to produce large leaves for cooking, sow the seed in a seed flat and plant out the seedlings once they have germinated. Space them about 18in. (45cm) apart. Sow in late spring for summer and fall picking, and in late summer for a winter crop, although the first sowing will often keep producing well into winter, and sometimes even overwinter to produce a crop again in spring. Sowings for cut-and-come-again plants should be made directly in the ground. Make a wide drill and sow the seeds thinly across it.

SWISS CHARD comes in such a flashy, startling range of colors that it's often given a prime spot at the front of a flowerbed or in containers.

WHEN HARVESTING CHARD, use sharp pruners or scissors to snip away the leaves, not cutting too close to the plant.

Caring for the crop

Swiss chard is one of the easiest vegetables to grow. It takes any amount of neglect and still looks good and produces leaves. Weed and keep the soil moist during dry weather for the best leaves, but the plant will withstand some drought once it's established.

Plants may bolt or develop tough leaves in warmer weather or if they are not regularly cut, but they are so vigorous that they can just be chopped back and they will start producing good, tasty leaves again.

Over winter, you will get the best-quality crop if you cover the plants with hoop houses and mulch around them to protect them from the worst of the weather.

At harvest time

Harvest large leaves for cooking individually as you need them, but do not cut too close to the plant. You can also cut the whole plant for cooking but make the cut 2in. (5cm) up the stem so that the plant can resprout. It will do this several times.

With plants that are not covered over winter, the outer leaves may be damaged, in which case you can just harvest the inner ones, leaving the outer ones as protection against the elements.

Storing and cooking tips

Raw chard leaves can be used in salads or as a flavorful substitute for lettuce in sandwiches, especially grilled panini. Large leaves can be frozen when raw or having been blanched, but do not freeze leaves for salad. They can also be steamed whole, but the tougher leafstalks take longer to cook than the more tender leaves. Ideally they should be cooked separately, or the leafstalk should be chopped up and added to the steamer a few minutes before the leaves are added; both then take a few minutes.

Selected varieties

Bright Lights
This is a good, colorful mixture of reliable varieties, including reds, yellows, and whites. Very ornamental and decorative.

Rhubarb Chard
The strikingly deep-red leafstalks of this variety are a good uniform color and the yields are high. A very pretty leaf crop.

Perpetual spinach

Beta vulgaris subsp. *cicla* var. *cicla*

Perpetual spinach, also known as leaf beet or spinach beet, will grow well in even the toughest, most northerly conditions and will continually produce nutritious, tasty leaves. Less well known than regular spinach, this makes a good alternative in summer when spinach bolts, and it can be overwintered in mild-winter regions such as the Pacific Northwest.

Where to grow

Perpetual spinach tolerates a little shade, particularly in summer, and grows well in moist soil, though it puts up with drier conditions than true spinach. Fertility is important, and you will get stronger growth and better-quality leaves if there are lots of nutrients in the soil. Before sowing, dig the ground over well, adding plenty of well-rotted organic matter and a dressing of a balanced fertilizer. Rake the fertilizer into the soil, leaving the seedbed as smooth as possible.

COLOR OR TASTE?

Perpetual spinach is easy to grow and quite heat-tolerant, but it has a milder flavor than Swiss chard (pages 188–9). Chard, with its more distinctive flavor, also has great ornamental value. Ordinary spinach (see pages 186–7) is the kind most likely to suffer when grown in the heat, but its superior flavor and texture definitely make it worth including in your vegetable garden if you have the right conditions.

Sowing and planting

A spring sowing will keep you in leaves all summer, but the more important sowing is in mid- to late summer, which will produce plants to keep you in leaves all winter long and right into the following early spring.

For summer plants, you can sow seed indoors in cell packs in early spring. Plant outside once the soil has started to warm up. An even easier way to start perpetual spinach is just wait until the soil is warm enough to sow directly outside.

If you are growing large leaves for cooking, keep the plants fairly far apart, to let them spread. Sow seed in rows 18in. (45cm) apart, with 12–15in. (30–38cm) between plants, putting a few together as a precaution in case some don't germinate. Good spacing also helps prevent downy mildew, which can occur with poor air circulation if plants are too close together. When seedlings appear, thin to leave the strongest in each group.

For small leaves in salads, grow as a cut-and-come-again crop. Make a wide drill a few inches across,

THE SHINY, CRINKLY LEAVES of fresh spinach are rich in iron and folic acid. Sowing in mid- or late summer provides an excellent supply for the kitchen over winter.

and then scatter seed thinly along and across it, letting the plants grow closer together.

Caring for the crop

Perpetual spinach can be picked year-round from just two sowings a year. Although it will produce leaves all winter without any special treatment, the leaves are more tender if they have some protection. Either use a cold frame or small hoop house, or cover your row with floating row cover supported on hoops or wires. If plastic or floating row covers are simply draped over the plants, this could lead to damaged leaves—in icy weather they can freeze where there is direct contact with the material.

At harvest time

Leaves are ready for harvesting from eight weeks after sowing; pick them when they have reached the required size. On large plants, you can either cut

YOU CAN GROW all kinds of spinach and chard in containers, along with your favorite herbs such as basil. Use a good-quality potting soil.

OTHER TYPES OF SPINACH

Two other vegetables commonly known as spinach—although not botanically in the same family—can also be grown for their leaves. Malabar spinach (*Basella alba, B. rubra*) is a heat-loving, vigorous vine that can reach 6–14ft. (1.8–4.5m) and must be trained on a sturdy support such as a bean teepee. New Zealand spinach (*Tetragonia tetragonioides*) is another heat-lover, doing well in hot, dry conditions. Plant from seed in rows 2ft. (60cm) apart and thin to 1ft. (30cm) between plants. The leaves of New Zealand spinach should be blanched before eating.

the whole plant, or take a few leaves at a time. If you harvest the whole plant, take care not to cut too low down, which will give the plant the chance to resprout. It should do this several times.

To harvest cut-and-come-again crops for salads, hold the tips of a handful of leaves with one hand and use a pair of scissors to cut the base of the leaves. Again, don't cut too low down: Leave a little stalk behind so that it can grow again. Harvest leaves for salads when they are still small, even just a few inches long, and use them as soon as possible. Harvest little and often, taking only what you need for each meal.

Storing and cooking tips

Leaves will keep for a couple of days in the refrigerator and can be frozen either before or after being cooked. They need to be cooked for a little longer than true spinach, but still the leaves don't take long to collapse and become tender.

Pests and diseases

Birds may nibble on your spinach plants, so cover with netting for protection. Slugs, snails, and cutworms may also snack especially on young seedlings, so handpick these pests, ideally in the evening when they are most active. Aphids may cluster on leaves; remove them with a strong blast of water from the hose. Rabbits love all kinds of spinach and only barriers will keep them away. Prevent downy mildew by giving the plants good air circulation and keeping water off the foliage.

Squash, pumpkins, and corn

Although squash and corn are not related, they make excellent neighbors in the vegetable garden and are often grown as companion plants. They both have their origins in Central and South America, where they have been cultivated for thousands of years. Although they are from the same family, for convenience squash are divided into two categories: summer squash, which are harvested before the rind has thickened; and winter squash and pumpkins, which develop hard rinds on vigorous, spreading plants.

Summer squash and zucchini

For quick results and a bumper yield, zucchini and summer squash must win first prize. From the moment the first seedlings push their twin leaves through the soil surface it is clear that these are plants to be reckoned with. Your biggest challenge, especially with zucchini, is to find takers for your abundant harvest.

Summer squash comes in various shapes: Some are like disks with scalloped edges; others are crooknecked; other varieties look very much like zucchini. Colors range from the familiar green and yellow to white, cream, black, and orange. Elongated, striped bush types known as marrows in England are a colorful addition to the garden; these can be harvested late in the season and baked more like winter squash.

Seed can be sown in early spring, but the plants grow vigorously and may run out of steam by midsummer, so be prepared to sow more to keep generating a crop into fall. And because they are loved by snails and slugs, don't put these succulent plants out until they have a fighting chance.

Zucchini and summer squash flowers and fruit are both edible. When in full growth, inspect your plants everyday. The fruits grow very quickly and are best when young and small, because the sweet flavor dissipates as the fruit—with its high water content—expands. Use recipes that are simple and quick: Try diced zucchini or squash in a pasta sauce, for instance. Experiment with different cooking methods to take advantage of your garden bounty: Zucchini can even be used in baked treats such as bread or muffins.

SUMMER SQUASH and zucchini are incredibly prolific vegetables, which keep producing fruit right through the summer months.

Summer squash and zucchini *Cucurbita pepo*

Even a single plant in this easy-to-grow and highly productive group will produce fantastic yields. Zucchini usually refers to the long, cylindrical fruits with green or yellow skin; round types are also available. Summer squash has different shapes, and they include pattypan types (a flattened fruit with scalloped edges) and crookneck types (with a kinked end to each fruit).

Where to grow

Summer squash and zucchini thrive in hot summers and need the sunniest position available. They are at their best in fertile, moist soil, but a range of soils is fine as the plants are very robust. A good site can be improved by the addition of plenty of well-rotted manure or garden compost, as well as a dressing of balanced fertilizer.

Sowing and planting

Zucchini are notorious for producing an unmanageable glut all at once. Two plants (they take up quite a lot of space) should keep you well supplied.

A ZUCCHINI PLANT takes up a big chunk of space, but smaller bush varieties can be planted in compact gardens.

THREE-CROP COOPERATION

Squash and corn constitute two-thirds of the 'three sisters' growing system developed by Native Americans to interplant their primary crops. The squash plants cover the ground, keeping the soil cool and moist, while the corn towers above. Because they have differing growth habits, the plants do not compete for space, and both get adequate sunlight. The third member of the trio is the bean, though many modern varieties are too vigorous for modern corn plants. Select varieties carefully or interplant the corn and beans rather than allowing the beans to scramble up the corn stalks.

If starting indoors, sow about four weeks before the last frost date for your area. Early sowing indoors or out is rarely of much benefit as the seeds may not germinate if the soil is too cold, or cold temperatures may damage young plants. Because the large seedlings do not transplant well, sow them individually into small pots to minimize root disturbance. Harden off and plant out when the seedlings have two or three leaves.

Outdoors, sow where the squash is to grow, two seeds at a time, thinning as soon as possible to one seedling. Such sowings often overtake indoor-raised plants. You can also buy transplants from the local nursery or garden center.

Check the seed package for spacing; bush zucchini types are usually spaced about 3ft. (90cm) apart.

Summer squash is more likely to be trailing plants, and can take up much more room, needing a space of up to 6ft. (1.8m). Alternatively, plant squash on hills 3–4ft. (1–1.2m) apart. Build up the planting mound with compost, leaf mold, or a rich planting mix. Plant 4–6 seeds per hill, then thin the seedlings to the two or three most vigorous young plants. If the soil is very poor, dig a planting hole to about a shovel's depth, width, and height. Mix lots of well-rotted manure or compost into the soil before you refill the hole.

To help retain moisture in the ground and suppress weeds, you can plant through a black plastic mulch or landscape fabric. However, plastic is a breeding ground for slugs, so be vigilant if you use this method, particularly when the plants are small and vulnerable to attack. Another alternative is to place mulch over the surface after watering the plants well.

In the variable and often cool weather of spring, plants benefit from the protection of a cloche or a floating

THE BULBOUS FRUITS of marrow-type squash are easier to stuff than zucchini, and they keep well if sun-ripened.

row cover to provide warmth. Once the weather is reliably warm, the covering can be removed. Do not leave the plants covered once flowers start to form, as insects must reach the flowers to pollinate the plants.

Caring for the crop

Male flowers form before female flowers and these can be picked for eating stuffed and baked, or you can coat them with batter and then fry them. When you are picking squash flowers to eat, be sure to leave some male flowers on the plant for pollination.

Where space is limited, check the spread of trailing types by pinning down the growth in a circle, or by training them over a sturdy support. As the fruit starts to form, feed with a liquid fertilizer every week or two. If outdoor plants fail to thrive, sprinkle nitrogen-rich fertilizer near the base of the plant and water. Watering is most important as the fruit is starting to form; the more the plants are watered at this time, the better quality the fruit will be. From then on,

ZUCCHINI PLANTS ARE THIRSTY in hot weather, and they should never be allowed to dry out when new fruit is developing. Regular irrigation guarantees quality fruit.

THE TASTIEST ZUCCHINI are picked when young and thin. Slice them off using a sharp kitchen knife or pruners. Never try to twist and pull them off, as it will damage the plant.

water plants generously every 10 days in dry spells, being sure to soak the soil thoroughly, but too much water leaves the plants prone to powdery mildew.

At harvest time

To keep fruit clean, mulch under the plants or place developing fruit on tiles or boards, rotating them once in a while, but taking care not to twist the fruit off the stalk.

Always use a sharp knife to cut zucchini and summer squash cleanly from the plant. If you are tempted to try to twist or pull the fruit off, you may damage the plant or the fruit. Pick the crop when it is young and tender. If left, zucchini and squash can quickly grow much larger, losing flavor and becoming watery as they do so. They'll also suppress further cropping.

Selected varieties (zucchini)

Golden Delight
Deep golden, highly productive fruit that grows to 7in. (18cm). Stems have very few spines. Is disease resistant.

Eightball
Dark green, shiny, rounded zucchini with a bushy growth habit and a long picking period. Was a 1999 AAS winner.

Selected varieties (summer squash)

Papaya Pear
Semibush plant with pear-shaped, yellow fruit that grows 3–4in. (7.5–10cm) long. An AAS winner in 2003.

Balmoral
Compact vines with 6in. (15cm), scalloped, white fruit that develops along the stems. Can be grown in containers.

Storing and cooking tips

Summer squash and zucchini are among the essential tastes of the season. They can be lightly sprinkled with olive oil and herbs, then barbecued. Or try slicing the fruit and roasting in the oven with peppers and eggplants. When picked tiny, the fruit can even be eaten raw in a salad. The flowers can also be used raw or cooked and are sometimes stuffed, dipped in a light batter, and deep-fried. Summer squash and zucchini will store for only a few days, and once picked they must be kept in a refrigerator where they will last for up to a week, if kept hydrated and in good condition.

Marrow-type squash can be eaten fresh or stored for a month or two. They can be stuffed (for example with

POLLINATION

In cool summers, you may notice that fruit on your squash plants is not setting, which is due to inadequate pollination. If this happens, remove a male flower and brush the central parts against the center of a female flower. Female flowers are easy to identify because they have a small developing fruit behind them, while male flowers do not have such a swelling.

rice mixed with cheese and vegetables, or ground beef with tomatoes and herbs) and baked.

Pests and diseases

Several pests can be problems for summer squash. Squash vine borers can cause plants to collapse suddenly, and cucumber beetles can spread the disease bacterial wilt; destroy the pests by hand or protect with floating row covers. Squash bugs can also be handpicked; look out for their bronze eggs and the nymphs, which look like gray aphids. Powdery mildew is common later in the season; keep plants well watered and plant resistant varieties if the disease continues to be a problem in your garden.

SQUASH AND ZUCCHINI FLOWERS are quite a delicacy and need to be picked just as they are opening, going straight into the kitchen. They can be stuffed or coated in batter and fried.

WHEN HARVESTING SUMMER SQUASH, it is best to wear gloves in order to protect your hands from the spines along the stems. Harvest frequently for the best fruit.

Winter squash and pumpkins

Cucurbita maxima

They're just what you want in your root cellar as the weather turns cold: Perfectly cured fruits, worth growing for their looks alone. Pumpkins in general are not as tasty as winter squash, nor do they store as well. The latter come in all shapes and sizes from the round and onionlike to the long and thin, with skin colors of blue, deep orange, pale yellow, or dark green.

Where to grow

Long, hot summers are ideal in fertile, moist soil. Use the sunniest, most sheltered spot in the garden and before planting amend the soil with compost or well-rotted manure as well as an application of balanced fertilizer.

Sowing and planting

Because winter squash and pumpkins need a long growing season to develop fully, look for varieties that will have enough time to ripen in your region. You must also time your sowing or planting to give plants the maximum growing time outdoors. In colder areas or where seasons are short, sow seed indoors or in a frost-free greenhouse about one month before the last expected frost. Plant outside when the risk of frost has passed. Water well, then mulch; protect in any cold spell with a cloche or floating row covers.

In warmer areas, sow directly in soil 1–2in. (2.5–5cm) deep once the soil temperature rises above 60°F (16°C). Sow four seeds per planting and thin later to

TO PROTECT DEVELOPING FRUIT from pests and other damage, place each pumpkin on a tile or board.

one or two plants having checked the seed package for spacing. Bush and semitrailing types usually need 3–4ft. (1–1.2m) between plants but vining types may need up to 6ft. (1.8m). Pumpkins and squash can also be grown on individual soil hills, planting four seeds per hill, then thinning to one or two.

Caring for the crop

Apply liquid fertilizer every couple of weeks, or scatter a balanced granular fertilizer around the plant soon after planting. Water only during particularly hot and dry spells. Weed regularly until the growing foliage outcompetes the weeds. If you are growing large varieties, remove the growing tip once three fruits have set, which gives the fruit a better chance of ripening.

At harvest time

Winter squash may lack flavor if harvested too early. Because of the vast varieties of sizes and colors, the rule

SEEDS FROM A PUMPKIN or squash can be extracted from the pulp by crushing it and cutting it open. Soak the seeds in water to remove the pulp, then dry out and store.

A NUMBER OF WINTER squash varieties are a striking blue color and make attractive fall displays with orange pumpkins.

of thumb is to wait until the fruit is full sized, has a deep rich color, and the rind is hard. Fruit for eating fresh can be cut off the plant as required. Otherwise, leave the fruit on the plant for as long as possible, and it should develop a tough skin that will prevent rotting for up to six months. When you decide the fruit has adequately ripened, cut it off the plant, taking with it as much of the stalk as possible, or by cutting on either side of the stalk. Because rot starts from the stalk end, the longer the stalk, the longer rotting is delayed. Once the fruit has been cut from the plant, it needs a further 10 days to cure. Ideally, this should be in full sun outside, but the

MAXIMIZING YIELDS

Pumpkins and squash like lots of nutrients and water, and they are often planted out on old compost piles. The rich soil leads to productive and healthy plants, although robust varieties usually do well on any good garden soil. A planting hole or mound with plenty of well-rotted manure or a rich growing mix might be necessary for really poor soils. Feed with fertilizer every two weeks.

ACORN SQUASH is a favorite winter vegetable and can be baked in the oven with a little brown sugar or maple syrup. This variety—'Cream of the Crop'—develops a creamy white skin, and it stores well. Before storage, cure acorn squash for 10 days in full sun outside, as long as it stays dry; if wet weather is forecast, shelter the squash in a cold frame or greenhouse.

Selected varieties (pumpkins)

Orange Smoothie
A great Halloween pumpkin for carving that can also be used in the kitchen. Globe-shaped fruit to 8lb. (3.5kg). This 2002 AAS winner has compact growth.

Rouge Vif d'Etamps
A really stunning pumpkin with red, ribbed skin and moist, orange flesh that is good for pies. Its fruit is very ornamental, both in the garden and indoors. The growth is vigorous and trailing.

Selected varieties (winter squash)

Honey Bear
Acorn-type squash that reaches up to 3ft. (1m) tall and 4ft. (1.2m) wide. Fruit, to 1½lb. (0.75kg), has orange flesh. This AAS winner in 2009 is resistant to powdery mildew.

Bonbon
A buttercup variety with deep green, smooth skin lightly striped with silver and sweet, deep golden flesh. Individual fruits may grow to 5lb. (2kg).

weather at this time of year is unpredictable, so it is often done in a greenhouse or cold frame, or indoors.

Storing and cooking tips

Once it is well cured, store winter squash in a dry place with temperatures under 60°F (16°C) but never where there is a risk of freezing. If you have a large crop, don't stack fruit too high on one another as they need plenty of air to breathe. Another option is to cut the flesh into chunks and store it in the freezer; it is advisable to use your frozen fruit quickly to maintain flavor.

During the coldest months when the garden produces little else, it is a real treat to pull out a large, heavy winter squash and slice into it, revealing the dense, orange or yellow flesh inside. Larger varieties are best chopped into chunks and roasted in oil and garlic until slightly caramelized, while smaller ones can be baked whole and eaten with butter and salt and pepper.

Pumpkins are usually grown for decorative purposes and carved at Halloween, but some varieties also produce flesh that are good for roasting and eating.

THE TREMENDOUS VARIETY in winter squash includes rounded acorn types, club-shaped butternut squash, white-and-green striped delicata squash, and blue-skinned hubbards.

TO GROW LARGE PUMPKINS or winter squash, leave one fruit on each plant and give it extra water and fertilizer.

Culinary or 'pie' varieties, such as 'Jack Be Little' and 'Rouge Vif d'Etamps', combine good looks with the sweet taste that characterizes rich, warming, golden pumpkin soups and traditional pumpkin pie.

Pests and diseases

Squash bugs and vine borers can attack winter squash and pumpkins. Try to control them by hand or by covering the plants with floating row covers; these techniques will also help control flea beetles and cucumber beetles (which spread bacterial wilt).

Corn

Maize, the precursor to modern sweet corn, has been grown since people began cultivating the land in North America. Its origins are in Mexico, where it was grown as long ago as 5,000 BC. From there it spread both north and south throughout the Americas. When the first Europeans arrived in North America, they learned how to grow corn from Native Americans, and by the early 19th century seed companies were selling sweet corn for home cultivation. Since then, breeders have developed varieties with sugar-enhanced kernels and 'supersweets', whose sugar content stays high for longer. Extra tender varieties have sweet, thin-skinned kernels and can be eaten raw right off the plant.

Sweet corn is one type of corn; gardeners can also grow popcorn—the type of corn that breaks out of its kernels into a puffy treat when heated. These are available with red, pink, black, yellow, or white kernels. Other types include decorative corn with multicolored ears or long fibrous tassels. Children find growing corn to be quite a magical process, and it's a crop that almost all kids are happy to eat.

Because fast-maturing corn is a tender crop, it can be damaged if planted out before the last frost date in spring. Corn plants need to be planted in a block rather than in lines or individually. Because they are pollinated by the wind, planting them close to one another ensures that the pollen produced on the apical heads of the male flowers ends up on the female flowers (the tassels borne halfway down the stems) which will eventually swell to produce the ear.

Harvested at its peak, the flavor is superb. Grasp the stem with one hand and push the fat ear downwards. Then peel down the outside casing, exposing the plump, golden kernels stacked on top of each other in a tightly packed cylinder. Strip off any remnants of the tassel and plunge the cob into boiling water. In a few minutes it is cooked. Drain and, as soon as it is cool enough to hold, eat and enjoy.

FRESH SWEET CORN from the garden is a late summer treat that can be boiled, roasted, or cooked on the barbecue.

Corn *Zea mays*

There is an enormous difference between freshly harvested corn on the cob and those that have been stored. The sugars start turning to starch as soon as the corn is picked, and it quickly loses its tenderness and tastiness. No matter how hard they try, supermarkets can't compete with sweet corn that has been harvested, boiled, and eaten within the hour.

Where to grow

Choose a sheltered, sunny site for planting. Corn is not fussy about soil, and will grow well provided the soil is well drained and has average fertility. If in doubt, amend with a general fertilizer.

Sowing and planting

Supersweet varieties are thought to have the sweetest taste and the most tender, juicy kernels. If you choose to cultivate these, you mustn't also grow the older varieties at the same time, because cross-pollination causes the kernels to turn starchy. Supersweet varieties are also more difficult to germinate and the seed is more likely to rot in cool, damp conditions.

Corn needs a warm season with no hint of frost for its fruit to mature. Wait until all danger of frost has passed and the soil temperature reaches 55°F (13°C). In areas with short growing seasons, choose varieties that are listed as 'early'; these need as few as 65 days to harvest.

Male flowers shower pollen down from the top of the plant to the females below, which capture it. Pollination is therefore most successful when plants are grown in blocks, because the pollen is more likely to land on the female flowers, and not be blown away from its target. Make blocks at least four plants deep and wide, with each plant 6in. (15cm) apart, thinning seedlings to 1ft. (30cm) apart. Underplant with squash and beans if you'd like to try a traditional 'three sisters' planting (see page 196).

Caring for the crop

Watering is particularly key while the plants are getting established and as the kernels are swelling, although it should not be necessary to water much in between, except during particularly hot, dry weather. Apply a balanced fertilizer when the young plants reach about 1ft. (30cm) in height. Mulch the plants once they are established. If you notice them starting to rock in high

Selected varieties

Silver King
Sweet, sugar-enhanced, white variety that has good resistance to a number of diseases. Each ear is up to 8in. (20cm) long, and the plants grow to 6ft. (1.8m) tall.

Brocade
Sugar-enhanced, bicolor sweet corn with 8½in. (21cm) ears and dark green husks. Plants reach 6½ft. (2m) tall.

Pink Popcorn
Early maturing variety with 6in. (15cm) ears. Rose-colored kernels are also highly decorative. Plants grow to 5ft. (1.5m) tall.

SHORING UP SWEET CORN

1 AS WELL AS MULCHING the sweet corn, you should add some more earth around the plants if your site is exposed to strong winds.

2 GENTLY SCOOP the new earth around the base of each plant, protecting each one from damage and encouraging the growth of adventitious roots.

winds, shore them up to foster the growth of stabilizing roots. Otherwise, cultivation is simply a matter of keeping the area around the plants weed-free.

At harvest time

Corn starts to mature from midsummer on. Once the silks on the ends of the ears turn brown you can start testing for maturity. Peel back the husk to check the corn; a milky liquid will appear when a kernel is pricked. It is vital to pick the ears when they have just reached ripeness, or they will not be at their best. To remove the ear, pull downwards to snap it off.

Storing and cooking tips

Sweet corn does not store well, although it can be eaten a few days later if kept refrigerated. Pick only what you want to eat that day, preferably as close to cooking time as possible. Corn can be sprinkled with olive oil or butter, wrapped in aluminum foil, and cooked on the grill. Or throw it in a pot of boiling water for a few minutes, drain, and serve with butter and a little salt and pepper.

Decorative corn that is grown for drying should be left on the plant beyond ripeness, until it starts to dry on the plant. You can then harvest and continue to

dry it indoors. Hang it in a well-ventilated spot for a few weeks.

Pests and diseases

European corn borers, corn earworms, and armyworms all love to feast on developing ears; handpick the caterpillars, or spray with an appropriate strain of *Bacillus thuringiensis* (Bt)—ask at your local Cooperative Extension Service. Raccoons, deer, and other wild animals enjoy ripening corn; barriers are the only effective deterrent. If rust or blight diseases are present in your area, plant resistant varieties.

GROWING POPCORN

Leave popcorn varieties on the plant until their stalks turn brown. The kernels will pop well only if they are completely dry, and this takes 4–5 weeks. When they're ready, test a few kernels in a pan of hot oil first. Once they are fully dried you can remove the remaining kernels from the ear and store them in airtight jars for several months. Cook the kernels in hot oil, or place the whole cob in a sealed paper bag in the microwave.

Heat-loving vegetables

Some vegetables are bellwether plants, refusing to grow until temperatures warm up enough to keep them happy. They just crave the sun. Peppers, okra, and eggplant are among these plants. In cooler climates, gardeners employ a wide range of techniques to grow these tropical perennials as annuals, from starting seeds indoors with extra heat, to using hoop houses and heated cloches, or even growing the crops in grow bags or containers in the greenhouse. Whatever the extra effort, it's worth it for the bounty they provide.

Eggplant

Solanum melongena

Eggplant gets its name from varieties that ~~are white and egg-shaped~~, even though the larger, purple types are more familiar to most gardeners. The fruit of these plants is versatile enough to be used in Mediterranean, Asian, and Indian dishes, and there are varieties with different shapes, sizes, and skin colors. The texture and taste are like no other vegetable.

Where to grow

Choose a sheltered site with free-draining soil to which plenty of organic matter has been added. Good drainage is essential, so if your soil is heavy clay consider growing eggplant in raised beds or large containers, which also helps prevent the soilborne diseases to which eggplant is susceptible along with tomatoes, peppers, and potatoes. Don't grow any of these crops in the same spot for more than two or three years in a row.

Sowing and planting

Eggplant needs up to three months of temperatures that don't dip beneath 65°F (18°C) to ripen. Although you can start eggplant indoors 8–10 weeks before the last frost date for your area, it may be easier to set out transplants purchased at the garden center or by mail order—specialty nurseries may sell them as plug plants. If growing from seed, start plants in trays or cell packs and keep the seeds warm, using bottom heat if necessary. Floating row covers and black plastic mulch

TO MAKE EGGPLANT sturdy and stable, pinch off the growing tips once the stems reach 12in. (30cm) long. Support plants with stakes or canes to prevent them from flopping over.

can help warm the garden soil for young plants. When the soil has warmed and all danger of frost has passed, plant out, at a spacing of 24in. (60cm) between seedlings or transplants.

Caring for the crop

If growing large-fruited varieties, pinch off the first fruit to form, and thin out subsequent fruit to leave 3–5 per plant (smaller-fruited varieties can be left unthinned). Water plants regularly and mulch to retain moisture in the soil. Feed plants regularly with a liquid fertilizer high in potassium.

At harvest time

Harvest the fruit as soon as it reaches full size and develops its particular skin color. Don't allow the fruit skin to dull on the plant because this is a sign of over-maturity, and the flesh will be leathery and dry. To encourage the remaining fruit to ripen at the end of the season, remove any that forms after late summer, because it's unlikely to mature. This will channel the plant's energy into ripening the larger fruit. Covering plants with floating row covers or plastic on cooler nights will also help with the ripening process.

Storing and cooking tips

Fruit can be stored in the refrigerator for a few days. Eggplant is extremely versatile and can be fried, roasted, microwaved (pierce the skins first), or added to curries and casseroles. Sprinkle slices with salt and allow to rest for 15 minutes before frying to stop the flesh from soaking up too much oil. The flesh discolors quickly after cutting; to prevent this, slice eggplant with a stainless steel knife and sprinkle the slices lightly with lemon juice.

SPECIALTY SEED SUPPLIERS provide the widest range of eggplant, such as long, slender Asian types. Start seeds indoors in all but the warmest zones.

Pests and diseases

Apply biological controls or insecticidal soap to control red spider mites. Check for aphids; squish small colonies with your fingers, blast away with a strong jet of water, or use biological controls. Flea beetles and Colorado potato beetles are common pests; floating row covers can keep them off plants.

Verticillium wilt is a disease that affects eggplant as well as tomatoes and peppers. Rotate crops so that you don't grow these plants in the same spot.

EGGPLANT makes a lively, decorative addition to the container garden, and it is not either black or purple. Container plants grown in good-quality potting soil are not subject to damaging soilborne diseases.

Selected varieties

Black Beauty
A popular variety that reliably produces glossy black fruit on strongly growing plants. The crop is quick to mature, and the large, pear-shaped fruit is tasty.

Moneymaker
A really good variety with large, deep purple fruit. The plants can be very productive, and the flowers are an attractive purple-blue.

Okra

Hibiscus esculentus

Traditionally a Southern favorite, okra was brought to America from Africa about 300 years ago. The fleshy seedpods have a gelatinous texture when cooked and are a staple in Cajun specialties such as gumbo. With their delicate, creamy flowers, the okra plants are highly ornamental and can grow to 6ft. (1.8m) high.

Where to grow

Okra needs free-draining soil in full sun. It demands a hot, humid environment with soil temperatures of 71–86°F (22–30°C) to produce succulent pods. Gardeners in the North can grow okra by selecting the right varieties and starting seeds indoors. Rotate plantings from one year to the next, because okra can suffer from nematode damage. Plant it away from pathways and patios, as the prickly pods can be irritating to the skin of passersby, especially when the plants are wet.

Sowing and planting

Okra seed doesn't remain viable for long, so buy it fresh or save your own each year. Because okra seedlings will collapse in cold, wet soil, sow in spring when soil temperatures have risen to about 70°F (21°C). Don't let the soil dry out before germination occurs, but then lighten up on watering. Sow seeds at a depth of 1in. (2.5cm) about 3in. (7.5cm) apart in rows that are 18–24in. (45–60cm) apart.

DON'T BE FOOLED by young okra plants. They can reach quite a size—about 6ft. (1.8m) high—and they need plenty of space.

In cooler areas, start seed indoors in a heated propagator about 4–6 weeks before planting out. Sow more than you need, as okra doesn't transplant easily. Harden off the plants carefully when they are 12in. (30cm) tall, pinch off their growing tips, and plant them 12in. (30cm) apart.

To warm the soil, you can lay down sheets of black plastic, then plant through slits cut in the sheets—do this very carefully, because okra roots are delicate. Floating row covers can also warm the soil and the young plants, as can individual cloches.

Caring for the crop

Keep well watered, and remove any weeds regularly. Mulch around each plant to preserve moisture in the soil. If plants are flopping over, support them with bamboo canes and string, or even tomato cages.

At harvest time

Each pod takes 3–5 days to develop after flowering, and grows 3–6in. (7.5–15cm) long. They can quickly become stringy and tough, so it is important to pick pods frequently.

Harvest okra with a sharp knife or pruners when pods are bright green, firm, and dry. Dull and yellowing fruit are past their best, but must still be picked. Handle pods carefully, because they bruise easily and any damage will affect their shelf life. Wear gloves if the spiny leaves cause any skin irritation when you are harvesting the pods.

Some gardeners like to leave some dried pods on the plant at the season's end for winter interest in the garden and as a treat for the birds.

WITH THEIR UNUSUAL appearance and attractive flowers, okra can be a decorative member of the summer kitchen garden.

Storing and cooking tips

Ideally, okra should be eaten as soon as it is harvested because it doesn't store well. However, pods can be kept dry for 2–3 days in the refrigerator in a plastic bag; do not freeze them as this affects their eating quality. Very young pods can be eaten raw. Mature pods can be boiled, fried, or added to soups and casseroles.

Pests and diseases

Aphids and red spider mites can be a problem on okra plants. Check carefully for aphids and, if they appear, act quickly to squish small colonies between your finger and thumb, or use a soap-based spray. Red spider mites can be deterred by maintaining high humidity, and you can also blast aphids from the leaves with a sharp jet of water from the hose. Use crop rotation to avoid nematodes.

Selected varieties

Clemson's Spineless
A vigorous and heavily cropping variety ideal for Asian cuisine. As the name suggests, the dark green seedpods are spineless; they are best picked when young.

Cajun Delight
A fast-growing variety that produces a generous crop even in Northern gardens. Pods are succulent and grow 3–4in. (7.5–10cm) in length.

Peppers

Capsicum annuum

Sweet peppers are mild and sometimes quite succulent and sweet. Chili peppers, on the other hand, contain high levels of the chemical capsaicin, which is what makes them hot—in some cases, very hot indeed. Immature fruits of both types are generally green, and do not develop their bright colors of red, yellow, orange, or purple until ripening time.

Types of peppers

The pungency of a pepper is often the first consideration when deciding what to plant in your kitchen garden, but there is more to peppers than spiciness. Many peppers have distinct flavors that range from smoky to fruity. They are also highly decorative plants, with dark green foliage and fruits in colors from red through orange, yellow, purple, and chocolate to mahogany.

There are two main kinds of sweet peppers. Bell peppers are the ones sold in supermarkets; they are square in shape and typically green, yellow, orange, or red, although purple varieties can also be found. Banana peppers are long and tapering and can be pickled or added to chutney and relishes. They are yellow, orange, or sometimes red if left to ripen fully.

Chili peppers are usually categorized by their shape and hotness, with specialty catalogs offering a huge selection of plants that range from mild to fiery. The standard scale for hotness is the Scoville rating, which is measured in multiples of 100. Bell peppers start at zero, and the heat rises from there. Some chili peppers are rated in the tens of thousands on the Scoville scale, and the hottest habañeros may have 200,000 units or more! Some seed catalogs use the Scoville scale, while others have their own rating systems; in any case, the tolerance for heat varies from one person to another, so use the catalog descriptions as a guide and experiment to find your own preferred types and varieties of pepper.

Some hot chili peppers to try include the small, slender Thai chilis, cayenne peppers (which have medium heat and are good for drying), and lantern-shaped habañeros (which are very fiery and grow best in hot-summer regions). Jalapeños and serranos are favorites for Mexican dishes and salsas, and poblanos (also called ancho or pasilla) are an essential ingredient in sauces such as mole. Anaheims are Southwestern favorites and are often stuffed and roasted. Hungarian wax are mild chili peppers that can be pickled or used in stews. They resemble banana peppers, and the names are often confused but Hungarian wax peppers have a bit more bite.

Where to grow

Both sweet and chili peppers need a sunny, sheltered site and high temperatures. When grown in a garden bed, the soil must be well drained and moisture-retentive, so dig in plenty of well-rotted organic matter before planting. In cooler climates, choose a site that gets nice and warm, such as a sheltered raised bed, or plant against a south-facing wall, which will radiate the sun's heat back onto the ripening fruit.

Peppers are subject to the same soilborne diseases as tomatoes, eggplant, and potatoes, so choose a site where none of these crops has been grown within the previous three years. Prepare the planting site by incorporating some balanced fertilizer up to four weeks before planting.

Peppers also grow well in containers filled with lightweight potting soil, which is another way to

SWEET PEPPERS can be sown indoors about eight weeks before the last spring frost.

avoid disease and provide good drainage for the plants. Raised beds are another good option; they also drain well and can be filled with planting mix that provides good drainage. Raised beds also offer the advantage that they warm up more quickly than regular garden beds.

Many sweet and chili peppers are decorative, so you can mix them in summer flower borders along with other annuals and grasses. Small varieties liven up window boxes; pair them with variegated ivy or other trailing plants.

Sowing and planting

Growing from seed offers by far the widest choice of varieties, although you can buy ready-grown plants if just a few are needed or you can't provide the high temperatures needed at the beginning of the growing season. Some mail-order nurseries offer plug plants of peppers that can be shipped around the best planting date in your area.

If starting plants indoors, sow seed with bottom heat in flats or cell packs filled with all-purpose starting mix. Sow the very hot chili varieties 10–12 weeks before the last frost date. Sow milder chili and sweet

GREEN BELL PEPPERS are generally not as sweet as red, yellow, or orange peppers, but they have a fresh taste and crunchy texture, whether eaten raw or cooked.

Selected varieties (sweet peppers)

Gourmet
A beautiful, bright orange bell pepper with a long cropping season. The flavor is sweet and the variety is well suited to growing in containers.

Gypsy
An early-cropping, bright red banana pepper with a good flavor and a tapered shape. The yields are good and the plants show some resistance to tobacco mosaic virus. 'Bell Boy' is similarly good.

Sweet Banana
A mild sweet pepper that produces yellow-green, pointed fruit, 6-7in. (15-18cm) long, which ripens to crimson.

California Wonder
The standard in bell peppers, this variety has large, block-shaped fruit with thick walls that start out green and can mature to red. Grows well in cooler areas.

peppers eight weeks before the last frost date. Thin seedlings to 2in. (5cm) apart and keep the flat or cell packs warm. Feed with a liquid starter fertilizer if seedlings are not growing well or are showing yellowing in the young leaves. Transfer into individual pots when they are large enough to handle by their leaves, and grow in a warm place.

Once the seedlings are 5–6in. (12.5–15cm) tall and outdoor temperatures are 60°F (16°C) or higher at night, begin gradually hardening off the plants to prepare them for planting outdoors.

In cooler areas, you can warm the soil with black plastic mulch or landscape fabric and plant peppers into slits or circles cut into the material. Not only will this help warm the soil, but the plastic or fabric will also keep down weeds.

Caring for the crop

Pinch off the growing tips of chili peppers when plants are 8in. (20cm) tall, to encourage bushiness and to prevent plants from becoming top-heavy; you can do this on sweet peppers, too, but it may lead to later cropping. The sideshoots on chili plants can be pinched back again if lots of small fruit is needed.

PIMENTO PEPPERS are among the many kinds of peppers available for growing in the garden. Some varieties are as sweet as bell peppers; others are hot.

Water pepper plants regularly when in full growth. Dark patches on the fruit can indicate blossom end rot, which is caused by insufficient or inconsistent watering, especially when the fruit is first developing. Mulch plants to help conserve soil moisture.

Train plants up stout canes, secured with loops of string tied in a figure eight, especially if the fruit is going to be large and heavy.

Feed plants regularly with a balanced fertilizer until flowers form, and then apply potassium-rich liquid fertilizer while in flower. Fruit sets easily and abundantly, but if growth flags go back to using a balanced liquid fertilizer.

If you have unripe fruit at the end of the summer and temperatures are starting to fall, cover plants with floating row covers or clear plastic to help them continue ripening.

At harvest time

Peppers can be picked while they are still immature, or be left to change color on the plant. This difference in harvesting time affects both their flavor and their heat. You can experiment by picking your peppers at different stages and see how you prefer them, keeping in mind that the heat will vary somewhat from season to season. However, leaving the fruit to mature on the plant does reduce yield.

Use caution when harvesting chili peppers, as the capsaicin can burn exposed skin and eyes.

Pick the fruit that grows low on the plant first. Rather than picking the fruit individually, you can also uproot the entire chili pepper plant and hang it upside-down in a greenhouse or dry shed .

Storage and cooking tips

Many kinds of peppers are suitable for pickling, including bell, Hungarian wax, banana, cayenne, and pimento. There are many different recipes, typically using salt and vinegar, but be sure to start with blemish-free peppers.

Sweet peppers can be eaten raw in salads or with dips, added to stews and sauces, or stuffed and baked in the oven. Brush them with oil and cook on the barbecue or roast in the oven with a few cloves of garlic.

A WIDE RANGE of chili peppers are now available, from the throat-blasting, hottest kind to the milder, fruitier type, with colors ranging from bright yellow to blackish-purple.

You can cook chili peppers when fresh in sauces and add them to salsas. The heat in chili peppers is in the seeds and the membrane inside the pepper; to retain the flavor of the pepper without as much of the heat, you can remove these parts before cooking. Chili peppers can be roasted and frozen for future use, or dried in a warm, dry place or in a food dehydrator before storing. Thread the peppers onto strings and hang in the kitchen so you can use as needed—chili strings add a flair to your décor, too.

When handling hot chili peppers, it is important to remember to wear rubber gloves and ensure that you do not allow any juice to get in your eyes or on other sensitive parts of your body.

Pests and diseases

Look out for aphids on young shoots, and squish small colonies or spray off plants every few days with strong blasts of water from the hose. Handpick caterpillars, including European corn borers, corn earworms, and hornworms, which can devour leaves and fruit. If infestations are severe, spray with *Bacillus thuringiensis* (Bt). Tobacco mosaic virus can cause yellow leaves and distorted fruit. Look for resistant varieties and rotate crops to prevent infection with viruses.

Blossom end rot can occur when peppers don't receive sufficient water when the fruit is developing. It appears as darkened patches on the ends of the fruit. It can also occur as a result of insufficient calcium in the soil. Test your soil pH and add lime if needed. White spots on the plants can be caused by sunscald; if this shows up repeatedly on your peppers, provide extra shade and control insects that can defoliate plants.

Selected varieties (chili peppers)

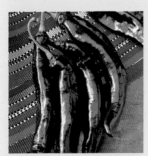

Holy Mole
A poblano pepper with slender, 9in. (23cm) fruit that ripens to a deep glossy chocolate-brown. As the name suggests, this virus-resistant variety is used in mole sauce.

Mariachi
Similar to a Hungarian wax pepper in appearance and size, 'Mariachi' produces cone-shaped, fleshy, 3–4in. (7.5–10cm) fruit that can ripen to red. A 2006 AAS winner.

Thai Dragon
A very hot red chili pepper. The crop is borne in great quantity on short plants, and the peppers themselves are up to 4in. (10cm) long. They dry well for future use.

Dulce
A jalapeño pepper with a mild, sweet flavor from dark green fruit that turns red if left to ripen. Ready to be picked when the fruit makes a crunching sound when squeezed.

Glossary

AAS
The All-America Selections are vegetable varieties chosen for their quality and suitability for a wide range of conditions.

Adventitious
Arising fromn places where growths do not normally occur on a plant. For example, adventitious roots may develop from the stems.

Bolting
The premature production of flowers and seed.

Cloche
A low glass or plastic covering used to protect young plants from adverse weather conditions.

Cold frame
An unheated outdoor frame in which young (often tender) plants are placed to acclimate them to outdoor conditions.

Compost tea
A liquid made by steeping or brewing compost in water. Used as a liquid soil amendment.

Crop rotation
Growing annual vegetables in a different area of the vegetable garden each season, primarily to prevent the buildup of pests and diseases, and maintain the nutrients, in the soil.

Damping off
When a fungal disease destroys emerging seedlings by rotting the stems at soil level.

Drill
Groove or furrow for planting seed.

F1 hybrid
Plants or seeds that have been bred under strict conditions to create a crop that is uniform, vigorous, and high yielding. Seeds gathered from F1 hybrids will not come true, so you will need to buy fresh stock for the next year.

Hardening off
The process of acclimating cool-season plants raised under glass to outdoor conditions by gradual exposure to lower temperatures.

Hardiness
The ability of a plant to withstand or resist frost or freezing temperatures. Non-hardy plants are also called 'tender.'

Intercropping
Growing a quick-maturing crop between slower growing ones.

Mulch
A thick covering over the soil, usually of well-rotted compost. Its many advantages include locking moisture in the ground in spring, ideally after a period of heavy rain, by reducing evaporation; insulating plants' roots in cold winters; blocking out weeds; and improving soil structure.

Offset
Young plant attached to the parent, which can be separated and grown on.

Pinch out
Remove the growing tip by nipping it off with finger and thumb, encouraging the growth of sideshoots.

Successive sowing
Making sowings at regular intervals to ensure a continuous supply of the crop and avoid one big glut.

Thinning
Removing some seedlings or plants to make sure that those left are evenly spaced with enough room to grow and access adequate light and food supplies. Also refers to removing some flower or fruit buds to improve the size and quality of the fruit that's left.

Transplanting
Moving a seedling, or plant, from a small to a larger pot or out into the garden.

Variety
A variant of a specific vegetable bred or selected for particular qualities. Also known as a cultivar (cultivated variety).

Further information

Mail-order vegetable suppliers

The following companies and organizations offer good-quality vegetable and herb seed through mail order. Some also offer young vegetables for transplanting.

Baker Creek Heirloom Seeds
Mansfield, Missouri
www.rareseeds.com
417.924.8917

Botanical Interests
Broomfield, Colorado
www.botanicalinterests.com 720.880.7293

W Atlee Burpee & Company
Warminster, Pennsylvania
www.burpee.com
800.333.5808

The Cook's Garden
Warminster, Pennsylvania
www.cooksgarden.com
800.457.9703

J L Hudson
La Honda, California
www.jlhudsonseeds.net
(no phone number)

Johnny's Selected Seeds
Winslow, Maine
www.johnnyseeds.com
877.johnnys (564.6697)

Nichols Garden Nursery
Albany, Oregon
www.nicholsgardennursery.com
800.422.3985

Park Seed
Greenwood, South Carolina
www.parkseed.com
800.213.0076

The Pepper Gal
Fort Lauderdale, Florida
www.peppergal.com
954.537.5540

Renee's Garden
Felton, California
www.reneesgarden.com
888.880.7228

Richter's Herb Specialists
Goodwood, Ontario
www.richters.com
905.640.6677

Salt Spring Seeds
Salt Spring Island, British Columbia
www.saltspringseeds.com
250.537.5269

Seeds of Change
Santa Fe, New Mexico
www.seedsofchange.com
888.762.7333

Southern Exposure Seed Exchange
Mineral, Virginia
www.southernexposure.com
540.894.9480

Stokes Seeds
Buffalo, New York
www.stokesseeds.com
800.396.9238

Territorial Seed Company
Cottage Grove, Oregon
www.territorialseed.com
800.626.0866

Thompson & Morgan
Jackson, New Jersey
www.tmseeds.com
800.274.7333

Totally Tomatoes
Randolph, Wisconsin
www.totallytomato.com
800.345.5977

Veseys
York, Prince Edward Island
www.veseys.com
800.363.7333

West Coast Seeds
Delta, British Columbia
www.westcoastseeds.com
888.804.8820

Your climate

The USDA plant hardiness zone map divides the United States and Canada into 11 zones based on average winter temperatures. It can be found on line at www.usna.usda.gov/Hardzone/index.html

Natural Resources Canada has further information on hardiness and climate zones at www.planthardiness.gc.ca/

In the West, Sunset has a system of zones that takes into account factors other than cold hardiness www.sunset.com/garden/climate-zones/

For information specific to your area, find your local Cooperative Extension Service. A list of regional offices can be found at www.csrees.usda.gov/Extension/

Index

Page numbers in *italic* indicate an illustration away from its text. Page numbers in **bold** indicate a main section.

Acknowledgments

SPECIAL THANKS TO THOSE WHO HAVE CONTRIBUTED TO THIS BOOK

Thanks to Carol Klein for her time, passion and energy.

Text written and compiled by: Carol Klein, Fiona Gilsenan, Guy Barter, Alison Mundie, Amy Lax, Andrea Loom, Lia Leendertz, Sue Fisher, Lucy Halsall and Simon Maughan

Royal Horticultural Society: Guy Barter, Alison Mundie, Amy Lax, Niki Simpson and Debbie Fitzgerald

RHS Publications: Susannah Charlton, Simon Maughan, Rae Spencer Jones and Lizzie Fowler

Mitchell Beazley: David Lamb, Helen Griffin, Joanna Chisholm, Victoria Easton, Juliette Norsworthy, Giulia Hetherington and Susan Meldrum

Bridgewater Book Company: Jonathan Bailey, Michael Whitehead, Robert Yarham, Diane Pengelly, Richard Rosenfeld, Liz Eddison, Jane Sebire, Kim Sayer, Laurie Evans. Thanks to Cathy and Jean from the Green Lane Allotment Society for assisting Jane Sebire with location photography

PHOTOGRAPHIC ACKNOWLEDGMENTS:
APM Studios: Andrew Perris 62 a, 64 a, 66 a, 76 a, 78a, 80a, 84a, 88a, 102 a, 106 a, 110 a, 116 a, 120 a, 124 a, 126 a, 130 a, 134, 136 a, 142 a, 146 a, 150 a, 154 a, 156 a, 162 a, 167 a, 170 a, 172 a, 174 a, 178 a, 186 a, 188 a, 190 a, 196 a, 200 a, 206 a, 210 a, 212 a, 214 a

Corbis: Staffan Widstrand 213 a

Fotolia: Anne Kitzman 70 inset, auremar 6, Barbara Delgado 145 b, Blake Courtney 9, CHG 32, David Gilder 63 b, David Whitfield 59 inset, Dennis Debono 120 b, DLeonis 160, forestpath 92 b, Ghost 209 inset, hensor 176, Horticulture 33 r, Igor Dutina 72 al, Frank Jr 178 l, Hazel Proudlove 95 inset, Ints 128 inset, Jack Kunnen 93 c, jojobob 114 inset, Kadal 147 a, kai-creativ 29, Karin Lau 204, Laurent Renault 165 bl, Lianem 159 inset, Liz Van Steenburgh 131 bl, Matevz Likar 33 l & c, MAXFX 201 a, monamakela.com 89 bl, nito 216, onionhead 93 a, naffarts 8, 148, Nathalie Dulex 183 inset, NCBateman1 23b, Nick Osborne 91br, nTripp 144 b, Olga Lipatova 215 a, Paul Paladin 152 a, Paweł Burgiel 198 br, Philip Syme 91 bl, phoenix 139 a, Rajeshwar Hundal 7, Ralf Siemieniec 175 cl, Robert Lerich 77 cr, Roslen Mack 144 a, Scott Griessel 145 a, Silvia Bogdanski 171 br, South12th 91 cl, TMLP 104, 194, Tootles 138, trombax 105 a, tsach 192 inset, Uros Petrovic 85 ar

The Garden Collection: Andrew Lawson 169 bl, Derek St Romaine 24, 31, 127 l, 164 cl, 166 al, 202 cr, Gary Rogers 126 b, Jonathan Buckley 169ar, Liz Eddison 168 ar, Nicola Stocken Tomkins 169 br, Torie Chugg 41 r, 169 al

Garden World Images: Botanic Images Inc 137 br, C Jenkins 124 br, G Kidd 82 cbr, T Sims 136 b, 164 bl, 166 bl, Tyrone 117 a, 165 a

iStockphoto.com: AtWaG: 157 br, blowbackphoto 153 c, carterdayne 67 cr, cjp 127 b, funwithfood 181 br, GomezDavid 79 br, 215 br, hipokrat 107 r, img85h 92 a, kcline 181 cl, ktmoffitt 181 cr, leopardhead 152 cl, lighthc patty_c 215 bl, stieglitz 135 br, 213 br, suzifc thepalmer 131 br

Jane Sebire 12, 13, ..., 18, 19, 21 all, 30, 35, 37 a & b, 39, 41 l, 43 al & ar, 44, 45 a, 46, 49, 50, 51, 52, 53 r, 54, 55, 60, 62 c, 63 al & ar, 64 bl & br, 66 b, 67 a, 68 al, ac & ar, 69 al & ar, 72 ar, 73 ar, 74, 80 bl, bc & br, 83 a, 89 al & ar, 96, 98 c, 99 l & r, 103 l & r, 108, 110 bl & br, 112 b, 113 a & b, 118, 121 a, 122, 125 al, 127 ar, 130 b, 131 a, 132, 135 a, 137 al, 140, 142 b, 143 a, 153 al & ar, 162 l & r, 167 bl & br, 174 b, 175 a, 179 all, 181 a, 184, 187 l & r, 188 b, 189 a, 191, 197 a & b, 198 a, 199 l & r, 203 a, 207 l & r, 210 b, 211 al & ar, 214 b

Jupiter Images: 45 bl

Laurie Evans: 61, 75, 87, 97, 101, 109, 119, 123, 125 ar, 133, 141, 149, 161, 163, 177, 185, 195, 205

Photolibrary: Garden Picture Library/Brian Carter 42, Garden Picture Library/David Cavagnaro 154 b, Garden Picture Library/Michael Howes 146 b, Garden Picture Library/Sklar Evan 150 b, Garden Picture Library/Tim Spence/Lightshaft Ltd 155 a, Westermann Studios GbR 157 a

RHS Collection: 16 a & b, 25 all, 26, 38, 76, 77 al & cl, 79 a, 83 b, 86 b, 100, 106b, 107 l, 137 ar, 143 br, 153 b, 155 br, 164 br, 166 ar & br, 171 bl, 181 bl, 189 bl, 200 b, 201 b, 212 b, 215 cl, Harry Smith 180 bl, Paul Bullivant: 23a, 36 l & r, 48, 49, 71 bl, 151 Tim Sandall 20, 22, 34, 40, 43 b, 47, 53 l, 78b, 116 b, 170 b, 171 al & ar, 172 b, 173 a, 178 br, 190 b, 196 b, 203 b, 217 a

Suttons Seeds: 62 bl & br, 65 b, 77 bl, 82 br, cal & car, 85 al, bl & br, 89 al & ar, 96 bl, 102 br, 112 al & cr, 121 bl, 124 bl, 127 br, 135 cr, 137 bl, 147 br, 165 br, 175 cr, bl & br, 186 bl & br, 189 br, 211 bl & br, 213 bl, 215 cr

Thompson & Morgan: 69 bl, 77 ar, 82 bl, 135 bl, 147 bl, 173 bl, 180 cl, 217 bl

All-America Selections (AAS): 192 l, 105 bl, 111 bl, 135 cl, 180 br & cr, 198 bl, 202 a, 202 cl, bl & br, 217 cl & cr

FG Images: 15, 86, 90 a & b, 111 br, 112 ar, 139 br, 165 cl & cr

Johnny's Selected Seeds: 68 b, 71 br, 121 br, 139 bl, 156 b, 157 bl, 173 br & cr, 217 br

Stokes Seeds: 65 a & c, 67 al & ar, cl & bl, 82 al, ar & cbl, 89 br, 91 al & cr, 112 cl, 164 cr, 173 al, 198 cl & cr, 206 ac

WCS Images: 67 br, 69 br, 79 bl, 93 b, 98 br, 105 br, 117 bl, 143 bl, 152 ar, bl & br, 155 bl, 206 b & bc